DANCE, MODERNITY
CULTURE

In *Dance, Modernity and Culture*, Helen Thomas provides an original, inter-disciplinary approach to the study of dance. By examining the development of modern dance in the USA during the 1920s and 1930s she develops a framework for analysing dance from a sociological perspective.

In applying her approach to the works of St Denis, Ted Shawn and Martha Graham, among others, she relates the emergence of modern dance to contemporaneous artistic developments, and locates dance within a wider social and economic context. Thus, she draws attention to the importance of popular culture in the development of modern dance, music and painting, and the crucial role women played in establishing dance as an art form.

Dance, Modernity and Culture explores an area of art practice that has long been marginalised by sociologists of art. As an important contribution to dance scholarship this book will be essential reading for all those interested in the performing arts.

Helen Thomas is Senior Lecturer and Deputy Head of Department in Sociology at Goldsmith's College, University of London. She has published numerous articles on dance in *Dance* and *Issues in Architecture, Art and Design* and is the editor of and a contributor to *Dance, Gender and Culture* (Macmillan, 1993).

Dance, Modernity and Culture

Explorations in the Sociology of Dance

Helen Thomas

London and New York

First published 1995
by Routledge
11 New Fetter Lane, London EC4P 4EE

Simultaneously published in the USA and Canada
by Routledge
29 West 35th Street, New York, NY 10001

© 1995 Helen Thomas

Typeset in Bembo by Florencetype Ltd, Stoodleigh, Devon
Printed and bound in Great Britain by TJ Press, Padstow
Ltd, Padstow, Cornwall

British Library Cataloguing in Publication Data
A catalogue record for this book is available from the
British Library

Library of Congress Cataloguing in Publication Data
A catalogue record for this book has been requested

ISBN 0-415-08793-7 (hbk)
ISBN 0-415-08794-5 (pbk)

CONTENTS

For Paul and David, and Edith and Frank

ILLUSTRATIONS

ACKNOWLEDGEMENTS

This book is based on my PhD thesis which was completed in 1986. I did try to get it published at the time and several publishers (Routledge included) expressed a strong interest, but, in the end, they decided that there was not a market for this type of work on dance. Clearly, at least as far as a few publishers are concerned, things have changed and I am very grateful for that.

In order to take account of developments in the field and to remove the 'thesis speak', I have written a number of new sections for this book and developed others. This entailed omitting aspects of the original work, such as the appendix on movement notation, the majority of the endnotes and the more detailed discussion on the body. Despite the fact that the shape of the book is somewhat different, I think that the general thrust of the original thesis, which argued for an interdisciplinary approach to the study of dance, remains in place.

Although I am aware that, in the final analysis, the responsibility for the work lies with me, I would like to acknowledge and thank the following people for their invaluable help, guidance and support in its development. Stephanie Jordan, with whom I sometimes write and often discuss dance issues, read the whole manuscript with her dance historian's eye and made a number of important critical comments, which, hopefully I have addressed. My colleague at Goldsmiths, Don Slater, read and commented on the first chapter and helped me to rethink the relation of women to consumer culture in the nineteenth century. Andrew Ward has discussed a number of ideas with me for this book and other dance projects on our many outings to dance performances over the years. My editor Julia Hall, who encouraged me to take out the thesis, dust it down and get to work on it, when I had thought that it would never see the light of day, has displayed a strong commitment to the work from start to finish. Her colleague, Emma Cotter, processed the manuscript through to publication in a fast and efficient manner. I am also grateful to Paul Filmer, the supervisor of the original thesis, for his guidance and sustained defence of a project that was not deemed to be within the bounds of 'proper' sociology in the early 1980s; to Dave Walsh for sharing with me his knowledge of musical theatre; to Peter Bassett, the Librarian at the Laban Centre, for giving me his time and passing on his knowledge of current dance resources; to Valerie Preston-Dunlop for bringing to bear her considerable movement analysis skills on a section of *Appalachian Spring* which I had found perplexing; to Bonnie Bird for giving me a brilliant interview which enabled one particular section to fall into place, and to my students at Goldsmiths and elsewhere who have taken my Sociology of Dance courses, who not only helped me to be clear about my ideas but also enabled me to indulge my 'magnificent obsession' – dance. Finally, I need to thank David and Paul for putting up with what must have appeared to be an action reply of someone writing up a PhD.

Helen Thomas
March 1995

1 FORMULATING A SOCIOLOGY OF DANCE

My intentions in writing this book are threefold. To begin with, I wish to set out a case for generating a systematic (although not all inclusive) approach to the sociology of dance. Second, I shall argue that as dance is simultaneously a feature of the socio-cultural context of its emergence, creation and performance and a reflexive practice realised through the medium of the body, such an approach needs to be inter-disciplinary in character. Third, in order to move beyond a programmatic level, this framework will be exemplified by means of a case study focusing on the emergence and development of American modern dance, partic-ularly through the work of Martha Graham. This case study also typifies the development and establishment of modernism in the arts in America and it heralds its decline and the subsequent emergence of postmodernism.

When people ask me what my research area is and I reply, 'the soci ology of dance', their usual response is, 'mmm . . . interesting . . . how unusual . . .', accompanied by raised eyebrows and a quizzical look which implies, 'What is it and how do you do it?' When I go on to explain that my research is in performance dance they are even more nonplussed. This is because, more often than not, they assume that an interest in dance would take me to some other (usually non-western) culture or that I am busily observing 'raves' or some other 'exotic' subcultures which are seen through the lenses of moral panics. The reason for this is that dancing is thought to be more visible in these contexts and therefore to have more relevance. These commonsense assumptions, although correct to a certain extent, are underpinned by certain attitudes towards dancing and those who dance, which, as I shall discuss below, are naive on the one hand and racist on the other, and in part, they have contributed to the lack of serious attention given to dance within sociology. At the same time, that unspoken question is important and requires to be addressed in some detail if the aims which I set out at the beginning of this book are to be achieved. But in order to do this it is necessary first to indicate the kinds of contexts in which dance takes place in contemporary western industrial cultures before moving on to consider sociology's address of dance.

The activity which commonsensically we understand as dancing does in fact take a number of different forms and occurs in a variety of social contexts which straddle the spectrum of the high art/popular culture divide in contemporary western industrial formations. As an art form, like the other arts, dance is a minority concern (and a minority concern within the arts), which is participated in by a minority and viewed by a minority of the public. As such it can be seen to reside within the confines of the tradition of 'high' culture. But it is not as simple as that because even its most classic or traditional form (ballet) slips across into the domain of popular (mass) appeal, as consumer capitalism extends its grip into the traditionally exclusive arena of high culture (Jameson 1985). Think, for example, of the Royal Ballet's summer performances under the big top at Battersea Park, or the now frequent visits of the Bolshoi, the Kirov or some other ballet company from the former USSR, with their ballet spectaculars which, performed in large arenas, would not have been out of keeping with a David Belasco extravaganza in the popular American theatre of the 1900s. Even contemporary or modern dance, whose formal codes are perhaps less familiar to the wider public than ballet and less well subsidised or patronised, is attempting to lose its former avant-gardist status and is moving out of the few existing tradi- tional dance venues and into the commercial theatre. The blurring of the traditional high/popular culture boundaries in terms of form and context is a feature of much new or postmodern dance, a tendency which can also be observed in the other arts.

Starting from the other end of the spectrum, dance can again be found in a diversity of shapes and forms in those products of popular (mass) culture which have been dubbed traditionally as 'light entertainment' (Dyer 1992), musical theatre, films, television and pop videos. While the favoured dance styles and genres exhibited in this diverse cultural arena have their roots in popular culture, drawing often on black cultural forms, they have also been influenced by and fed back into 'art' dance and popular dance forms.

Dancing, however, is not just something that we look at, it is also an activity that takes place in different social contexts, in mainstream popular culture and in subcultures. For example, in the current era of the body beautiful, dance, from jazz to ballroom to ballet, has come to be seen as means of keeping fit, in addition to any consideration of the particular aesthetic components involved. Dance-style routines and movements are a feature of the highly populated adult 'aerobics' and 'step' classes which are held throughout the day, almost every day of the year, in leisure centres and fitness clubs throughout the country. Similarly, from an early age, numbers of young children (particularly girls), whose parents can afford it, assiduously attend ballet and tap classes. And if 'Come Dancing' (the longest running television series in Britain) is anything to go by, there are people in every pocket of the country who are dedicated to learning the requisite dancing skills and advancing their style and technique to compete in ballroom, Latin-American and formation dancing competitions. Dancing is a social activity which has a tradition of popular appeal. Social dance forms, like performance dance, are expressed in a variety of codes and bodily aesthetics, some of which are relatively stable while others are in a state of continuous flux. It is a bodily activity in which many people participate at various stages of their lives, sometimes by themselves, in couples, or in groups, in a range of social settings, from street dancing to dance halls, discos and raves, to parties, dinner dances, weddings and church socials.

Although dancing is not something that most of us do or watch every day, it is most surely a cultural product which has a place in our cultural tradition. As such, it might reasonably be expected to have come under the gaze of sociology. Until quite recently, however, the study of dance as a performance art, a leisure pursuit, or as a representational form within contemporary western industrial societies has been a generally neglected area of sociological concern. Indeed, the sociological tradition has had its eyes closed to the subject. The late 1960s and the 1970s witnessed the publication of a few sociological monographs specifically about dance or dancers such as: Francis Rust's (1969) structural functionalist analysis of the history of social dance; Edith Cope's (1976) interactionist account of the group dynamics of a small dance company, while Simon Frith's (1978) sociological analysis of rock music contained numerous passages on the role of dance in youth culture. Janet Wolff's (1975) study on hermeneutics and the sociology of art included a long programmatic passage on the sociology of dance. This work, however, did not lead to a more sustained programme of sociological study and in 1983 Peter Brinson attempted to set out the parameters of a sociology of dance from within the confines of a developing dance scholarship in the UK.

The 1970s and 1980s witnessed the growth of cultural studies which celebrated the convergence of a range of intellectual disciplines applied to the hitherto denigrated forms of popular culture. Dancing, as Frith (1978) showed, plays an important social role in the lives of young people and, therefore, it is not surprising that cultural analysts' increasing fascination with youth culture in the late 1970s and early 1980s led them to stray into the domain of dancing. For example: David Robins and Phil Cohen (1978) on disco dancing; Geoff Mungham (1976) on the role of dancing in working-class youth culture, Dick Hebdige (1979) on punk dancing and Angela McRobbie (1984) on dancing and gender identification. McRobbie also indicated the need for more substantive and detailed analyses.

Although subsequent studies on youth culture have continued to pay lip service to the importance of dancing for young people they have seldom analysed in any detail the activity of dancing in relation to the flow of urban life (McRobbie 1991). For example, Iain Chambers' (1985) detailed discussion of the dance halls and clubs which have formed a vital setting for post-war urban youth culture and popular music, highlights the importance of dancing as a leisure activity ('the freedom of Saturday night'). He also points to the influence of black music and dance on the dancing of white youth. The enduring influence of black music, dance fashions and styles of dress on white urban youth culture is also documented in Paul Gilroy's (1987) work. Chambers, unfortunately, like Frith (1978) before him, shies away from carefully situating the popular dance styles from the shake to body popping within the context of culture, in preference for a more critical examination of music. This privileging of music (and other aspects of culture) over dance is also evidenced in Simon Jones's (1988) study which charts the influence of black culture on white British youth. In Paul Willis's celebration of the 'symbolic work' expressed through the cultural activities of young people, dancing is once again subsumed under music and Jones states that 'dancing is the principal way in which musical pleasures become realised in physical movement and in bodily grounded aesthetics' (Willis *et al.* 1990: 65).

Despite the recognition that dancing is a crucial aspect of 'leisure activity, entertainment and sexuality' (McRobbie 1984), discussions of dance in cultural or subcultural analyses have taken up little space in comparison to other more carefully considered cultural phenomena. Moreover, the persistent interest that cultural studies has shown in forms of popular culture has meant that it does not often stray into the enclaves of 'high' art and thus has maintained a virtual silence on performance dance. Peter Wollen's (1987) essay on the import of Diaghilev's Ballet Russe productions to the aesthetics of modernism stands as an exception here.

The net result of all this is that the specificity of dance and, hence, its difference has not been addressed in a sustained and systematic manner. According to Andrew Ward (1993) cultural studies' unspoken commitment to particular forms of rationalism has helped to keep 'dancing in the dark' (a topic that will be discussed later in relation to sociology). Ward implies that the influences of poststructuralism and postmodernism in cultural studies and the theoretical shifts created by the opening up of the categories of gender and race, which call into question the canons of rationality, provide the possibility for bringing the activity of dancing out into its *own* light (again these are considerations that will be addressed later in relation to sociology).

The neglect of dance in sociology and the latent interest in cultural studies find an echo in another recently developed area, feminist studies. There are several reasons why dance might have been taken out of the shadows by feminist social and cultural research. To begin with, as the studies on youth culture have indicated, dance is not only an important leisure activity for young people, it is also bound up with the processes of gender roles and identification, particularly in relation to girls and young women (Frith 1978, McRobbie 1984, Mungham 1976). Although feminism has been concerned to open up the categories of gender, dancing has not been used as a significant resource.

Feminist interests in dance, however, need not have been confined to 'popular' dance. Female performers have been the central protagonists on the classical ballet stage since the nineteenth century. Despite the negative puritanical sexual connotations associated with dancing (and this is worthy of exploration in terms of race and gender representations), dance history (Kendall 1979, Sorell 1981) demonstrates that this was one of the few areas in public life which afforded women an opportunity for self-expression and for some limited social advancement, particularly for working-class girls. Given feminists' interest in rectifying the androcentric bias in historical analysis, particularly in the initial phases of feminist scholarship, it is rather curious that this 'women's realm' of activity was not given more than a passing glance. Influential commentators such as Germaine Greer (1971) dismissed ballet as something for middle-class women to watch, while female dancers were viewed as 'eternally feminine' stereotypes. Yet, these 'eternally feminine' ballet dancers which Greer cast aside often confronted conventional (patriarchal) representations of women's bodies through their expansive use of space and their attire. This was even more the case with the emergence this century of the modern dance movement, whose founders were mostly women who not only created but also controlled the productions of their dance images. These dance images can incorporate a body aesthetic which has negative under-tones. For example, the desire to attain the perfect slim prepubescent ballet body demanded by the system, can lead the dancer into an obsessive relation with her body, which, in turn, can lead to such eating disorders and illnesses as anorexia and bulimia (Buckroyd 1989, Kirkland 1987, Novack 1993, Vincent 1979). Given the preoccupation of feminist scholarships with representations of women's bodies, it is even more curious that it has not generated a thoroughgoing consideration of the character and forms of dancing.

Although there has been lack of detailed attention given to dance in feminist scholarship and cultural analysis, a number of dance scholars have seized upon the theoretical and methodological insights which these areas have opened up (a concern with textual/intertextual analyses, interdisciplinary frameworks, diversity of cultural forms/practices, putting gender/race issues on the cultural agenda), in order to generate a more cultural and textual basis for dance studies. For example, Susan Foster (1986) draws on the work of cultural critics such as Roland Barthes and Michel Foucault for her decidedly 'intertextual' analysis of the work of four choreographers. Ann Daly's (1987) discussion of the dancer's body in Balanchine's work relies heavily on feminist and semiotic notions of representations. Cynthia Novack's (1990) anthropological analysis of contact improvisation is influenced by developments in cultural studies as are a number of papers in Stephanie Jordan's and Dave Allen's (1993) collection of media representations of dance. Christy Adair's book *Women in Dance* (1992) and a number of papers in the collection I edited (Thomas 1993) also draw explicitly from both cultural studies and feminist cultural criticism and sociology. Although the flow of ideas has remained largely one way from social and cultural analysis to dance rather than the other way round, the very existence of some of these texts (this one included) within mainstream academic publishing signifies that dance is currently being seen (at least by the publishers) as an emergent area of interest for the social and cultural sciences. But before we get too obsessed with the lowering of the drawbridge, I want to consider further the hitherto marginalisation of dance by sociology.

One of the central problems in analysing dance from a sociological perspective is that, like painting and sculpture as opposed to literature or poetry, it expresses itself non-verbally. However, while the artwork can stand independently of the artist, the dance and the dancer cannot be separated (Hanna 1980). This is because the body is the primary instrument and means of expression and representation in dance, at least in the West. In part, the key to understanding sociology's neglect of dance lies in the way that the body and dance have been perceived within western culture.

The mind/body dualism inscribed in Descartes' first principle of philosophy in his *Discourse in Method (1637)*, 'Cogito, ergo sum' – 'I think, therefore I am' (Hampshire 1956: 68) has been of central importance to classical thought and to developments and achievements in scientific thought. For Descartes, 'the essence or nature' of human beings 'consists only in thinking' and is not 'dependent on any material thing'. The human subject, is constituted through the mind and 'the mind . . . is wholly distinct from the body' (Hampshire 1956: 69). Western cultural thought since the enlightenment has been dominated by the privileging of the rational thinking subject and the negation or relegation of the 'other' to a subservient position. Rationality takes precedence over the emotions, idealism over materialism, culture over nature, objectivity over subjectivity. In a rationalised and technocratic culture such as ours, the mind and the body stand in binary opposition, with the former being placed under the category of culture and the latter under that of nature. Commonsensically, we treat the body as pre-linguistic, and/or expressive of some inner-emotional state. That is, the body becomes viewed as existing outside language and, as such, is not subject to the (cultural) conventions of discourse. While we think that speech as an exemplar of language and culture can cover over the 'real' attitude of the speaker, body movement, it is thought, does not; it reveals it. Here, speech becomes the representation and body movement the material reality. These commonsense perceptions are given voice in those pop-psychology 'body language' features in the tabloids which seem to resurface every other year and in popular manuals like *Body Language* (Fast 1970) and *Intimate Behaviour*

(Morris 1979) where the tools of ethology are dragged in to provide an air of scientific legitimacy and to reveal the behaviour of the 'human animal'.

But the representation/reality, culture/nature, mind/body associations of speech/movement are also to be found lurking in the background of theories that seek to call into question the Cartesian mind/body dualism and reinstate the power of the body into the cultural frame. For example, they are inherent in Rodolf Laban's (1971) theories of movement, in Louis Horst's idea that 'the body is the most dangerous of instruments' (Lloyd 1968: 92), and in Martha Graham's famous statement that 'movement is the one speech that cannot lie' (Graham 1968b: 99). Sigmund Freud (Freud and Bruer 1974) also considered that the 'abnormal' bodily attitudes and bodily eruptions of his (predominantly female) patients were related to their unbalanced state of mind.

It is not surprising that the body has been treated as being more akin to some 'primitive' ('natural') or unconscious state of being in a dominant cultural tradition, which, underpinned by enlightenment philosophies celebrating the power of reason, and the word, has sought to distinguish itself from nature through the mastery and transformation of it by means of science and technology. As Norbert Elias (1978) has shown, with the acceleration of the 'civilising process' which began with the rise of individualism and the Renaissance and was given further impetus with the breakdown of the feudal social order and the rise of Puritanism, science, urbanisation and industrialism, 'natural' or 'instinctive' behaviour came to be seen as coarse and impolite. The distancing from nature also entailed a distancing from the body. The cultural codes of polite society increasingly came to be directed towards the control and privatisation of the body. The body becomes shrouded in manners, adornments and implements and its (natural) functions become privatised and concealed. So the body comes to be classified as the dangerous 'other' to culture; as a thing that speaks of nature, it has to be surrounded by (private) rituals and controlled through manners and covered in appropriate dress and adornments, in order to prevent it seeping out or breaking through into and contaminating its privileged 'other', culture, reason, civilisation. Dress, which operates at the interface between the 'natural body' and the 'social body' (Douglas 1975) has been used as a symbolic battle-ground for cultural supremacy and counter-hegemonic attacks. Dominant cultural groups or classes have attempted to maintain their position in the social structure by controlling what can and cannot be worn (e.g. sixteenth-century sumptuary legislation, the banning of the kilt in Scotland after the battle of Culloden in the eighteenth century). Dress has also been dragged into play by groups and individuals seeking to combat the dominant hegemony (subcultural oppositional dress and demeanour, dress reform movement, second wave feminism's assault on the dominant body politic).

The perceived nearness of the body to nature rather than culture has consequences for dance. As Sparshott (1988) has argued, there is a long tradition of considering dance to be one of the oldest or indeed the oldest of arts. It was viewed as existing prior to language and the other arts and, as such, was situated on the cusp of prehistory and humanity. For example, the eighteenth-century enlightenment philosopher, Condillac, considered that music and poetry were associated with dance and existed prior to them. As 'the art of gesture', dance constituted the first symbolic activity from which language and music stemmed and as such Condillac supposed that 'at all times and among all peoples, some kind of music, dance and poetry might have been observed' (Sparshott 1988: 3). Dance came to be associated with formal ritual and rites of passage, which, in turn, were viewed as essential components of 'traditional' structurally simple, pre-literate cultures. In nineteenth-century sociological and anthropological texts, these forms of social organisation are viewed as standing in binary opposition to those of 'modern' complex industrial cultures. Durkheim's (1964) analysis of 'mechanical' and 'organic' solidarity which has been influential in both normative sociology and in anthropology, is a prime example of this typology.

In sharp contrast to sociology, anthropology can at least lay claim to a considerable body of data on dance in relation to so-called 'primitive' cultures, despite the cries of dance anthropologists (Grau 1993, Kaeli'-inohomoku 1983, Royce 1980) to the contrary. When anthropology started out in the first half of the nineteenth century it was concerned to delineate humans from non-humans. Its focus of attention was directed towards the study of non-literate, non-Christian societies. The idea that dance belongs to the past or to structurally simple societies was revived by speculative evolutionary approaches in the latter half of the nineteenth century. The evolutionists rejected Christianity's view of the man (*sic*) being made in God's image, in favour of the idea that humanity is made up of diverse species and that the European variety constituted the more fully developed rational type. It was assumed that these pre-literate, non-European societies represented an earlier phase of human development, i.e. 'primitive' societies. Dance was treated as an essential component of primitive culture, a world inspired by fear and dread, which the primitives attempted to explain and control by magic and ritual means. In trying to explain and control events in the world by means of magic, it was construed that they were in fact operating at a primitive level of scientific thought; they were trying to make sense of the world but they were getting it wrong (Douglas 1970a). As Royce (1980) has indicated, a cursory glance at some of the early evolutionary accounts such as *The Golden Bough* (Frazer 1957) or *Religion in Primitive Culture* (Tylor 1958) leaves the reader in little doubt that the authors considered that the primitives were so steeped in magic that they could hardly perform a task without dancing or partaking in some other associated formal ritual. It was also assumed that as cultures developed and became more 'civilised' and 'rational', then dancing would become less important. Although this mode of analysis was abandoned by anthropology in the early part of the twentieth century, the concept of dance that it sustained, as a number of commentators (Kaeli'inohomoku 1983, Williams 1977, Youngerman 1974) have demonstrated, continued to persist long afterwards.

Sociology, like anthropology, also began in the nineteenth century but, by contrast, its focus was directed towards the problem of modernity. That is, the historical shift from a feudal society to a modern industrial market society, with the concomitant increase in the processes of specialisation, rationalisation and the development of science on the one hand and the decline of ritual and religion, and the marginalisation of the arts and dance on the other. It was also concerned to understand the problem of 'social order', to comprehend how people operated in what was often perceived to be an inhospitable and rapidly changing social environment. Because it was interested in analysing the major issues and features of 'modern' industrial society, sociology paid scant attention to such topics as art and dance, which were becoming increasingly marginalised with the march of industrialism. Indeed, the term sociology which is derived from the Latin word *socius* and the Greek *logos*, literally translated means the word of the social. But if the arts have been marginalised within sociology, dance has been marginalised threefold: first as an art, second as a practice which places the body at the centre of its discourse, and third as an activity which is viewed as a predominantly feminine mode of expression and representation. The anthropology of dance, as Royce (1980) has demonstrated, has been developing for over a hundred years and can be divided into five main categories of approach. There has also been a considerable amount of research interest in the body within anthropology, while classical sociology did not generate a thoroughgoing analysis of the body in society. The dualisms which enabled anthropology to direct its attention towards the body and dancing in traditional cultures, were contributory factors in sociology's neglect of the body and dance. It is interesting to note that where a concern with dance has occurred, it has largely emerged from the focus on working-class subcultures and youth. While dancing is marginalised in the dominant cultural tradition, it is a central interest to these structurally marginal groups whose ideas and practices are generally seen as (morally) suspect (sex, drugs and rock 'n' roll). The discussions of dance in subcultures and youth studies, as Ward (1993) points out, are generally couched in terms of the functions dance performs: escape from the boring routine of work (Chambers 1985, Frith 1978); a means of getting a sexual partner (Mungham 1976); an escape through 'fantasy' (McRobbie 1984); a primary symbol of 'resistance' for black youth (Brake 1985). This tendency to see dance in terms of something else is reminiscent of the treatment of dance in primitive societies summarised above. Although such authors as Frith, Chambers and McRobbie can hardly be called functionalist, and they do also recognise the expressive sensual character of dancing (the site where 'zones of socialised pleasures and individual desires entwine . . . in the "reason of the body" ' (Chambers 1985: 17)), there is a creeping functionalist rationale lurking beneath their discussions of dance. As such, there emerges a remarkable similarity between the analytic relation of subculture and dominant culture in subcultural analysis and that of 'primitive' and 'modern' culture which the rationalist accounts outlined above sustained: in other words, in relation to dance, subculture is to dominant culture as primitive is to modern culture: a dangerous, exotic, non-rational, marginal 'other'.

The marginality of dance within sociology is reflected in other academic fields. The philosophy of art, for the most part, has paid scant attention to dance in the past, often subsuming it under the wider heading of theatrical or performance arts. But dance, as I have indicated – and the literature seems to indicate this also – is very slippery and its meanings as Sparshott (1988) has argued are equivocal. Part of the problem in analysing dance lies in its transient quality: as you see it, so it has gone. As a result of this the reality of dance seems more elusive than painting and literature, which are relatively fixed in appearance. Although drama and music, like dance, are performance arts, they too appear to be more accessible to study than dance by virtue of the fact that a researcher can consult a text or a score. The absence of a universally accepted system for the recording and preservation of dances contributes to the difficulty of fixing dance's identity, and of grasping a strong sense of its tradition (Ziff 1981).

One of the most influential philosophical theories of dance this century is that by Susanne Langer (1953, 1957) which proposed that dance be viewed as a 'symbolic form' (see the Appendix for a discussion of Langer's theory of dance as a symbolic form). Langer's approach to dance aesthetics was extremely influential in the realms of dance theory in the 1960s and 1970s, largely I suspect because it enabled dance to gain a degree of autonomy and legitimacy in the arts. Langer's ideas have often been used uncritically by dance scholars because for some years they represented the most, and for some the only, comprehensive corpus of work in the philosophy of art. Moreover, the idea of dance as a symbolic form appeared to be based on truth because American dance at the time was dominated by an emphasis on non-literal movement. This view of dance as transformational began to be called into question by Sheets-Johnstone (1978) and Selma-Jean Cohen (1981), partly as a result of the emergence of the 'anti-illusionist' post-modern dance movement in the late 1960s and 1970s. Although philosophical inquiry of dance remains marginal to the philosophy of art, dance aesthetics can lay claim to a small but growing tradition (for example, Fancher and Myers 1981, McFee 1991, Redfern 1983, Sheets-Johnstone 1984, Sparshott 1988,).

Dance's peripheral status in sociology and philosophy reflects its marginal institutional position within contemporary culture. Art or performance dance remains largely a minority concern, in spite of the recent so-called 'dance boom' and attempts at mass marketing aspects of it. Other arts, such as painting and drama, are also minority concerns but, unlike dance, they have been extensively considered in literature from sociological and philosophical viewpoints. Fine art, drama, literature and music, are viewed as forms that have made significant contributions to the life of society, enriching its fabric and expressing the life of the times. Sparshott considers that it is naive to be surprised by the absence of philosophical literature on dance. In order for a philosophy of a particular art to emerge, he states that: 'It is necessary that the art should occupy at the relevant time a culturally relevant position, or that the ideology of the art could be integrated with a culturally prevalent ideology' (Sparshott 1988: 95). He argues that dance, unlike the other arts at various times, has never fulfilled the above criteria, and therefore, has not generated a significant corpus of philosophical literature; philosophical discourse is therefore conducted and proceeds through debate on particular areas of interest within the total field. The same argument can be applied to sociology. Its interests from the outset were focused on the problematic character of modern industrial society, and dance did not seem to feature strongly in that; and as long as that situation persisted the neglect of dance would endure, although there might be no sound grounds for persisting to ignore it. The fact of neglect, as Sparshott (1988) points out, is not as important as the consideration of what has occurred to bring this neglect into focus. Sparshott, of course, is referring to recent philosophical interest in dance, but the point is equally relevant to sociology. Dance, which straddles the high art/popular culture spectrum – as Brinson (1983) has argued and as the preceding discussion has indicated – is a 'social fact'. As such, it is an appropriate object of sociological inquiry, despite its hitherto marginalisation by sociology. However, if sociology is even to begin to address its neglect of dance, certain shifts in its discourse would have to take place. A space does seem to be opening up for such recognition to take place (McRobbie 1991, Thomas 1993, Ward 1993) and it is important to consider how this has been made possible.

To a large extent, the aforementioned gap has been created through the challenges to mainstream sociology, philosophy and cultural analysis emerging from poststructuralism, postmodernism and feminism entering into the critical frame. The discussion that follows does not constitute a detailed map of these areas; rather my concern is to provide an indication of the kinds of ideas and issues they have raised, which, in turn, have reverberated through sociology and cultural analysis.

Over the past twenty-five years, feminists have challenged the most cherished assumptions of sociology (see Harding 1987, Mitchell and Oakley 1986, Segal 1987, Stanley 1990). Mainstream sociology has come under attack before from different theoretical and political standpoints such as radical liberalism, phenomenology and neo-Marxism (exemplified by the work of C. Wright Mills in the 1950s, Alvin Gouldner in the 1960s, Harold Garfinkel in the 1970s, Jürgen Habermas in the 1970s). But, with the exception of Marxism perhaps, and even that has now fallen away, these critiques have not had the same impact on the spectrum of the social sciences and cultural criticism as those raised by feminists. Feminist sociologists have demonstrated the inherent androcentrism in sociology's choice of topics, methods and analyses. Classical sociology's legacy of value-freedom, it has been argued, has directed the focus of sociology in particular ways which have contributed to women's invisibility in sociological discourse (Millman and Kanter 1987, Sydie 1987). Feminist researches have challenged the privileging of such categories as objectivity over subjectivity, reason over emotion, mind over body, men over women, public over private (the dualisms of the Enlightenment legacy). Feminism, in its various strands and theoretical perspectives (see Harding 1987, Stanley 1990) has sought to bring women into the realms of visibility in sociology as knowing subjects, on both sides of the research fence – the researched and the researcher, the theory and the practice – and has advocated a reflexive practice. The concern to bring women into the discourse of sociology and to enable their voices to be heard entailed (a) a critical reappraisal of the dominant (patriarchal) representations of women in sociology and the wider cultural formation and (b) a consideration of those areas which had been traditionally associated with women and which had received little attention in sociology and cultural analyses. By insisting that women be brought into the critical frame, feminist writings have helped to push new and different aspects of cultural experience to the centre of these discourses. The kinds of issues and ideas that postmodernism and poststructuralism have generated have also impinged on sociology and cultural analysis.

The word 'postmodernism' is highly contentious. The issues surrounding postmodernism became the subject of much discussion and debate in the 1980s in a number of discursive arenas, including the arts, sociology, anthropology, philosophy and literary criticism, feminist analyses, cultural studies, geography and economics. Anyone who tries to delineate what postmodernism *is*, is immediately confronted with a variety of different levels of meaning and usage. However, a number of attempts have been made to set out and clarify the puzzling and often 'messy' issues that surround the thorny related terms of modernism/postmodernism and modernity/postmodernity (Bauman 1992, Boyne and Rattansi 1990, Featherstone 1988, Huyssen 1986). Although certain variations in emphasis and references are used in these 'maps' of modernism and postmodernism and in their relative differences, it is generally agreed that during the period since the end of the Second World War there has been a 'slowly emerging cultural transformation' in western societies for which the term 'post-modernism' may be suitable to describe the 'shift in sensibility, practices, and discourse formations' (Huyssen 1986: 186).

The *post* in postmodernism, as Andreas Huyssen (1986) notes, should provide a caution for those wishing to define the meaning of post-modernism within closed boundaries because it indicates its relational character. Boyne and Rattansi (1990), similarly, recognise that the 'distinctiveness' of postmodernism in relation to modernism is inescapably fuzzy around the edges. But they also point out that although the term lacks conceptual coherence, a certain unity is to be found in 'the paradox of a set of cultural projects united by a self-proclaimed commitment to heterogeneity, fragmentation and difference' (Boyne and Rattansi 1990: 9) and in the reaction to modernism. For Frederic Jameson (1985), the most salient stylistic features of postmodernism are: the erosion of 'key boundaries and separations', particularly the high/popular culture divide, 'pastiche', diversity, and a heightened awareness or 'schizophrenia', brought about through a reaction against 'established forms of high modernism . . . which conquered the university, the museum, the art gallery, the network, and the foundation' (Jameson 1985: 111).

Postmodernism is generally used in connection with developments in the arts and cultural products while postmodernity is characterised as a 'social, political and cultural configuration of which "postmodernism" is a constitutive element' (Boyne and Rattansi 1990).

Although the philosophical roots of postmodernism can be traced back to the late nineteenth century to the writings of Nietzsche, the word postmodernism first appeared in the 1930s to point to a slight resistance to modernism (Featherstone 1988). In the late 1950s it was used in literature to denote a concern for the loss of the cutting edge of the modernist movement. It was taken up in New York in the 1960s by literary critics and artists from different fields (Ihab Hassan, Leslie Fielder, Susan Sontag, John Cage, Robert Rauschenberg, Yvonne Rainer) as a response to the institutionalisation of modernism in the arts and in literature. In America in the 1970s and 1980s the term became commonplace across the arts, encompassing architecture, dance, theatre, painting, film and music. Huyssen (1986) suggests there is a historical distinction between the postmodernism of the 1960s, 1970s and 1980s. Postmodernism, according to Huyssen (1986), played itself out in the arena of popular culture and the critique of modernism's hostility towards mass culture has been a recurrent theme in aesthetic postmodernism. In the 1960s the postmodernists tried to revive the European tradition of modernism of the 1920s (like Duchamp) but they wanted to give it an American form (Warhol, Cage, Rauschenberg). As modernism became institutionalised in the 1950s, it came to be associated with conservative ideology and was used as a weapon in the propaganda war against communism. Although the postmodern imagination of the 1960s took a similar shape to that of European avant-gardism like dada and surrealism of the 1920s, Huyssen (1986) insists that it has to be seen against the backdrop of a specifically American socio-political arena of protest movements in the 1960s. The avant-garde edge of 1960s postmodernism was lost by the 1970s. The iconoclasm of pop had disappeared under the pressure of commercial culture, the counter-culture movement was increasingly seen as naive, and the merging of high/popular culture was cemented. Feminists in the arts and the cultural sciences and other minority groups began to explore their 'hidden', 'silenced' traditions and in so doing provided a different impetus to the critique of high culture and to the generation of alternate forms of cultural production (Huyssen 1986).

The ideas encapsulated in aesthetic postmodernism are perhaps more visible in architecture than in some of the other arts. Charles Jencks dates the symbolic death of modernism and the transition to postmodernism as having occurred at 3.32 p.m. on 15 July 1972 when the Puitt–Igoe Housing complex in St Louis was dynamited because it was considered to be an unfriendly environment for its low-paid inhabitants (Harvey 1989). Built in 1952, this development was a prize-winning variant of Le Corbusier's 'machine for modern living'. The 'tradition of the new' (Rosenberg 1962) in architecture which emerged out of the ashes of the Great War and the Russian Revolution, incorporated a vision of the renewal of society and wanted to create buildings which would contribute to that regeneration. Modernist architecture turned its back on the past and set out to design rational streamlined buildings for a new rational society using the tools and materials of modern technology. The social idealism embodied in modernist architecture was largely lost after the Second World War and the large-scale (public) housing projects which came to be built under the rubric of modernism became 'symbols of alienation, and dehumanization' (Huyssen 1986: 186), like the Puitt–Igoe housing project. After 1972, the ideas inscribed in 'high modernism' gave way increasingly under the sway of a diversity of new ideas and possibilities. The concern focused on designing for people rather than prescribing theoretical ideals and plans. The starkness of those 1950s and 1960s concrete tower blocks – which had neither decoration, focal point nor individualism, and had helped to create vast landscapes of urban blight rather than renewal – increasingly gave way to ornamentation and a mixing and matching of different styles and materials.

If postmodernism emerged in America in the 1960s it travelled to Europe in the 1970s and was taken up by such writers as Jean-François Lyotard, Julia Kristeva and Jürgen Habermas. In the US critics also began to discuss overlaps between postmodernism and poststructuralism, a recent import from Europe (Harvey 1989).

Although poststructuralism and postmodernism are often used inter-
changeably, they are not necessarily the same thing (see Boyne and
Rattansi 1990, Huyssen 1986, McNay 1992, Phillipson 1985, Smart 1993
for the distinctions). Just to complicate matters further, there is also
diversity of thought and approach sheltering under each of the terms
(see Eagleton 1983, McNay 1992, Smart 1993).

The term poststructuralism usually refers to a number of initiatives in
French intellectual thought (literary criticism, philosophy, history) which
began to gain ground after the collapse of the socialist led student revolts
in 1968 which had swept across Europe. Like postmodernism, poststructuralism is a relative term. 'Poststructuralism', according to Terry Eagleton
(1983: 142), 'was a product of that blend of euphoria and disillusionment,
liberation and dissipation, carnival and catastrophe, which was 1968.
Unable to break the structures of state–power, poststructuralism found it
possible instead to subvert the structures of language.' Among the names
associated with poststructuralism are Jacques Derrida, Michel Foucault,
Jacques Lacan, Julia Kristeva and Jean Baudrillard. Despite differences in
the projects and the analyses of the various thinkers who are dubbed as
poststructuralists, there are particular suppositions regarding 'language,
meaning and subjectivity' that they share in common (Weedon 1987).

Central to poststructuralist thought, as Lois McNay (1992) has argued,
is the critique of the human subject or *cogito* which was inscribed in
Cartesianism and hitherto has dominated western cultural thought. The
idea of the individual as a self-reflecting, rational, unified, fixed subject
is rejected in favour of a dislocated, contradictory, fragmented subjectivity
which is not fixed but is reconstituted in language on each and every
occasion we speak. The subject, in poststructuralist theory, contrary to
the dominant western humanist tradition, is constructed in and through
language. Poststructuralism takes its starting point from Saussure's struc-
turalist linguistic theory (1974) in which language is viewed as an abstract
system of relational signs which are arbitrary and extra-individual. Saussure
conceived of language as a closed system where the signifiers (sounds)
and the signifieds (meanings) are arbitrary, and the arbitrary relation of
the signifier to the signified is fixed by social convention. Poststructuralism
rejects the idea of language as a closed system and the relative fixing of
the elements of the sign in preference for the notion that the signifieds
of language are never fixed but are always in the process of being
'deferred'. The signifiers and the signifieds are 'continually breaking apart
and reattaching in new combinations' (Harvey 1989: 49). The focus
moves away from the 'logocentrism' of the speaking subject (the word)
to the 'text', thus the speaking subject is decentred. Cultural existence
is seen as a succession of texts which converge with other texts that,
in turn, produce other texts. Writers create texts on the basis of all
other texts they have ever come across and readers read texts on the
same principle. This 'collage/montage' effect or 'intertextuality' has an

existence of its own which gives rise to multiple (unintended) readings and meanings (Harvey 1989). This heralds the 'death of the author', traditionally cast as the privileged speaking subject who creates the text and is the sole arbiter of meaning and, in turn, gives rise to the notion of 'birth of the reader' (the consumer) as 'deconstructing' and combining the elements in any way they like (Harvey 1989: 49). Thus, the idea of 'real', 'true', 'fixed' meanings is called into question.

In the late 1970s poststructuralist theories, particularly those of Derrida and Barthes, crossed the Atlantic and became entwined with a rekindled interest in philosophical pragmatism in philosophy and literary and cultural criticism. The battle cry of philosophical discourse was raised against humanism and the enlightenment tradition, although the critical thrust of the poststructuralist enterprise melted into a form of neo-conservatism (see Eagleton 1983, Huyssen 1986 and McNay 1992). The critique of the enlightenment project (modernity) is a pivotal theme in the modernism/postmodernism debate, as are notions of intertextuality, difference, plurality, reflexivity. For some, such as Habermas (1985), who wishes to reinstate the emancipatory potential inscribed in the enlightenment project into late twentieth-century culture, postmodernism and poststructuralism represent neo-conservatism. For others, like Lyotard (1984), on the other hand, the erosion of the 'metanarratives' or 'grand narratives' of rationalist scientific discourse after 1945 points to a new mood or the 'postmodern condition'.

By the 1980s the modernism/postmodernism debate in the arts and wider cultural arena and the modernity/postmodernity debate in the cultural sciences became a highly contested area. The terms modernity and postmodernity, as Mike Featherstone (1988) has noted, suggest an epochal meaning. The idea of modernity came into being around the Renaissance period. It was defined in terms of the relation between modern and ancient. The more familiar use of modernity is that which I discussed above in relation to classical sociology's concern to understand the processes of development which led to the collapse of feudalism and the emergence and establishment of modern industrial capitalist society. These processes were not always viewed from a promodernity standpoint. Max Weber (1976), for example, viewed the gathering processes of rationalisation which constituted the cornerstone of modern capitalism as a potential 'iron cage' from which there could be no escape. Emile Durkheim, too, despite the obvious positive attitude towards industrialism exhibited in his early work (1964), nevertheless recognised that the increasing differentiation within society could lead to 'anomie', or an erosion of sociality.

The notion of postmodernity intimates a shift or a break with modernity, a different social world ordered on different or new principles – a postmodern industrial order organised around the changes and developments in technology and information – moving from a 'productive' to a 'reproductive' social formation in which distinctions between appearance and reality are being rubbed out (Featherstone 1988: 198). The idea of an 'epochal' shift is evidenced in the writings of Lyotard and Baudrillard. Although Jameson (1985) sees that there has been a shift in the global economic order since 1945, he rejects the idea of a total epochal shift to postindustrialism or postcapitalism. Rather, for Jameson, capitalism is not dead, it has developed new energies and strategies. The emergence of postmodernism is closely related to the emergence of this 'new moment' of late capitalism. In consumer or multinational capitalism, according to Jameson (1985), representation has become a central focus of economic activity. Culture has become commodified; style, images, representations, no longer embellish economic products, rather, they are themselves products. The eruption and expansion of cultural commodities and representations leads to what Baudrillard calls a 'political economy of the sign' where the signs have lost their referential function (as indicators of the economic) and instead there is a 'continuous play of signifiers' which have their own logic (Connor 1989: 51-2).

The idea of a postmodern mood or attitude, 'the aestheticisation of everyday life' (Featherstone 1991b), directs attention towards another meaning of modernity/postmodernity. In Lyotard's work the meaning of the experience of modernity ('modernité') is taken on board (Featherstone 1991a). Here, the quality of modernity in modern life gives rise to the notion of a break with time, of ephemerality, of a break with tradition in favour of constant renewal. This sense of being modern resonates with one aspect of Baudelaire's much quoted definition of modernity published in 1863, 'Modernity is the transient, the fleeting, the contingent; it is one half of art, the other being the eternal and immutable' (Harvey 1989: 10). Postmodernism, by and large, however, was founded on a specific image of modernism represented by high modernism and as a consequence can be criticised for offering an all too unitary view of modernism. Some of the features of postmodernism which are seen as a mark of its otherness to modernism, are also to be found in the wider view of modernism captured in Baudelaire's writing. 'The basic features of modernism' as Featherstone has argued, are:

> An aesthetic self-consciousness and reflexiveness; a rejection of narrative structures in favour of simultaneity and montage; an exploration of the para-doxical, ambiguous and uncertain nature of reality; and a rejection of the notion of an integrated personality in favour of an emphasis upon the destructured, dehumanized subject.
>
> (Featherstone 1988: 202)

As most of these features are encapsulated in many definitions of postmodernism, it becomes questionable whether it is appropriate to speak of postmodernism as an aesthetic and/or cultural configuration that is distinct from and oppositional to modernism. What is clear, however, is that if postmodernism started out as an aesthetic project in the 1960s, it permeated into the discourses of philosophy, social sciences and cultural analysis and latterly feminism in the 1980s, contributing to a trend running through these frameworks which Roy Boyne and Ali Rattansi (1990) suggest is characterised by 'a series of crises of representation' where:

> older modes of defining, appropriating and recomposing the objects of artistic, philosophical, literary and social scientific languages are no longer credible and in which one common aspect is the dissolution of the very boundary between language and its object, this in turn being related to the acceptance of the inevitability of a plurality of perspectives and the dissolution of various older polarities (popular/elite forms, subject/object) and boundaries (for instance between disciplines such as philosophy, sociology, history and psychoanalysis).
>
> (Boyne and Rattansi 1990: 12)

Prior to the mid-1970s, sociologists who were interested in the arts and culture were situated on the margins of the discipline. Moreover, such interest was 'often considered eccentric and dilettantish' (Featherstone 1991a) and not quite proper sociology. At the same time there was little cross-over between the sociology of art and culture and, say, art or literary criticism, aesthetics, and art or cultural history. For the most part, when sociology did examine art, it approached the work extrinsically; that is, it typically viewed art in terms of a reflection of something outside itself, such as the social conditions of existence; the author's biography and/or intentions; composition of the audience, or 'taste' (see Eagleton 1977, Filmer 1978, Wolff 1981 for critical appraisals of these early studies). What was lacking in extrinsically oriented studies is the factor that Herbert Marcuse (1979) termed, 'the aesthetic dimension'. Marcuse's critique was directed specifically at reductionist Marxist analyses but his observations are also appropriate to the early, largely positivist analyses. When art is treated in a definite and somewhat mechanical relation to society, as in these early studies, the examination becomes overloaded in the direction of content to the neglect of the form. The specific qualities of the art form or of the particular art work were not discussed, because, generally speaking, the nature of the aesthetic was not considered sociologically significant, or was taken as unproblematic.

This essentially reductionist outlook was called into question in the late 1970s by some sociologists and social historians of art (Kristeva 1980, Marcuse 1979, Williams 1977) who argued that an understanding of the specificity of art should be included in the discussion of art in society. Although the theoretical perspectives of writers who sought to include the aesthetic dimension varied, there was general agreement that art has some kind of relative autonomy and that an analysis of the work itself can lead to insights which a purely extrinsic approach could not but fail to reveal (for a discussion of the various ways in which the notion of specificity of art has been used, see Wolff 1983: 95–104). At the same time, these writers pointed to the fact that the very notions of the aesthetic with which we work are in themselves historically constructed; they have a social dimension.

Although theoretical considerations in the realm of art and culture were situated in the margins of sociology in the 1970s, they have become a legitimate area of sociological inquiry. The relaxing of traditional disciplinary boundaries in sociology has been accompanied by a shift of interest towards the theorisation of culture. Culture is the common thread that runs through the range of meanings which prevail under the banner of postmodernism (Featherstone 1988). In postmodernism's armoury the conceptual tools and justificatory strategies for analysing and critiquing texts are aesthetic and its models for life are organised around the aesthetics of life (the aestheticisation of everyday life; art as life/life as art) (Featherstone 1991a). Cultural questions and aesthetic considerations have been propelled onto the sociological stage by postmodernism's aestheticism. But it is important to note that the rise of interest in other areas such as feminism, psychoanalysis, semiotics, Marxism and cultural studies have also contributed towards putting cultural issues on the agenda.

The elevation of culture to the centre of sociological theorising and the interest in pursuing interdisciplinary frameworks have helped to make way for dance as a cultural product to emerge into the sociological frame. Earlier I argued that the peripheral role of dance in contemporary culture was contingent upon the marginalization of the arts, the body and women, through the processes of modernity. Women, as Huyssen (1986) has argued, have been also associated with the *mass*, which is modernism's other and they have been located and represented in terms of their bodies. Part of the potential of postmodernism and poststructuralism lies in their emphasis and celebration of difference(s) which, in turn, opens up the possibility of other (marginal) voices to be heard and accepted as legitimate (dance, women, bodies). The other side of the coin, however, is that this plurality lends itself well to the idea that 'anything goes' (a criticism often levelled at postmodernism by its detractors). But in that case an appeal could still be made for a sociology of dance. If other aspects of culture are coming under the scrutiny of sociology, why not dance, which, as I have argued takes place in a variety of socio-cultural contexts?

But that emergent space has also been given impetus by an upsurge of interest in the topic of the body in a range of disciplines. If postmodernism was the buzz word of the 1980s, the subject of the body must be close on its heels. The body has entered into the titles of a number of recent books, journal editions, and academic papers in such diverse areas as: 'social history, clinical practice in psychiatry and psychoanalysis, anthropology, and cognitive science and philosophy' (Frank 1991:37). Sociology, as I have indicated, did not develop a systematic analysis of the body, unlike anthropology. Although sociology has been slow to topicalise the body in comparison with other academic discourses, nevertheless, the body is being dragged into its theoretical sights (Featherstone *et al.* 1991, O'Neill 1985, Shilling 1993, Synott 1993, Turner 1984).

In part, the emergence of the body into the discourses of sociology is tied up with the 'crises of representation'. Poststructuralism, postmodernism and feminism have instigated their respective attacks on the human subject, the enlightenment project and patriarchy, by focusing their telescopes on the body. They have revealed the centrality of the body as a site of discourse and of social control. They have elucidated how bodies have been objectified and subjectified through a range of discourses. Poststructuralist feminists like Luce Irigaray and Hélène Cixous, for example, have argued for a rewriting of the body on the grounds that the feminine has been devalued and repressed through the logocentric structure of language in patriarchal culture (Fraser and Bartky 1992). By elucidating how bodies have been objectified and subjectified through a range of discourses, poststructuralism and postmodernism have contributed further to the possibility of dance being afforded a more substantial cultural voice. The body in western theatrical dance is the primary means of expression and its representational form, at least since the nineteenth century, has been associated with the feminine body. A substantial part of the discussion of this book focuses on the development of American modern dance in the 1920s and 1930s. It could be suggested that through their material rewriting of the dancing body, modern dancers such as Martha Graham and Doris Humphrey were breaking through the dominant symbolic order of both dance and language. Their iconoclastic images worked against tradition in an aesthetic modernist fashion (the 'tradition of the new' (Rosenberg 1962)). As the work became codified and merged into the dominant corpus, so a new generation of postmodern dancers began in the 1960s to launch their attack on modern dance on the grounds that it had lost its cutting edge through its institutionalisation into the dominant culture. Postmodernism and poststructuralism are seductive because they create spaces for dance, the body and women. As I indicated earlier, several of the new generation of dance scholars have been drawn to these theories (Adair 1991, Dempster 1993, Foster 1986, Sanchez-Colberg 1993). In part, the appeal of these theories is somewhat akin to the interest that Susanne Langer's work generated in the 1950s and 1960s. Langer's concept of dance as a symbolic form afforded dance the possibility of a status (as an art in its own right) that it had seldom been accorded in academia. Postmodernism and poststructuralism have entered the dance arena through a new generation of dance scholars jostling to find their place *vis-à-vis* the old garde.

Although the central tenets of these frameworks offer dance the possibility of a new found legitimacy, I do not want to suggest that the analysis of dance *should* be launched from within a postmodern/

poststructural sociology. Postmodern sociology, it would seem, is a contradiction in terms. No matter how blurred sociology has become round the edges, it is nevertheless a product of modernity; part of the enlightenment legacy, postmodernism's reviled other. As Featherstone (1988) has argued, any attempt to construct a postmodern sociology is ultimately doomed to failure because it could not be other than a flawed attempt to construct another grand narrative. Moreover, although I am intrigued by postmodernism, I am most certainly not a convert. In agreement with Huyssen (1986), I consider that it tends to offer an all too unitary view of modernism. While I welcome the critique of absolutism, I do not wish to ascribe to the view that *any* account will do; both of which can be derived from the relativisation of accounts inscribed in the celebration of the seemingly endless play of signifiers. Although I do not wish to fall victim to the rationalist accounting procedures that have bedevilled cultural studies discussions of dance, I am concerned, none the less, to demonstrate dance's sociality and, in so doing, propose it as a legitimate area of sociological inquiry. As Featherstone (1988) has argued, although a postmodern sociology would have to 'abandon its generalizing social science ambitions', the implications of its critical analytic mode can be instructive. It invites us to question how analytic models are constructed, to question the ideas that underpin them, and the authorial voice (the sociologist) that speaks of and on behalf of the 'other'. Like Zigmund Bauman (1992), Featherstone (1988) considers that in order to understand the changes in contemporary culture, it is necessary to forego the 'attractions of a postmodern sociology' in favour of the development of a sociology of postmodernism.

The subject under discussion here, however, is the sociology of dance, not postmodernism. One of the central concerns of this book is to offer a sociological approach to the study of performance dance in western culture that provides a concrete working model for empirical study. One of the major problems in analysing dance is that, like painting or sculpture, it expresses itself non-verbally. In a rationalised and word-oriented culture, the non-verbal also comes under the scrutiny of rationalism (as we have seen with, for example, cultural studies and early anthropological approaches to dance). Indeed, the very wording that is used to describe the form of communication of dance, *non*-verbal, implies that dance's identity and difference are defined in terms of a lack *vis-à-vis* the dominant mode of communication, the verbal. Sociology, in the past, as I have pointed out, has typically approached the study of art extrinsically. However, following on from the earlier discussion of the idea of a sociology of art that guarantees the specificity of art, dance is viewed, here, as a reflexive bodily practice which inheres sets of emergent meanings (the aesthetic dimension). The intention is to generate an approach that seeks to elucidate these meanings and thereby preserve dance's reflexive character. The concern is not simply to set out a theoretical framework for a sociology of dance, but also to indicate the use of this framework for analysing dance forms and dances by using the early development of American modern dance and Graham's *Appalachian Spring* (1944) as the focus of discussion. It should be pointed out, however, that I am not advocating that theatre or art dance should have a privileged status in the development of a sociology of dance. In fact, as discussed above, when sociologists or cultural analysts do turn their attention to dance they tend to be interested in looking at popular dance forms rather than performance dance. There is no intrinsic reason for not choosing postmodern dance, dance on television or film, current trends in popular or disco dance and so forth. Nor do I wish to claim a higher status for 'western' art dance to the neglect of other 'ethnic' or cultural forms. The selection of this case study is a matter of personal interest, but, as I shall argue below, there are sound sociological grounds for examining this period of development and Graham's dance. Clearly, these are important in making the topic a legitimate area of sociological investigation.

It should be clear from the preceding discussion that sociologists who wish to pursue an interest in dance can still expect little direct guidance from the discipline. The absence of a significant corpus of sociological material on dance to guide an examination such as that described above entails that certain choices have to be made concerning how the analysis should proceed. When sociology set out to establish itself in the late nineteenth century, it presented itself as a way of seeing the social world and a mode of analysis which could be applied to a number of other disciplines such as history, philosophy and ethics. As a result, as E.P. Thompson (1982) has pointed out, it has sometimes been criticised by, and encountered resistance from, other disciplines for its so-called sociological imperialism. It should be stressed from the outset that I am not arguing for a kind of sociological imperialism and that in order to take account of dance as a social, cultural and artistic force, the approach which I seek to develop here is interdisciplinary in outlook. It draws on related areas such as dance aesthetics/dance theory, movement studies, dance cultural history, art cultural history, American cultural history, dance anthropology and social study of the body and everyday movement. Indeed, I would want to maintain that dance offers an interesting site for sociological study precisely because it encompasses a number of different elements and can be studied from other viewpoints. And it is here that postmodernism is most instructive because it seeks to show that there is (positive) strength in the margins.

The major thrust of the discussion that follows is to offer an approach to the sociology of dance to, in this instance, the emergence and early development of modern dance. But before I go on to do that I want to pause for a moment and draw attention to the areas which have particularly informed my thinking: anthropology of dance, dance aesthetics and, in particular, the phenomenological approach and the social study of the body and everyday movement (see the Appendix for a fuller discussion of the issues and insights which these areas offered). Anthropology provides a much more integrated approach to the study of dance in society than sociology. None the less, because anthropology began in the last century by studying small-scale 'exotic' societies (usually the societies of the 'other') and, for the most part, has continued to do so to the present day, there are certain problems attached to using its framework as a model for a sociological analysis of dance in a western industrial culture. Nevertheless, it does offer certain insights into the study of dance in society that are illuminating for a sociology of dance. Similarly, the philosophy of dance, by its very complexion, directs its concerns towards questions of the nature and meaning of dance, the relationship of form to content and so forth and not, as a overtly sociological inquiry would demand, to a consideration of the relation of dance to a particular society at a given point in time. But, again, as Wolff (1983) has argued, the sociology of art ignores the aesthetic dimensions of art at its peril. The body is the primary medium of expression in western theatrical dance. Although there is a lack of sociological material on dance there is nevertheless a great deal of work on the body and everyday movement in society, largely from the area of cultural and social anthropology, which can contribute to an understanding of the way in which the body is perceived and represented in western dance (see Thomas 1993 for a discussion of this in relation to the social construction of gender).

The analytic approach to the sociology of dance proposed here is situated within the broad span of what is generally referred to as the 'interpretive' tradition of the social sciences (see Geertz 1975: 3–33 for an illuminating discussion of this tradition and his approach which he terms 'thick description'). The intent is to maintain the integrity of an interpretive sociology as a mode seeing and analysing the social world on the one hand and, on the other, the specificity and reflexive character of dance as an art form. With these considerations in view, the remainder of this chapter sets out to argue for an examination of, in this instance, early American modern dance which incorporates a sociological approach from two perspectives: *extrinsic* and *intrinsic*. The extrinsic approach examines the social context of the development of American modern dance: it contains the sociological element. By contrast, the intrinsic approach considers the qualities that are specific to dance form itself, and this addresses the aesthetic components. On first view, these two perspectives appear to be almost diametrically opposed to each other but, none the less, as demonstrated below, both are crucial for a fuller understanding of the topic in question.

The extrinsic approach takes its point of departure from the consideration that dance is a social fact and, as such, it is generated from and within a particular social milieu and on a number of different but interrelated levels, it speaks of the life of a culture. That is, dance stands in a social relation to the wider cultural formation, to the other arts, and to the tradition of dance itself. Anthropological studies of dance provide sufficient evidence to support and sustain this view (Boas 1972, Kaeli'inohomoku 1979, Radcliffe-Brown 1964, Royce 1980).

American modern dance began to develop in the late 1920s and early 1930s through the work of a group of individual iconoclasts, the most notable of whom were Martha Graham, Doris Humphrey, Charles Weidman and Helen Tamiris. The term modern dance is rather misleading because it implies a uniform system, whereas one of the most striking features of its development was that of a diversity of forms. Although there were marked similarities throughout the modern dance field, as John Martin has stated: '[The] modern dance is not a system; it is a point of view' (Martin 1972: 20). In general, modern dance refers to performance art dance that is not founded on the *danse d'école* (ballet) nor in the various forms of 'popular' dance entertainment, although, as we shall see, it does stand in relation to these.

Modern dance began to germinate in America around the turn of the century, at a time when rapid technological advances were taking place and America was beginning to become conscious of the fact that it lacked significant art forms and cultural institutions that it would rightly call its own. From around the turn of the century, Americans became increasingly concerned to understand the origins and distinctive characteristics of the American way of life. This concern reached its peak during the period of isolationism after the First World War. It is evidenced in most of the arts and in academic fields such as history at the time. The 'compulsive desire' for Americans to understand their own character and tradition, as Schlatter (1962: 28) has argued, 'is a function of the shortness of the American past', the polyglot composition of its people and 'the derivative nature of American culture'.

Unlike the creative dance iconoclasts of the 1920s and 1930s, who established themselves firmly in America before they took their dance works to Europe, the major forerunners of American modern dance, Loïe Fuller, Isadora Duncan, Maud Allan and Ruth St Denis, had to go to Europe to gain acclaim for their dance. Of these four, only St Denis, who returned to live and work primarily in America, became accepted wholeheartedly by the American public.

In 1914, St Denis and another American dancer Ted Shawn formed a partnership, established the Denishawn company and in 1915 they formed the first company school in Los Angeles, California. From this institution there emerged a significant number of figures of American modern dance: Martha Graham and her musical director Louis Horst; Doris Humphrey; her partner Charles Weidman and their costume designer Pauline Lawrence. Although St Denis had a direct influence on American modern dance, Fuller, Duncan and, to a lesser degree, Allan are also important in this context. In their different ways all of these dancers wanted dance to be treated as a high art. That they had to leave their native soil for the shores of Europe in order to be treated seriously, indicates something of the position of dance in America during the latter part of the nineteenth century.

Theatrical dance in late nineteenth-century America was confined overwhelmingly to the field of popular entertainment, such as the minstrel shows, chorus lines and speciality acts in vaudeville, and the elaborate extravaganzas like *The Black Crook* (1866). Nineteenth-century America did not develop a 'serious' dance tradition. The codified form of serious western theatrical dance, the ballet, did not take root in American soil to a sufficient degree to enable the establishment of a sustained tradition (Banes 1980). Although dance traditionally was afforded a low social status and dancers were treated as social outcasts in America, it would be erroneous to assume that serious theatrical dance was entirely unknown there before the twentieth century (for examples see Magriel 1978, Ruyter 1979, Swift 1980). None the less, as Nancy Ruyter (1979) has argued, it was not before the advent of modern dance and the emergence of an American style of ballet in the late 1930s and 1940s that dance began to emerge as a significant feature of American culture. By the 1950s, dancers, e.g. Graham, were asked to represent the country abroad. This shift in the role of dance in America, from one of social outcast to that of cultural ambassador, is significant enough to warrant a sociological investigation of its emergence and development.

In order to understand the sociological implications of something like American modern dance it would be necessary to consider: the role of dance in American culture prior to its emergence; why it emerged in the late 1920s and early 1930s; how it related to what was happening in the wider social formation and other arts in America at that time; how it stood in relation to the classical and romantic tradition of dance; and how it developed over time. The focus of the extrinsic approach, then, is directed overwhelmingly towards a consideration of the socio-institutional features of dance. To put it in simple terms, the idea is to peel away the layers to look under the surface to uncover interconnections that are not immediately available to the eye in order to build up a composite (but not complete) image or a photo-montage of the role of dance in America.

As indicated above, America did not give rise to a sustained art dance tradition until the third decade of the present century. The extrinsic approach in this instance would seek to explore the contingent features that contributed to this predicament. An examination of the relation between theatrical dance and American society prior to the twentieth century, as I shall argue later, can point to the consideration that, in part, a combination of the legacy of Puritanism and frontierism prevented the establishment of a sustained art dance tradition modelled on European ballet. Many of the features that Puritanism and frontierism promoted, and that helped to form the mythic idea of the 'American character', were a negation of the élitist character of European culture out of which ballet was forged. At the same time, as I hope to show, in major features of its foundation, American modern dance reflected dominant aspects of the idea of the American character which had been fostered by Puritanism and frontierism: non-conformism, individualism, equalitarianism and functionalism. These were not only features of non-academic dance in America but also of twentieth-century American art (Rose 1967). Dance, as I shall argue, began to come of age in America when it incorporated some of the striking features of the culture. One of the salient features that made modern dance distinct from Denishawn, Duncan and the other interpretive dancers was that it invoked systematically the desire to draw on and communicate, to the American public, what they perceived to be their difference and specificity from other cultures – particularly European culture. This desire to communicate the American experience became particularly important to many artists and writers during the 1930s during the depression. But dancers like Graham and Humphrey also wanted to make dance an independent art, and in accordance with the canons of modernism, they emphasised the primacy of movement over all other aspects of theatrical performance. Therefore, their work can also be examined in terms of a wider international modern art movement and its consequences for American culture.

The discussion above is intended to give an indication of some of the issues that an extrinsic examination of American modern dance would be required to address. It should be clear from this that the extrinsic approach addresses its questions to the socio-historical context of the emergence and development of American modern dance. But if the examination were to be left at this point, dance would be being viewed, here, as little more than a reflection of aspects of society. This would result in a somewhat reductionist and mechanistic approach to the study of dance in particular and, by implication, to art in general. Although both modern dance and American art reflected dominant aspects of the idea of the American character, they were not exhausted by them, nor did they mirror them in a correspondential sense. Art and reality (itself a social construction) are not interchangeable; rather, as Marcuse (1979) has argued, the former retains an essential otherness to reality.

In agreement with Wolff's (1983) idea of a sociology of art that guarantees the specificity of art, I want to propose that the socio-historical and the aesthetic dimensions of a phenomenon like American modern dance cannot and should not be reduced to a single dimension. This irreducibility follows on from the contention that dance is primarily a mode of reflexive bodily communication that generates meanings through its specific form. That form, as Sheets-Johnstone (1979) has argued, exists in its own space and time. That is, unlike a painting or a novel, the dance work is never fixed at any one point in space and time but is always in the process of becoming the work itself, from the beginning to the end. In that sense each and every dance is unique. The view taken here is that dance does not simply reflect reality but, rather, it creates its own life-world through its form; it transforms reality into its own particular context. For example, Graham's *Primitive Mysteries* (1931) is not a re-enactment of the primitive religious rituals of the Southwest American Indians. The dance can be seen to fall under the category of primitivism. The primitiv-*ism* of *Primitive Mysteries* is generated through the idea of formal ritual, the solemnity of the procession, moving in a circle in unison, and the use of whole body movement juxtaposed with segmental movement. The dance takes the core of the rituals and transforms them into the context of a choreographic format through distortion, stylisation, rhythm and so on. Similarly, although Humphrey drew heavily on aspects of the rituals and beliefs of the Shaker sect for her dance *The Shakers* (1931), the work does not constitute an authentic reflection of the reality of Shakerism. To begin with, the ritual practices of the Shakers, as Edward Andrews (1967) has shown, changed and developed over some hundred and fifty years. Humphrey managed to condense the essences of these into a symbolic movement form in the space of about nine minutes in 'real' time. Moreover, the dance movement is not an exact copy of the Shakers' movement practices. Yet again Graham's *Appalachian Spring* (1944), which will be discussed more fully towards the end of this book, should not be viewed as a reflection of a nineteenth-century frontier wedding, just as the musical folklore that pervades Aaron Copland's music for the work is not an authentic rendering of the Shaker hymn *Simple Gifts*. However, almost from the opening of the dance it is recognisable as a piece of Americana. Its created world is founded on conceptions of American frontier life in the last century. These conceptions are not individual but are shared, which, in part, allows for the almost immediate recognisability of the dance. There would be little possibility of anyone vaguely familiar with American culture locating the thematic content of *Appalachian Spring* in terms of, for example, Japanese culture. At the same time, the dance does not depict the real pioneer life 'out there'. It creates its own life-world through its specific interpretive medium, which in the case of American modern dance is 'significant movement' (Graham 1968b). In dance works such as *Appalachian Spring*, as in the works of the majority of early modern dancers, the emphasis is placed on non-literal movement. Ordinary movement or gesture is taken from its source and is trans-formed through a movement idea into the dance context and developed into a condensed symbolic form. On the one hand, then, as I hope to demonstrate, *Appalachian Spring* is locatable in terms of the context of American culture, in that sense it is denotative; but, on the other hand, its movement form is symbolic and in that sense the work is connotative.

Dance does not easily lend itself to realism, because of the transformative character of movement involved (see Prickett 1992 for an interesting discussion on this issue with regard to revolutionary dance in America in the 1930s). Although we might have difficulty in defining precisely what dance is, and of course, concepts change over time, it is recognisable, none the less, as an encoded system which inheres particular stylistic qualities. As Margaret Lloyd (1974) pointed out, if anyone tried to walk down the street using, for example, a Graham walk, he or she would be looked upon as extremely odd by other pedestrians. Conversely, if dancers moved completely 'naturally' in the dance context, it would not be treated as dance. The idea of transformation, I would argue, stands for aspects of postmodern dance which stress 'natural' movement as well as consciously created symbolic forms like modern dance.

In order to uncover its symbolic character and thereby elucidate its potential for meaning, it is necessary to examine the intrinsic qualities of the dance. In the case of American modern dance this would involve a consideration of the movement, music, decor and so on. But I want to go further than this and propose, on the basis of the evidence provided by dance anthropologists such as Judith Lynne Hanna (1980) and Joanne Kaeli'inohomoku (1979), that through its interpretive and connotative features, dance is reflective upon the social world. This means that dance is being viewed as not only speaking *of* the social milieu in which it is created and performed, but also as speaking *to* it. It follows from this that if the dance itself can provide a point of reference for interpretations of culture, it is appropriate that a sociological inquiry be extended to an examination of dance works.

The extrinsic perspective that involves analysing the social, denotative features of dance and the intrinsic perspective that considers the aesthetic, connotative features, stand in a tense relation to each other. One way of exploring the tension between the extrinsic and intrinsic perspectives is to examine the relationship between everyday movement and dance movement. As a consciously articulated movement form American modern dance shares certain important variables with everyday movement. Both have the same substance, movement created in time and space; in both forms, the body is the medium of expression. Modern dance, however, is readily recognisable as an encoded system. It has particular stylistic qualities that are understandable as dance.

In everyday life, ordinary movement, for the most part, is not perceived of as an encoded system. The work of Hall (1969, 1973) on proxemics, Birdwhistell (1973) on kinesics, and that of the Durkheimian-oriented thinkers, such as Douglas (1970a,b, 1975, 1978) on body symbolism, clearly demonstrates that everyday movement is not quite as 'natural' or 'individual' as is commonly thought. The Durkheimian tradition of thought is particularly pertinent to the present discussion because it directs its attention towards the consideration of the social aspects of the human body. That is, a specifically sociological approach to the study of the human body and everyday movement, wherein the body is treated as a symbol of society.

American modern dance, as a symbolic art form, consciously attends to its bodily techniques through its encoded system. It is reflexive upon everyday movement. The work of the Durkheimians shows that 'natural' everyday movement is also a symbolic form with an encoded system, but it is treated by societal members as natural (non-social) behaviour. That is, its symbolism, unlike that of dance, is implicit. As an encoded system, everyday movement stands in a particular relation to the society in which it is expressed. In this light, everyday movement can be seen to be as much a socio-cultural phenomenon as American modern dance. Because everyday gesture is meaningful in its social context – although, for the most part, its signification remains out of awareness – it is possible to gain some insight into the emergent meanings that dance engenders by pointing to the transformation of everyday movement into dance movement. In order to consider how dance transforms everyday movement into its own context, a detailed examination of a specific dance is required; in this instance, a dance from the era of American modern dance under consideration, such as *Appalachian Spring*.

There are several sound sociological grounds for choosing to analyse *Appalachian Spring* (1944). To begin with, it can be seen as the culminating point of Graham's Americana period. On an extrinsic level, the dance can be analysed in terms of Graham's development away from a recital format, with the minimum of theatricality in terms of costume, music and setting, and towards that of an integrated dance theatre. It can also be viewed in terms of the wider concerns of modern dancers at that time to generate a strong American dance culture. Moreover, its thematic concerns resonated with a number of issues that engaged the country during the Depression years of the 1930s. Furthermore, this work is the result of a collaboration between two highly influential figures in the development of American modern dance and American art music, Martha Graham and Aaron Copland. These two prominent American artists collaborated with each other for the first and the last time with *Appalachian Spring*, although Graham did create a dance called *Dithyrambic* to Copland's *Piano Variations* in 1931. Copland and Graham, as I shall show, were not only ardent modernists in the late 1920s, they were also conceptual Americanists and both began producing Americanist works around the middle 1930s. As such, their work can be used to exemplify the concerns of many American artists in the 1930s and early 1940s. Therefore, *Appalachian Spring* provides a crucial siting for an examination of the history of modern dance and modern music in America.

Furthermore, *Appalachian Spring* offers a point of reference in exploring the relation between the *extrinsic* and *intrinsic* features of dance. Through its specific movement symbolism, the dance generates a set of emergent meanings concerning pioneerism, Puritanism and individualism, that provide for cultural interpretations of American history. The emergent meanings that the symbolism engenders stand in a relational tension to the various parts within the dance and to other external referents. As such, the totality of the dance is always more than the sum of its parts or the social conditions in which it emerged. This book, then, proposes a sociology of dance that elucidates not only how dance is understandable as a feature of the socio-cultural context of its creation, but also how it constitutes reflexively a significant resource for understanding that context itself.

Chapter 2 examines the history of theatrical dance in America from the eighteenth to the nineteenth century. The processes of change which, in part, enabled the beginnings of a serious theatrical dance to emerge in America are discussed in Chapter 3. Chapter 4 sets out the concerns of the major forerunners of American modern dance and their attempts to have dance taken seriously in their own society. Included in this chapter is an examination of the relationship of dance to the other arts in America and Europe around the turn of the century. The emergence of American modern dance in the late 1920s and its revolt against classical and romantic styles of dance are discussed in Chapter 5. Chapter 6 examines the major features of the development of modern dance which enabled it to become a significant aspect of American culture in the years to follow. The relationship of modernism in dance to the other arts is considered through a discussion of the revolt in the arts in America. Chapter 7 traces American modern dance's transition from a concert dance form to a theatre dance form. Attention is directed towards a consideration of the role of the New Deal Federal Arts Projects in the growth of the arts in America. In Chapter 8 the growth of modern American music is examined in terms of the relationship between modern dance and music, and through the work of Aaron Copland. The central focus of the penultimate chapter is an analysis of Martha Graham's *Appalachian Spring* which entails a detailed examination of a particular section of the work. The concluding chapter draws together the sociological issues raised by the examination of the development of modern dance in America in terms of both its *extrinsic* and *intrinsic features*.

2 THEATRICAL DANCE IN AMERICA FROM THE EIGHTEENTH TO THE NINETEENTH CENTURY

The major cause of the lack of any significant theatrical activity and development in America prior to the mid-eighteenth century and, therefore, by implication, the latent development of professional art dance, is often attributed to Puritan denunciations of the arts and entertainment (Cole 1942, Kraus and Chapman 1981). In New England in the seventeenth century the Puritans ruled with the stern hand of Calvinism, the principles of which were founded on the doctrine of predestination; that is, the idea that individuals are saved or damned before they are born and that only a few are 'chosen' (predestined for salvation). Although not all colonists in New England were Puritans, they were the most dominant group and often those who did not agree with their rules were either banished or severely punished.

> The Puritans had come to the New World to set up a society based on the Calvinist interpretation of the Bible. They believed that they were a chosen people; the early government of Massachusetts, for example, was a theocracy run by Puritan ministers who thought that the Bible was the disclosed word of God, and that its meaning and intention on every subject had been made explicit to them.
>
> (Kraus and Chapman 1981: 89)

In accordance with the principles of Calvinism, the Puritans maintained that individuals exist on earth for the sake of God and not God for individuals. The doctrine of predestination demanded that the followers should live out their earthly existence in terms of the 'calling', for to do otherwise would be a sign of imperfect faith and evidence of certain damnation. The faith decreed that the followers should engage in rigorous manual or mental labour for the furtherance of the Glory of God and resist all temptations of the world, particularly those of the flesh, which were perceived as the work of Satan. The German sociologist Max Weber (1976), in his influential and much criticised account of the role of ascetic Protestantism in the development of modern capitalism written in 1904–5 (see Giddens 1971, 1972), maintained that the central dogma of the doctrine of predestination resulted in an 'unprecedented inner loneliness' for the individual follower (Weber 1976: 104). Because no priest or religious sacraments could intercede on the individual's behalf as the means for the attainment of grace, as that issue had already been decided before the individual had entered the world, the individual follower was left utterly alone. With Calvinism, according to Weber (1976: 105), the gradual 'elimination of magic from the world' and the movement towards 'rationalisation' which began with the Hebrew scriptures, reached its logical conclusion. 'Wasting time', for the Puritans, was the first and 'deadliest of sins', because it deflected individuals from the ascetic pursuit of the 'calling' (Weber 1976: 157). Thus idle talk, sociability, contemplation, leisure and entertainment activities were condemned. In England, the Puritans closed the theatre at Stratford-on-Avon while Shakespeare was residing there in his final years and the Puritans who had fled to New England during the reign of the Stuarts, acted in a similar vein. In Massachusetts and Connecticut the Puritans banned games of chance such as 'dice, cards, quoits, ninepins' and in several colonies, theatrical entertainment was completely banned (Kraus and Chapman 1981: 89).

Weber (1976: 105) maintained that the key to Puritanism's antagonism towards the 'sensual and emotional elements in culture and religion', is contained in the inner loneliness of the individual, in combination with the doctrines of 'the absolute transcendency of God' and the belief that all things pertaining to the flesh are corrupt. The sensual and emotional aspects of life were rendered useless as a means to salvation by the dogma of predestination, but they were also viewed as dangerous because they promoted 'sentimental illusions and idolatorous superstitions' (Weber 1976: 105). Ascetic Protestantism's attitude towards sexual intercourse differed from that of monasticism only in degree, but not in principle. Sexual intercourse, within marriage, was tolerated by Puritanism in as much as it fosters the procreation of the species as God had commanded – 'Be fruitful and multiply' (Weber 1976: 158) – but it should not be enjoyed for the sake of earthly pleasure or desire. It should be a means to further the wishes of God, not of men or women. Dancing is an activity in which the instrument and means of expression is the human body and, for the Puritans, bodily indulgence or anything else connected with it was viewed as dangerous. It was likely to result in the emergence of baser instincts which would lead to 'an unclean life' and all that that entailed. Given the Puritans' distrust of the body, it is not surprising that they held strong views on dancing and performers. Moreover, this legacy was sustained long after Puritanism as a doctrine had diminished in importance (sex 'n' drugs 'n' rock 'n' roll).

Although the Puritans thought that most kinds of dancing would be likely to induce people into the excesses of sexual behaviour, they did not consider that all dancing was necessarily bad. In 1684 a group of Boston ministers, headed by Increase Mather, made clear their attitudes towards dancing in a treatise called *An Arrow Against Profane and Promiscuous*

Dancing, Drawn out of the Quiver of The Scriptures (see Miller and Johnson 1938: 411–12). While the tract condemned 'Gynecandrical' or 'Mixt or Promiscuous Dancing' (men and women dancing together), it also implied that dancing could be a means of teaching good body carriage, posture and grace, if it were taught by a stern teacher and the pupils were segregated by sex. The Puritans also objected to dancing in public places such as taverns, to professional performances, to maypole dancing (which they considered pagan) and to dancing and feasting (Chase 1955).

The Puritans, then, did not ban all dancing. They themselves had come from England where dancing was considered a necessary accomplishment of any gentleman or lady, as was poetry, literature and music (Kraus and Chapman 1981). Before they came to the New World, the Puritans, like other members of the English middle class, had studied dancing as a basic skill. For example, Playford's *The English Dancing Master* (1651) was published in England during the period of the Commonwealth and went through many subsequent editions. It was extremely popular in England and the American Puritans were familiar with it also. The Puritans, then, regarded dance essentially as 'a private matter to be enjoyed in the home and family circle, rather than in public spectacles or entertainment' (Kraus and Chapman 1981: 89). Entertainment is a leisure activity and, as such, went against the spirit of Puritanism, the work ethic and the distinction between public and private. At the same time, the Puritans considered that theatrical entertainment involved unnecessary expense, in terms of costume, setting, actors, etc., and the doctrine stressed simplicity and economy of form and content in both worship and daily life. In general, and perhaps for all of the above reasons, theatrical performers were regarded with suspicion in the early colonies, particularly in the north.

The view that the Puritans were anti-art in any form is a myth that was propagated by former 'pious Harvard historians' and, more recently, by the 'debunking' school of history that emerged in the 1920s (see Schlatter 1962). The common assumption that the Puritans hated all music apart from psalm-tunes, for example, is not borne out by the facts. Indeed, Gilbert Chase (1955), in his study of the development of American music from the Puritans to the present day, argues that it would be more appropriate to say that the Puritans held the 'art' of music in high esteem and that their attitude towards music was not antagonistic (anti-aesthetic) but moralistic. It was particularly valued as an aid to worship, although the use of instrumental music in churches was objected to on religious grounds. However, the Puritans did not object to the use of instrumental music on certain social occasions or in the home (see Chase 1955: 3–21). They decried singing when it was associated with 'bawdy' or 'obscene' songs and they opposed the use of music 'as an incentive to wanton or lascivious dancing' (Chase 1955: 7).

It is also clear that the Puritans regarded learning and literature in the highest esteem. In 1636, within six years of settling in the New World, the founders of the Boston Bay Colony established the foundations of Harvard College. Until well into the nineteenth century most of the colleges in America were in New England and were founded by Puritans and their descendants. American literature, until the middle of the nineteenth century for the most part, was written by New England Puritans and their descendants. Moreover, the 'renaissance of American literature' (Matthiessen 1969), which occurred in the middle of the nineteenth century (Hawthorne, Melville, Thoreau and James), emerged through the Puritan imagination in the field of letters (Bercovitch 1974, Schlatter 1962).

The evidence suggests then that Puritan denunciations of the arts and entertainment were not as pervasive or as strict as some historians and commonsense perceptions would have us believe. What does emerge, however, is that the Puritan attitude towards dancing, and indeed all the arts, was informed by a concern for rational conduct in everyday life based on moral grounds. Weber's (1976) thesis proposed that there was an 'elective affinity' between the regulation of conduct in daily life inherent in the Puritan ethic and the development of the rigorous economic calculus of modern capitalism. Puritanism opened up a gap for the process of rationalisation to proceed towards what Weber termed 'the disenchantment of the world'. For Weber (1976), Protestantism, and Puritanism in particular, played a crucial role in the development of modernity.

Although the Puritan backlash could result in harsh punitive treatment of dissenters, as in the celebrated trials of Salem, it is important to remember that not all colonists in seventeenth century America were of the Puritan persuasion. By 1667, the British territories in America ran in a continuous line from north to south along the eastern seaboard, and there were striking differences between them. Massachusetts, Connecticut, New Hampshire and Rhode Island made up Puritan New England. In the southern colonies of Virginia (the oldest British territory), Maryland, North and South Carolina, the Church of England was established by law. The central colonies, New York (formally a Dutch territory), New Jersey, Pennsylvania and Delaware, comprised heterogeneous elements, and a diversity of race and religion could be found in one or other of them. Puritan New England, although the most populated area, did not have everything its own way.

It is clear, for example, that the Puritans did not succeed in banning social dancing (see Chase 1955, Cole 1942, Kraus and Chapman 1981). There were enough settlers of different social classes and different denominations in the other colonies and in New England who did not view dancing as a moral threat and continued their respective native dance traditions. This was particularly so in the south, where dancing was positively encouraged as an essential part of the education of the élite. The social order of the south was based on a plantation economy involving slave labour imported largely from the west coast of Africa.

The British settlers in that part of the country were of a much higher social class than the Puritans in the north and training in dancing, balls and assemblies was an integral part of southern plantation society life. But, as Lynne Emery (1988) has demonstrated, dancing was also an integral feature of the traditions of the black slaves and of black Americans' experiences, which, for the most part have remained invisible in the cultural history of 'serious' American theatrical dance. Despite the fact that 'slaves had to dance aboard ship, and on the auction block, and *had* (my emphasis) to dance and play upon the command to entertain the white folks', it was in part through dance that 'a link was maintained with the past and an escape made temporarily from the present' (Emery 1988: 103). Although the later Protestant churches, like the Baptists and the Methodists which became established in the south, also frowned upon dancing as an aid to worship, they did not manage to abolish the desire of the plantation slaves to worship in this way. Rather, the black religious dance traditions of the Afro-Americans were 'improvised to fit in within the structure of the Protestant church' (Emery 1988: 120).

Care has to be taken, then, not to overstate the historical role of Puritanism and award it an overriding influence on the general development of America. The available evidence demonstrates that the Puritan strain considerably affected the development of New England culture, and most American historians concur that there was some link between the Protestant ethic and the development of capitalism in America (Schlatter 1962). In general, however, American historians emphasise that Puritanism represents but one feature of the history of that country, albeit an important one, and that the description of its influence on American life has to be seen in conjunction with other significant aspects of culture (Schlatter 1962). Thus, the contribution of the Protestant ethic to the lack of the development of theatrical dance in America prior to the mid-eighteenth century has to be examined in relation to other contingent features. Nancy Lee Ruyter (1979) has argued (following the historian Louis B. Wright) that the specific social environment of the early colonies was a contributory factor. Formal, 'cultured' entertainment such as stage plays, opera and concerts are features of and are supported by an established urban life. 'Moral scruples, combined with a lack of cities, postponed the development of professional performance arts in colonial America' (Ruyter 1979: 3). As modern American city life developed and became established, so too did the arts. However, as we shall see, the division between high art and popular culture in America was not so clear cut as in European culture.

The religious significance of Puritanism in America began to fade during the eighteenth century and other sects such as the Baptists and the Methodists emerged who could be equally unsympathetic to dancing. Cities began to develop and by the middle of the century theatrical activity began to grow in New York, Philadelphia and Charleston. Minstrel shows and circuses were usually performed outside the legitimate theatre and it was these that brought a sense of musical theatre to whole areas of the country where the legitimate theatre could not or would not venture (Mates 1985). Although the power of Puritanism as a religious creed diminished, the view of professional entertainers as morally dubious characters, which the Protestant ethic had inspired, continued until well into the twentieth century, and there were still the occasional outpourings against dancing by the clergy (Cole 1942, Kendall 1979, Kraus and Chapman 1981).

From the beginning of its development, theatrical dance in America, similar to other arts, was imported from Europe and remained under the control of Europeans in terms of style, personnel and direction until well into the twentieth century. Prior to the American Revolution the performers and dancing masters came from England. From reports of the current newspapers and advertising bills of that era, it appears that America was a 'dance conscious country' (Winter 1974). Theatrical dance in America developed in a hotch-potch manner and styles of dancing were not clearly articulated in the eighteenth century. It began as acrobatics, on a high wire, a horse or slack-rope dancing (Mates 1885). No matter how far it developed into a more abstract form, dance remained in touch with the dramatic musical theatre. Theatrical entertainment emulated the London convention of blending together the spoken play with music and dancing (Ruyter 1979). It was virtually impossible to single out dancers from singers or actors as the performers were supposed to be competent in all three areas (Mates 1985).

During the Revolution the theatre was prohibited by the first Continental Congress in 1774 and in 1787 an anti-theatre act was passed by Congress, but was repealed soon afterwards. One of the reasons for banning the theatre was that drama was considered to be politically subversive, particularly by the Puritans (Heinemann 1980). When theatrical activity resumed in the period immediately after Independence, the dancing emphasised patriotic themes. Harlequinades, pastoral ballets and scenes which employed the talents of speciality dancers, acrobats and tight-rope dancers, were also mounted (Ruyter 1979). After Independence, the British were superseded by a stream of French performers who were allied to the aristocracy and fled France to escape the Revolution there. With the inflow of French immigrants ballet began to appear as a distinctive form from other forms of popular dance entertainment. From the mid-nineteenth century, performers and teachers from other European countries, notably from Italy and Hungary, travelled to America to work (Ruyter 1979).

The first recorded serious ballet production in America was presented in Philadelphia in 1784. *La Forêt noire* starred the French dancer Madame Gardie and the only indigenous American dancer of note in the eighteenth century, John Durang, who was famous for his hornpipes and gigues. The distinction between popular dance entertainment and serious ballet was not clear cut. Ballets such as *La Forêt noire* included speciality dances such as the hornpipe and popular dance entertainment included some ballet type dancing. By the latter part of the nineteenth century, theatrical dancing in America would be confined overwhelmingly to the field of popular entertainment. The high point of America's enthusiasm for ballet, however, was during the period between 1830 and 1850, when the romantic era in ballet became dominant throughout Europe and the predominance of the ballerina, now *en pointe,* reached the heights of its supremacy over the male dancer.

The romantic era in ballet was part of a much wider artistic movement throughout Europe. It was characterised by a breaking of the formal classical rules, in favour of the expression of feeling, emotion and a yearning for the unobtainable. In part, it emerged as a reaction against the social upheaval that had been set in motion by the French and the Industrial revolutions. Romanticism, as embodied in the poems of Byron, the paintings of Delacroix and the music of Berlioz, combined realism with escapism. With romanticism, the emphasis moved to the subjective and the intuitive and away from the objective and rational. Romanticism, as Deborah Jowitt (1988) has pointed out, did not always entail a total rejection of neo-classicism but rather of futile academism: romantic ballet, and romantic poetry, for example, 'exploited and developed' their respective traditional forms. In ballet, as with the other arts, romanticism gave rise to new themes and ideas. Choreographers found inspiration in far-off exotic lands, nostalgia, legends and the magical world of fairies, elves and sylphs, reminiscent of Hans Christian Andersen's fairy tales.

The theatrical illusions of the supernatural and magic were made possible by the introduction of gas lighting into the theatres which 'permitted flickering contrasts of brightness and gloom appropriate to nocturnal or supernatural landscapes' (Anderson 1974: 44). The auditorium lights could now be turned off and the audience, sitting in the darkened auditorium, could be surprised by the eerie setting before them simulated by suspended gas jets. Gas lighting, along with the introduction of the romantic tutu, with its tight bodice and ankle length skirt of billowing layers of white gauze, and the illusion of anti-gravitation made possible by 'toe dancing', contributed to the rise of the ballerina into a position of supremacy on the stage. The romantic idealisation of woman but not woman, real but transcendent, was epitomised by Marie Taglioni in *La Sylphide* in 1832, the work that officially marks the entry of ballet into romanticism (Jowitt 1988, Sorell 1981).

Although the French ballerinas began to visit America in some numbers in the 1920s, Fanny Elssler was the first great romantic ballerina of distinction to make an extended tour of the New World from 1840 to 1842. Elssler, whom the balletomane Théophile Gautier described as 'a completely pagan dancer' in contrast to the 'ethereal Christian dancer' Marie Taglioni, was famous for her earthy dramatic interpretations and her character dances, such as *Cachucha* (Anderson 1974: 48). Despite the denunciations from the pulpits, and the usual disapproval of theatrical performers, Elssler was applauded by ecstatic audiences wherever she performed, by politicians and New England intellectuals such as Hawthorne and Emerson alike.

It was during this period that America produced some indigenous accomplished ballet dancers, most notably Mary Ann Lee, Julia Turnball, George Washington Smith, who danced opposite all of the leading visiting European and American ballerinas, and Augusta Maywood, who became the first American ballerina to gain international acclaim throughout Europe, including the mecca of ballet, the Paris Opéra (Ruyter 1979, Anderson 1974). These dancers were trained in the romantic style and performed its major masterpieces such as *Giselle* and *La Bayadère*.

By the middle of the nineteenth century, the romantic ballet had begun to go into decline in western Europe and America. Since its earliest beginnings in the high renaissance, ballet had gone through successive periods of growth and stagnation and the centres of interest had shifted from country to country. While ballet in most of western Europe continued its descent into decadence throughout the latter half of the nineteenth century (apart from relatively isolated Denmark where August Bournoville's romantic ballets survived intact), the centre for its future regeneration was to be found in imperial Russia.

In America during the latter half of the nineteenth century, ballet became incorporated into the spectacular extravaganzas of the popular theatre. The most renowned and well documented of these was *The Black Crook* which opened in New York in 1866. This production was so popular that it ran for a record 475 nights, making a great deal of money for the producers and the author. The play itself, although recognised as an extremely bad melodramatic adaptation of the Faust tale, was but a mere incidental to the real attraction of the spectacular, the ballet, or more appropriately, the all-female troupe of dancers, advertised in the advance publicity as a 'Great Parisienne Troupe' (Freedley 1978). The cast, billed in accordance with traditional ballet hierarchy, numbered eighty in all and included the Italian dancer Marie Bonfanti and other leading European dancers, plus 'Fifty Auxiliary Ladies' selected from the principal theatres of London and America (Freedley 1978).

The advance publicity for *The Black Crook* spoke of the enormous cost of the production, the elaborate settings and 'the ballet troupe whose premiere danseuse is bewitchingly beautiful and exceedingly graceful' (Freedley 1978: 66). The publicity and the attendant rumours led to the expectation that the dancers would be scantily clad, and women attending the show wore long veils so that they would not be recognised. The reviewer for the *New York Herald* added weight to the view that the ballet in the spectacular was 'nice but naughty', and exotically foreign (Freedley 1978).

So successful was *The Black Crook* that within a week of its closing in 1868, it was followed up with a variation entitled *The White Fawn*. There were numerous shows like *The Black Crook*, and its many revivals, and 'there were burlesques and many imitations of the most popular of these spectaculars' (Ruyter 1979: 7). Although *The Black Crook* helped to feed the rage for burlesque in America and contributed to the desire for girlie shows, it was not an originator of burlesque. The extravaganza became a separate stage form whose value was judged principally on its elaborate costumes, settings, crowd scenes and magical effects, rather than on its musical elements (Mates 1985). The spectacular aspects of the extravaganza form found their way into David Belasco's theatrical work at the turn of the century and Ruth St Denis' dance.

The Kiralfy family, who came from Hungary to live in America in 1868, gave further impetus to the ballet spectaculars in the American theatre, as the Ravel Company had done with their rope dancing and 'pantomime ballets' during the first half of the century (Ruyter 1979, Mates 1985). The whole Kiralfy family performed, and two of the brothers choreographed and staged elaborate productions throughout the remainder of the century (Senelick 1989). These extravaganzas, with their elaborate theatrical effects, were given an air of realism because their themes were based on actual historical events, like the 'triumph of electricity' or the 'fall of Rome', in contrast to spectaculars like *The Black Crook* with its 'white fawns' and 'nymphs of the rainbow' drawn from the romantic ballet tradition (Ruyter 1979: 8).

The extensive touring of America by both the romantic ballerinas and the later ballet extravaganzas not only brought American audiences into contact with theatrical dance, but also a number of American dancers were brought into contact with ballet (Ruyter 1979). Only the principal or lead dancers in these productions went on tour, the majority of dancers being drawn from the towns in which the productions were to be staged (Barth 1980, Mates 1985, Ruyter 1979). These American girls, unlike the Europeans, often had little or no formal dance training.

> Chorus dancers and supernumeraries were hired locally and given as much as six to eight weeks' training by the ballet master, who travelled ahead of the main company. For elaborate shows as many as two or three hundred local people might be engaged. Many of these were factory girls who had come from the farms to work in the cities and whose families were too far away to know what they were up to.
>
> (Ruyter 1979: 8)

During the latter half of the nineteenth century the opportunity to study ballet increased, particularly in major cities like New York. Many of the European dancers who came to America to perform stayed on to teach. For example, the Italian dancer, Marie Bonfanti, who was one of the stars of the original production of *The Black Crook*, settled in New York

to teach and included among her pupils were Isadora Duncan and Ruth
St Denis. However, the quality of ballet teaching in America at this time
was often less than desirable:

> Standards of training varied alarmingly, with some schools teaching acrobatic
> tricks to showgirls seeking jobs in Broadway chorus lines. At other schools
> ignorant teachers threatened children with serious physical injury by putting
> tiny children 'en pointe' before their feet were sufficiently strong.
>
> (Anderson 1974: 97)

During this period there were several alternatives available to dancers
who wished to work in the theatre (see Ruyter 1979: 8): they could
dance in the ballet extravaganzas; they could work as actor–dancers in
the theatre, as did Loïe Fuller, Isadora Duncan and Ruth St Denis; they
could perform dance speciality acts, or be in the chorus lines in variety
theatre or vaudeville. On rare occasions, when the opportunity arose,
such as the short-lived American Opera Company in the 1880s, they
could perform in more serious ballet productions. For the most part,
however, from around the middle of the century until Anna Pavlova and
Mikhail Mordkin took the Metropolitan Opera House in New York by
storm in 1910, there was little evidence of ballet as a high art on the
American stage. When these first Russian dancers began coming to
America, dancers such as Fuller, Duncan and St Denis had already rejected
the classical tradition and were in the process of clearing the ground for
the emergence of American modern dance.

It is clear that theatrical dance in pre-twentieth-century America had
not been as absent as some commentators would have us believe. Dancing
played a role in the musical stage, in pantomime, in minstrelry, in variety
theatre, extravaganzas and in vaudeville (Mates 1985). At the same time,
however, it is evident that dance as a high art did not establish the
beginnings of a sustained tradition prior to the third decade of the present
century. Jack Anderson (1974: 41) has argued that although the history
of American dance is scattered with the names of 'many illustrious
individuals', there was 'little sustained creative development' of the art
because, unlike Europe, there were no permanent American ballet
companies. At the beginning of this century, the Metropolitan Opera
House which opened in 1883 was almost the only theatre to stage
'serious' ballet productions. For these, the management imported the
dancers from Europe and a school was not established until 1909.

Most commentators, particularly the advocates of American modern
dance in the 1930s and 1940s such as John Martin (1967), have argued
that ballet could not have become established in America because it was
a foreign art form that had its origins in the hierarchical social order of
Europe, and America had long rejected the European order of rule in
favour of a democratic republic. In *American Dancing* (1967: 41), Martin
likened the presence of European ballet in nineteenth-century America

to a 'hothouse flower, unable to stand the native ways of thinking'. Nevertheless, nineteenth-century America did produce some indigenous dancers of distinction and national fame, all of whom adopted the European style as their dance model. For example, Mary Ann Lee, generally regarded as the first American prima ballerina to win nationwide acclaim in the romantic era, received her early training from a former member of the Paris Opéra who had settled in Philadelphia (see Ruyter 1979: 8). Later, Lee learnt all of Fanny Elssler's leading roles from the Austrian ballerina's partner and performed them extensively throughout America. In 1844, Lee went to Europe for a year to study at the Paris Opéra ballet school where she improved her technique in the romantic style and extended her repertoire to some considerable degree. This enabled her to provide American audiences with convincing interpretations of the major European ballet presentations.

Like most American performers of classical ballet, Lee was concerned to work within the canons of French ballet and match its ideals and standards, rather than 'seek or promote other ideals or other goals' (Ruyter 1979). Dance was not alone in this, most of the arts in America were derived from European forms. Aaron Copland (1953), for example, recalled that when he and other young American composers began to look for 'a usable past' upon which to develop an American style of music in the 1920s, they found that there was none. Academic music, in America, like dance, had been founded on the European tradition and American composers were generally considered second rate in comparison to the Europeans.

As we saw with *The Black Crook*, in order to attract an audience for dance in America during the nineteenth century it was deemed necessary to advertise the dancers as foreign, particularly French or Italian (in the twentieth century this dominance was supplanted by a Russian monopoly, much to the annoyance of such balletomanes as Lincoln Kristein who were trying to generate an American style of ballet in the 1930s). The appeal to Europeanism in American dance was double-edged. It was characterised by an almost love–hate relationship towards anything European. On the one hand, as Ruyter (1979) has indicated, European dance served as a legitimation for 'art' dance on the American stage. On the other hand, as Elizabeth Kendall (1979) has argued, nineteenth-century Americans looked on European dance as something utterly foreign, exotic and rather decadent, and the dancers were viewed in the same light. Furthermore, the American public did not quite realise that ballet constituted a disciplined system of movement or that the European dance academies in which the dancers were trained were highly disciplined training grounds.

> The featured ballet dancers – Italian, French and English ... might as well have been creatures from the moon as far as the public knew or cared – they seemed more like contortionists than actresses (and actresses were foreign

enough). If they were viewed as people, as women, at all, they were condemned as absolutely outside the pale of normal American social intercourse.

(Kendall 1979: 6)

However, if foreign dancers were considered less than respectable, in part, at least, they could be excused because they came from decadent Europe. The American dancers could not dance as well as their European counterparts, they had even worse reputations than the Europeans (Kendall 1979, Mates 1985) and, as a result, were socially ostracised. Most American theatrical dancers were 'probably without exception' either born into the theatre, from the poor urban areas, or from poor farming stock (Ruyter 1979: 10). Mary Ann Lee and Augusta Maywood, for example, came from theatrical families and George Washington Smith was a stonecutter prior to taking up dancing. In contrast, two of the forerunners to modern dance, Ruth St Denis and Isadora Duncan, came from poor middle-class families and the most important figures of American modern dance in the 1930s, Martha Graham, Doris Humphrey and Charles Weidman, came from 'respectable' middle-class backgrounds. Moreover, most of the dancers who were performing in the latter part of the century were from Catholic backgrounds whereas St Denis was one of the first Prostestants to go into theatrical dance of that generation (Kendall 1979).

Theatrical art dance in nineteenth-century America also suffered from the fact that it did not elicit support from the influential sectors of society.

Ballet never seriously engaged the cultural, social, political and moral leaders of America before the twentieth century. They might have attended performances and enjoyed them immensely, but as far as we know they did not subsidise the art with public or private funds. They did not argue its virtues and potential benefits for the nation. They did not marry dancers. And they certainly did not encourage their sons and daughters to become ballet dancers.

(Ruyter 1979: 10)

Not only did 'respectable' parents discourage their offspring from becoming dancers, it was not considered appropriate for 'respectable' women to attend performances, particularly the variety shows. In the 1880s and 1890s, however, variety theatre was becoming 'vaudeville': the variety houses began to 'clean up' their acts, redecorate the halls and introduce 'classy' elements such as skirt dancing, in order to attract middle-class audiences and women (Barth 1980, Kendall 1979, Mates 1985).

American attitudes towards dancers, the significant lack of American dancers from Protestant backgrounds and/or from respectable middle-class backgrounds prior to the end of the nineteenth century, can be viewed as part of the legacy of the Protestant ethic, or the 'iron cage' as Weber (1976) called it, that dominated America during the colonial period. That is, although the concept of 'the calling' ceased to have religious significance, the attitudes that ascetic Protestantism had fostered in individuals, particularly the antagonism towards the sensual, had continued unabated throughout the succeeding centuries. However, the years between 1890 and 1910 witnessed a vast influx of European immigrants to America from different cultural and religious backgrounds. It was hoped that these new groups, like the German immigrant farmers earlier in the century, would be assimilated into the dominant American cultural tradition which was underpinned by white Anglo-Saxon Protestantism (WASP). The 'melting pot' theory did not become a reality (see Chapter 4) and although the WASPs remained dominant in American society, the various new religious and ethnic minorities set out to maintain their own cultural and religious concerns within American society and to organise their own political lobbies.

Even if the above considerations had not been present, it is possible that nineteenth-century America could not have developed a 'serious' art dance tradition like that of Europe because the geographical history of America and its cultural significance was so utterly different (Martin 1967). The history of modern America is brief in comparison with Europe. It is a relatively short step in time from the date the first white settlements were made in 1607 to the Declaration of Independence in 1776: through to the bloody battles between north and south that ripped the growing (industrialising) nation apart in the civil war of 1861–5; to the subsequent emergence of the United States as the most powerful industrial nation of the twentieth century, and finally its political dominance on the western capitalist stage. The land itself, rich, fertile and inhospitable, totalling two million square miles, and the rapid mastery of it, played a significant role in the development of American culture.

In 1893, the year the American frontier was officially closed, Frederick Jackson Turner published his study of *The Significance of the Frontier in American History*. Turner's paper was set against a background of labour unrest, the rise of urbanism, the effects of new mass immigration, world recession and the final closure of the frontier which had been a symbol of escape from conformity. Turner wanted to explain these events and consider why they had not occurred before. He found the key in the 'Frontier Thesis', which entailed reworking a long-established myth and making it a significant heuristic device for social analysis (Susman 1984). Turner's frontier thesis (1945) proposed that the confrontation between civilisation and nature was the distinguishing feature of the American experience. From the very beginning, the settlers who crossed the Atlantic to the New World made clearings in the woods, carved a society out of wilderness, contended with harsh winters and the fear of what lay beyond the clearings. The Puritans erected barriers around their settlements to keep out the vagaries of the wilderness beyond the clearings. Because they believed that all events occurred as a result of Divine Providence, the Puritans both feared and extolled nature. In the New World, the French,

Spanish, English, Dutch, Germans and the Scots–Irish spread out like a great fan across the frontier towards the west, and they viewed the land as both a symbol of opportunity and of the enemy. For Turner (1945) it was the remote and hostile wilderness of the American frontier and the pioneer movement westwards towards the Pacific to conquer it, that made America unique from Europe. The central contention of the Turner thesis is that the frontier of America functioned like an active social force that, in effect, decivilised the European characteristics of the pioneers and led to the emergence of many of the characteristics that are associated with American society.

> It [the frontier] created a resourceful independent and egalitarian society with freedom of opportunity and free land to every man who had the energy courage and will to work it; it called for initiative, ingenuity and self-reliance; it was hostile to remote authority because it was remote and because it was authority; it was activist, un-intellectual and strongly optimistic.
>
> (Wright 1967: 5)

Although, by the early part of the nineteenth century, towns like New Orleans and Philadelphia vied with New York for theatrical importance, vast tracts of the country were yet to be penetrated and developed. The Atlantic ocean isolated America from the forms of amusement that filtered through Europe, and the frontier isolated the pioneers from the growing centres of amusement along the eastern seaboard. According to Turner (1945), the demands of the frontier, which led to the development of the American character, entailed the elimination of European cultural forms. He considered that America could not develop its own art until that anti-intellectual force had been conquered and finally put to rest.

> The American intellect owes its striking characteristics to the frontier. That coarseness and strength, combined with acuteness and acquisitiveness; that practical inventive turn of the mind, quick to find expedients; the masterful grasp of material things, lacking in the artistic but powerful to effect great ends; that restless, nervous energy; that dominant individualism, working for good and for evil; and withal, that buoyancy and exuberance that comes from freedom – these are the traits of the frontier, or the traits called out elsewhere because of the existence of the frontier.
>
> (Turner 1945: 37)

3 TRANSITIONS

As we have seen, the reasons why theatrical dance was not considered important in America before the twentieth century are highly complex and have to be considered on a number of different but interrelated levels. The social environment of the early colonies did not lend itself well to the development of formal sophisticated artistic entertainment. Although modern cities developed in the nineteenth century along with a heterogeneous urban population that could support such formal entertainment, there were still no permanent companies to enable the creative development of American dance. Such art dance that did exist was under the control of Europeans and Americans who were oriented to European ideals rather than those of America. Ballet to Americans was utterly foreign. During the romantic era, it presented a never-never-land of fairies danced by beautiful women, and later it presented fairy tales, with added special theatrical effects and a host of female dancers who were scantily clad. European ballet did not engage the imaginations of the leaders of America to a sufficient extent to entice them to support it and make it part of American culture. Moreover, the stigmas attached to theatrical dancing and dancers remained in the minds of the American public long after Puritanism had ceased to be a religious force.

Puritanism, however, according to certain proponents of American modern dance in the 1930s, need not be seen as a negative construct *vis-à-vis* the development of dance. Martin (1967) for example, considered that Puritanism in both its theological and non-theological sense promoted individualism, anti-authoritarianism, democracy and functionalism, and that these were essential characteristics of the American way of life. He argued that by hindering the development of European art forms in America, religious Puritanism made a positive contribution to the emergence of art forms that reflected the American way of life. In its widest non-theological sense, Puritanism emphasised that the American theatre should promote the ideals of the republic, 'virtuous simplicity, humility of demeanour and love of equal liberty', as opposed to tales of 'passionate kings, pouting queens, rakish princes and flirting princesses etc.' (Martin 1967: 48). In other words, Puritanism stressed that the American theatre should not model itself on the decadent authoritarianism of European culture, which America had rejected in favour of egalitarianism and the rights of the individual. American theatrical forms should be functional for the American character. Thus, ballet could not have captured the imaginations of American people because its form and content were antithetical to the American way of life. Martin maintained that when American dance began to emerge, it embodied those very characteristics that Puritanism had promoted: individualism, anti-authoritarianism, democracy and functionalism.

For Martin (1967: 63), it was not only Puritanism that played an important part in shaping the arts in America, but also the 'early conditions of its geography', the frontier. The differences between the geographical climate of Europe and that of America, which helped form the characteristics of the respective peoples, entailed that the American arts would be different from and not reducible to European art forms (Martin 1967). Certainly, when American modern dance began to emerge, its practitioners emphasised that it should reflect the American experience and the character of its culture. It also went against established codes of dance in favour of the development of individualistic dance metaphors. Furthermore, the qualities of early colonial life in America that Martin (1967: 42) describes 'as nothing luxurious, acquiescent' or 'indulgent', could be applied equally to the qualities of American modern dance in its initial stages of development. The modern dancers systematically stripped dance movement, costume and setting down to the bare bones, and required the audience to engage actively in the performance, as opposed to simply indulging their senses (see Chapters 5 and 6 for a fuller discussion of the Americanisation of dance).

To enable performance dance to become part of American cultural life, it had to undergo certain processes. The ground had to be cleared in order to generate the conditions which would facilitate the cultural reproduction of dance.

> The evils of dance had to be neutralised, grandiose ideals had to be established and promoted, and dance had to be brought in line with some part of American culture. Dance had to develop positive values for American society.
>
> (Ruyter 1979: 13)

As Raymond Williams (1981: 180–204) has argued, the concept of reproduction is crucial to a sociology of tradition or education. The term 'reproduction' has two meanings. The first, more common, usage of reproduction is associated with making a copy, as in the processes of mechanical or electronic copying. The second meaning is to be found in biology and refers to the making of something within the same species, which is *not* an exact copy. Mechanical reproduction in the sense of making exact copies is reproduction in a 'uniform sense'. In the process of biological reproduction, on the other hand, the forms or species are continued but in 'intrinsically variable individual examples', they are never quite the same; this is 'reproduction in a genetic sense' (Williams 1981: 185). The first sense of reproduction, as Williams points out, is more restricted and remaining within the bounds of mechanical reproduction can obscure change and relative autonomy. Reproduction in the genetic sense is preferable as a *metaphor* for the transmission of culture because it also entails *production*, the active process of making anew. It points to both the idea of replication and innovation which are characteristic of cultural forms. In order to establish the grounds for its own reproductive cycle American dance had to take up, and indeed reproduce in itself, some features, ideas, beliefs, etc., of the dominant culture. But it achieved this through the generation of an anti-formalist aesthetic, not by remaining within the canons of an established form. For its own ends dance took on aspects of the dominant culture – in order to lay claim to its emergent relative autonomy as an artistic and cultural institution.

During the *fin de siècle* there was a movement against formalism in all the arts in both Europe and America. The central concern was to look for 'real' expressions as opposed to creating artifices. In Europe, this entailed a shift away from formalism in favour of anti-formalist aesthetics like 'art nouveau'. In America at this time, the first programmatic attempt to develop a native style of painting was being mounted. A group of artists who called themselves 'The Eight' began to rebel against the academy and paint what they saw as 'real' American life. Although The Eight were opposed to the modernist movements of the French avant-garde, nevertheless they remained within the bounds of pre-impressionist European painting, while rejecting the staid American academy. However, when American dance began to emerge at around the turn of the century, it found its expression not in the formalised systems of European ballet but in the dances of other cultures (Kendall 1979, Ruyter 1979, Shelton 1981).

European ballet in the nineteenth century was dominated by the presence on the stage of the ballerina, but its direction remained under the control of the ballet masters and male choreographers. In contrast, the forerunners of American modern dance, and most of the later dance innovators, were women who not only performed but also created their own highly individual dance metaphors. Furthermore, in comparison with the earlier American 'ballet girl' dancers, these women came from middle-class backgrounds (Kendall 1979, Ruyter 1979, Shelton 1981).

To enable dance to become an occupation in which 'respectable' American middle-class women could engage, traditional attitudes towards the body – particularly the female body – had to be broken down. At the same time, dance had to be given different ends to enable it to transcend its traditional problematic moral representation (Kendall 1979, Ruyter 1979).

As Ruyter and Kendall have shown, the process of breaking down traditional attitudes towards the body was given impetus through the feminist reformists' concern with health and hygiene and the influence of Delsarte's system of expression, which took on the status of a fad in America in the late nineteenth century. Delsarte's influence, through the work of his American disciples, in part, also provided the spiritual ends to which dance needed to aspire to enhance its image and make it acceptable as an activity for middle-class women. In American dance, the influence of Delsarte can be traced through Isadora Duncan and Ruth St Denis, both of whom received some informal training in it, and directly through Ted Shawn who was taught by one of the leaders of the American Delsartian movement. Shawn wrote *Every Little Movement* (1974) as a tribute to Delsarte's ideas.

François Delsarte (1811–78) began his career as an opera singer. He began to develop his system of expression after he had lost his voice through poor training. Delsarte believed that through his observations and cataloguing of gestures, attitudes, tone and manner of voice, he had discovered scientific 'laws' that governed human expression. This positivistic approach to expression, however, was underpinned by an ornate quasi-mystical 'science of aesthetics' which originated from his particular representation of the Christian Trinity (Ruyter 1979).

Delsarte tabulated gestures in accordance with specific zones, head, heart and lower limbs, which, for Delsarte, corresponded to mind, soul and life. The gestures of the upper body were most important because they had spiritual significance. Delsarte designed his system for the stage and his students included many orators, singers, teachers and actors of the day, like Sarah Bernhardt. Delsarte's influence in Europe diminished after his death but it found a new lease of life in America through the efforts of his disciples such as Steele Mackaye, Genevieve Stebbins and Henrietta Russell (Kendall 1979, Ruyter 1979).

In Europe, in the 1890s, however, a concern for physical culture came into vogue and resulted in a renewed interest in Delsartism. The Dalcroze system of Eurythmics also gained popularity in Europe at this time. Both of these systems filtered through into German modern dance through the work of Rudolf Laban and Mary Wigman. The principles of Delsarte found their way into German modern dance through the influence of Duncan and St Denis, whose work achieved great acclaim in Germany (Shawn 1974).

Ruyter identifies three stages of American Delsartism:

> The first began in the early 1870s and was closely associated with the professional training of speakers and actors. The second phase coming to the fore in the 1880s, emphasised physical culture for the general public. It became particularly popular among women, in the third and broadest phase, which began in the late 1880s. Delsartian aesthetic theory was established and applied to all aspects of life.
>
> (Ruyter 1979: 18)

Although Delsarte designed his system specifically for the theatre, in America it touched many aspects of middle-class and upper-middle-class life. It was taught in the most important schools of speech and theatre training; it was incorporated into the curriculum of the newly emerging physical education schools, along with other systems such as Swedish Ling gymnastics. Numerous books and articles on Delsarte's system of expression were published at the height of its popularity in America between 1890 and 1900 (see Shawn 1974 for bibliographic details with commentary).

Delsarte rejected the artifice of convention by attempting to discover the 'real' relations of movement and meaning through observing ordinary behaviour. But by categorising gestures in terms of The Trinity, Delsarte's system of expression became a formalism in itself, particularly in the hands of some of his less competent followers on both sides of the Atlantic (Ruyter 1979).

In the work of the leading American Delsartians Mackaye and Stebbins, however, Delsarte's original rejection of formalism was continued. Both were sufficiently flexible in their approach to use Delsarte's system as a firm base and to incorporate other elements of their own design into the development of a physical training programme.

> The American Delsarte system developed new principles of movement based on relaxation, controlled and limited tension, easy balance, and natural flow of breath. It emphasised new or rediscovered design in movement; the spiral curve, successional movement, and a variety of movements suggestive of Greek art. And in order to train the students in the new principles and techniques, the American Delsartians compiled and created a body of exercises that could be used for both general physical culture and as a basis for further innovations in the art of movement.
>
> (Ruyter 1979: 29)

Steele Mackaye had been a student of Delsarte and he publicised the maestro's system in America through extensive lecture tours. It was largely through his influence that the Delsarte Method of Oratory became the most popular method of speech training in America until the 1920s. Mackaye was an innovator in theatrical production and was the first manager to introduce electrical lighting into the American theatre in 1883. He is also credited with extending the system into the field of 'harmonic gymnastics' (Kendall 1979, Ruyter 1979).

The major figure of the second phase was Genevieve Stebbins who aided the popularisation of the Delsarte system into the arena of physical culture and also carried it into the direction of dance (see Ruyter 1979: 29–34). She promoted the system through extensive lecturing, writing and performing. Her performances consisted of two of Delsarte's forms of expression, pantomime and statue-posing. These pantomimes were not of the traditional kind. They were interpretations of a poem, a story or an idea and were based on the Delsarte system of expression, Mackaye's

harmonic gymnastics and Stebbins' own innovations. Her movements
were brought into line with more traditional notions of dance by adding
steps and rhythmic elements (Kendall 1979, Ruyter 1979, Shelton 1981).
She identified her system of expressive movement with the sacred dance
of the Orient or the art of Greece, not the formalised ballet system that
had fallen into disrepute (Ruyter 1979). Later St Denis and Duncan
employed these sources for the development of their own dance forms
(Kendall 1979, Shelton 1981).

Apart from the field of public oratory and theatre training, the
American Delsarte movement was principally a women's movement, in
terms of both its teachers and the students. American Delsartism played
a contributory role in the liberation of middle-class American women
(Kendall 1979, Ruyter 1979, Shelton 1981).

During the period of reconstruction after the civil war, the dominant
agrarian economy began to give way to one of industrialism and in its
wake there emerged a crisis in social and moral values. With the end
of the civil war, the last emblem of America's popular religion, nature as
a source of society's ideals, was being cancelled out by the challenges of
science and industrialism. The vast expansiveness of the frontier, with its
attendant myths of the pioneer spirit and the healthy life, was giving way
to urban squalor and disease. In the period immediately after the civil war
it became increasingly apparent that American middle-class women were
being plagued by ill health, particularly those who had chosen to live a
life of the mind and not of the land. The poor condition of women's
health had been witnessed earlier in Europe around the 1820s–1830s when
urbanisation and industrialisation had increased rapidly. It was often the
women themselves who advertised their condition, and their major
concern was not to elucidate the causes (i.e. women's subordination) but
rather to find remedies to alleviate the condition (Kendall 1979, Kesselman
1991). Some, like Ruth St Denis's mother, who was a doctor, turned to
alternative medicine as a remedy for their ailments. They advocated cold
water cures and robust physical exercise, the antithesis of the 'prevailing
cult of ladylike delicacy and weakness' (Kesselman 1991: 497). Others,
like the radical feminists of the 1850s, incorporated clothing reform into
their campaigns for women's rights which led to the appearance of women
in trousers on the streets of New England. The loose-fitting trouser
garment, worn under a short skirt, was named after the American feminist
Amelia Bloomer, although it was not her invention. The bloomer, sometimes called the 'Turkish dress', 'the American costume', 'short dress' or
the 'reform dress', became associated with women's rights activists, but its
history has its roots in the health reform movement and the more radical
utopian socialist communities that were established in America from the
1820s to the 1860s (Kesselman 1991, Luck 1992).

The association of the bloomer with women's rights resulted in a great
deal of bad publicity for the reform dress. The press characterised the

bloomer as anti-feminine and reform dress came to 'stand as a symbol of everything that was threatening about feminism' (Kesselman 1991: 501). Moreover, it became clear that the antagonism to dress reform came not only from men but also from women. As Thorstein Veblen's (1970) study of 'conspicuous consumption' of the American leisure class in the 1890s demonstrates, middle-class American women were renowned for their enslavement to European fashions. Contemporary fashionable dress, for Veblen (1970), bore the 'insignia of leisure', it not only demonstrated that the individual had the financial means to consume expensive goods, it also confirmed that they could consume without producing. This 'conspicuous leisure' reached its height of expression in the restrictive and elaborate fashionable dress of women. In order to escape some of the public derision associated with the bloomer, the women's rights leaders abandoned the reform dress. They concluded that there would have to be more basic changes to women's condition before the issue of dress reform and conventional ideas of beauty could be confronted.

Although the women's rights movement gave up the bloomer, the dress reformers who stemmed from the water cure community carried on wearing the reform dress. The American dress reform movement was as much concerned with health and hygiene as with comfort. For example, it advocated the raising of the skirt, not only for a greater freedom of movement, but also to eliminate the germs that accumulated in the hems of the long skirts through continuous contact with dirt, mud, etc. At the same time, as Douglas (1970a) has argued, the removal of dirt is a symbolic act; it is an attempt to relate form to function.

The American Dress Reform Association was established in 1856 and was dedicated to reform in women's dress which was 'incompatible with good health, refined taste, simplicity, economy and beauty' (Kesselman 1991: 503). The dress reform movement stood for a different type of feminism than that of the women's rights movement. The dress reformers operated on the premise that the 'personal is political' and were concerned to inspire others through their individual action and principles of living. The women's rights leaders, on the other hand, were concerned to create a movement that would bring about social, economic and political change and they concluded that certain concessions had to be made in order to achieve this.

Delsartism also encouraged women to be more healthy by advocating physical exercise. In order to do exercise, restrictive clothing, such as the corset, had to be shed and thus American Delsartism formed a link with the clothing reform movement that re-emerged in the 1890s. In the 1890s, with the development of low wheel safety bicycles, women began to take to the streets on bicycles in large numbers and this also contributed to the acceptance of functional dress (Grossbard and Merkel 1990).

In its third phase, through the work of Henrietta Russell, American Delsartism advocated clothing reform for both men and women on aesthetic grounds as well as on the grounds of good health (Kendall 1979, Ruyter 1979). The aesthetic movement in dress, which was taken up by actresses such as Sarah Bernhardt and Ellen Terry and the women attached to the Pre-Raphaelite movement, helped to provide 'an acceptable alternative to fashionable dress' (Roberts 1977: 567). One of the significant features of American Delsartism is that it not only advocated physical exercise for women, it also gave them a spiritual purpose for moving expressively and for developing self-awareness.

> Delsartian statue-posing and pantomime – the ultimate in refinement and gentility – became the opening wedge for the entrance of respectable women into the field of theatrical dance. Delsartism made it possible for two middle-class women not only to become professional dancers, but to initiate and lead a far-reaching renaissance of the art.
>
> (Ruyter 1979: 29)

The two women Ruyter is referring to are Isadora Duncan and Ruth St Denis, both of whom started out as Delsartians but developed from there to create their own individual dance styles.

Plate 1 Painting by Toulouse-Lautrec of Loïe Fuller in *The Serpentine* (reproduced courtesy of the New York Public Library Dance Collection).

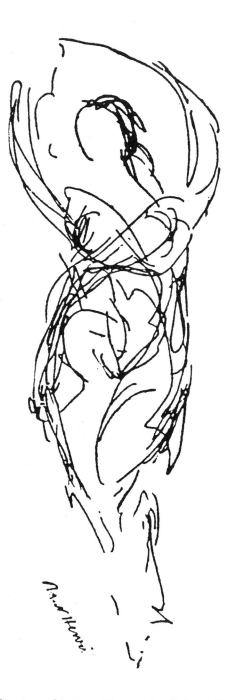

Plate 2 Pen drawing of Isadora Duncan by Robert Henri.

Plate 3 Isadora Duncan in the *Marseillaise* (reproduced courtesy of the New York Public Library Dance Collection).

Plate 4 Ruth St Denis in *Radha* (reproduced courtesy of the New York Public Library Dance Collection).

4 BEGINNINGS: DANCE AND THE PROCESSES OF CULTURAL REPRODUCTION

American Delsartism, along with the health and hygiene reformist movement and the fads for physical culture, helped to dissemble traditional attitudes towards the body and to promote a new anti-formalist body aesthetic. However, as Ruyter (1979) has pointed out, American Delsartism tended to remain within the confines of amateur salon performances and was not directed explicitly towards the creation of a new theatrical dance art. Nevertheless, as Kendall (1979: 30) has argued, in the 1890s Stebbins, Russell and others were representative of a number of new concerns that were beginning to enter the British and American theatre 'by the back door of art and reform'. The presence of a woman wearing a Greek or oriental style gown performing alone on the stage was becoming a consuming image on both the amateur and the professional stage around this time. Being in the forefront of the 'art as life' movement, Russell, who was similarly at ease in the 'fashionable salons of London, New York and Newport', dressed in loose Greek style robes, pinned by large brooches at the shoulder (which she called her 'brain costume') and 'served as an inspiration to rich Edwardian ladies on two continents' (Kendall 1979: 30).

The crystallisation of the Delsartian anti-formalist aesthetic in theatrical dance emerged first through Isadora Duncan and then through Ruth St Denis (Ruyter 1979). Before Duncan, however, another American dancer, Loïe Fuller, also contributed to the anti-formalist movement in dance and influenced the 'art nouveau' movement in Europe. Fuller, and the Canadian born dancer Maud Allan who, like Duncan, danced in a neo-Grecian style costume to the music of the great classical composers, have been paid scant attention by many established American dance writers in the past (see Sommer 1975, 1982). However, Fuller's contribution to dance underwent a process of reassessment after the emergence of postmodern dance in the 1960s. As Sally Banes (1980) has noted, a number of the concepts behind postmodern dance at that time were evocative of the radical changes that Fuller had made in dance in the late nineteenth century, many of which were rejected by the subsequent generation of choreographers:

Fuller eschewed the projection of emotion or personality of the performer, virtuosic dance technique, and even the appearance of physical beauty in the dancer. . . . There were rarely narratives in Fuller's dances; the text of the performance was the physical creation of an objective presence. When she danced with a group, she planned the dances so that the individual differences between the ways the dancers moved would be preserved. She often used untrained dancers in her works, and she gave performers a wide range of choices within the preset, imaginistic framework she created.

(Banes 1980: 2)

Banes's description of Fuller's ideas could refer equally to many of the dance concerns of the postmodernists who were reacting against the dance tradition that had been established by the first generation of modern dancers such as Graham, Humphrey, Weidman, etc. The postmodernists rejected style and the star image of the performer, in favour of natural movement and a decentring of the individual personality. They rejected narrative forms and the notion of meaning in movement in favour of an exploration of the possibilities of everyday movement as an activity in and of itself. Choreographers like Trisha Brown and Yvonne Rainer used untrained as well as trained dancers in their group dances. In the context of this discussion, it is not primarily because of the relationship of her work to that of the postmodern dancers that Fuller is important, but rather because it is often overlooked that much of the value accorded to Duncan's dance had its roots in Fuller's work (Kermode 1983). Furthermore, Fuller was the first American woman to set Europe alight with her dance images since Augusta Maywood captured the Paris Opéra during the romantic era in ballet. Fuller, however, took a popular form of dance entertainment and transformed it into a high art. She was the first American woman to put her hallmark on non-academic dance. Like Duncan and St Denis who followed in her footsteps, Fuller symbolised an emergent type of American female (Kendall 1979), the 'new' independent woman of the twentieth century; the woman who was crossing the boundary from the traditional female domain of the private sphere to the public sphere and increasingly becoming visible in the world of work and leisure in and around the city. She is, therefore, a good starting point to begin to tease out the many processes that contributed to the development of art dance in America. My intention is not to slip into what Lynn Garafola (1993) called the 'apostolic succession' (a term she borrowed from Lincoln Kirstein) in modern dance – that is, seeing the development of modern dance as a fan that spread out from a single point of reference: Denishawn. St Denis and Shawn are important figures in the generation of the processes of the cultural reproduction of dance in America, but they are by no means the only points of reference. Although the discussion that follows centres around the work of particular individuals, it is important to stress that my concern is to use these as pivotal points from which to generate a number of more general or structural, socio-cultural issues.

LOÏE FULLER

Loïe Fuller (1862–1928), actress, producer and former child temperance lecturer, stumbled almost accidentally on the dance form for which she became famous while she was rehearsing for a part in a play called *Quack M.D.*, in 1889. She wanted to convey a hypnotic and mysterious effect for her character in the play. In her autobiography Fuller (1913) recalls that she put on a long Indian silk skirt and, standing in front of the mirror, she held the skirt in her hands and began to wave her arms so that the cloth twisted and swayed and caught the sunlight coming through the window. And thus, her famous *Serpentine* dance was born. In the first performance of *Quack M.D.*, Fuller's skirt dance was greeted by gasps from the audience of, 'It's a butterfly!' and 'It's an orchid!' (Morinni 1978: 206)

Fuller's skirt dance achieved considerable popularity and by the time she left America for Europe it had taken on the status of a fad to the extent that often Fuller had difficulty persuading managers that she was the original. Fuller, however, was not the first to perform the skirt dance:

> It had long been popularly developed in English music halls from a compromise of a classical ballet variation of the Lancashire clog, or 'step dance'. Its leading exponent was Kate Vaughan, who first appeared as a skirt dancer in a 'Ballet of the Furies' at the Holborn Theatre in 1873.
>
> (Morinni 1978: 106–7)

Although the plays in which she performed, such as *Quack M.D.*, were failures, Fuller's dancing was so successful that she immediately abandoned her career as an actress in favour of that of a dancer. It was not so much that Fuller's dancing was a success, because, having had fewer than six dancing lessons in her life, she had little technical skill in this arena; rather, it was her imaginative use of lighting that enthralled the assembled audiences.

From the beginning of her dancing career Fuller became preoccupied with achieving the correct lighting effects. Through experimentation, she learned to place the lamps in particular positions so that they would project shafts of light across the darkened stage onto the skirt as it swirled and unfolded around her body. The actor-turned-dancer gave numbers not names to the early dances she developed. For example, the twelve dances she performed as a feature act in a spectacular called *Uncle Célestin*, were classified as 'twelve characteristic motions' and the first dance was given under blue light, the second under red, the third under yellow, and so on (Morinni 1978). Fuller became an innovator in the use of the electrical stage lighting that we now accept as commonplace. Her contribution to this field has been equated with the stage design innovations of Gordon Craig and Adolph Appia. She maintained a loyal band of electricians around her so that her lighting effects would not be stolen and in France she ran a laboratory where she experimented with electricity (Sorell 1981).

Fuller encountered considerable difficulties in advancing her newly chosen career in America. She was known as an actor to the managers and producers in New York and they paid her very little for her performance, left her name out of the programme and secretly trained a chorus girl to take her place. Ultimately, ambition and a well-publicised scandal surrounding a suit that she brought against her husband for bigamy, drove Fuller to Europe in 1892. She believed that in Paris her dancing would be placed in the 'realm of art' (Fuller 1913).

She travelled first to Germany and worked her way back to Paris. She went first to the Paris Opéra but, not surprisingly, the management was not impressed by her dancing. Although the Paris Opéra was no longer the centre of the ballet world it once had been, many dancers considered that they should be seen there prior to performing in Russia, and thus it managed to hold on to some of its former status (Sorell 1981). Undaunted, Fuller went to the Folies Bergère where she managed to secure employment, despite the fact that one of her imitators was already performing there. However, at that point in time, the Folies Bergère, unlike the Paris Opéra 'was practically taboo in respectable artistic society' (Morinni 1978: 209), although it was a regular haunt of modern or avant-garde artists and writers.

Fuller's dance images created a sensation in Paris and from there she progressed to capture most of Europe. Instead of the traditional ballet dancer clothed in tights and ballet skirt and the usual virtuosic performance, the audience witnessed the blurred form of a woman in a profusion of drapery whose image was magically transformed, through the manipulation of drapery and light, into an elusive materiality which took on the shape of natural objects such as 'a magnificent lily' or 'a huge glistening moth' (Morinni 1978: 209). Within a short space of time, Fuller's dance art helped to change the hitherto dubious reputation of the Folies Bergère into an 'artistic shrine', with even women and children attending her performances in the wake of writers such as Mallarmé and artists such as Lautrec (Morinni 1978).

In many respects, Fuller had the good fortune of being in the right place at the right time. In all the arts the revolt against the artifice of formalism was being mobilised and Paris was its centrifugal force. In addition, the Paris Opéra no longer provided the creative impetus for the art of dance and the vacuum was filled by 'the music halls, the Folies Bergère and the Moulin Rouge' (Sorell 1981: 303).

Fuller continued experimenting with lighting and creating new dances to which she now gave names, not numbers. One of her most spectacular dances, immortalised in Lautrec's lithograph of 1893, was called *Fire Dance*, and was accompanied by Wagner's *Ride of the Valkyries*. In this dance, Fuller performed her extraordinary manipulations of fabric on a pane of frosted glass and was lit from below the stage by a red lantern. The indirect lighting, an innovation at the time, caught the spiralling, swirling fabric and Fuller appeared to be enveloped in flames. One commentator described her as 'a nightmare in red clay'. She could be seen smiling through the flames, 'but she did not burn. . . . She was a flame' (Mazo 1977: 23). Frank Kermode has suggested that Fuller 'seemed to be doing almost single-handed what Diaghilev was later to achieve only with the help of great painters, musicians and dancers' (Kermode 1983: 151). Fuller, like Duncan and St Denis who followed in her footsteps, became the idol of artists and writers throughout Europe. She was painted by Mantelet, and the poet Mallarmé thought that Fuller's dance images in which the dancer herself almost disappeared, constituted an 'industrial achievement' and had significance 'for the art as a whole' (Kermode 1983: 155). Even the critic André Levinson, who believed that classical ballet was the ultimate in dance art, admired Fuller's work, although he despised Duncan, claiming that she had no technique, style or beauty (Kermode 1983).

Fuller's concern with exploring the possibilities of scientific discoveries of light for her art dance was paralleled in the visual arts of the time. Earlier, in the 1860s, the French impressionist painters such as Monet and Renoir, who began to advocate painting in the open air ('plein air'), became fascinated by the optical illusions and colour changes created by strong direct light. In Fuller's work, the dancer's actual bodily form practically disappeared under the array of light and colour on moving drapery. Similarly, in the works of the impressionist painters, who were also concerned with movement, the physical form of the subject (human or natural) becomes blurred under the intensity of light and vibrant colours. The neo-impressionist movement of pointillism, headed by Seurat, took the issue of light and colour much further than the impressionists and attempted to use the physics of light vibration as a method for painting.

Seurat rejected the technique of impressionism, which he perceived as empiricist and allied to the positivism of the biologist Bernard, in favour of finding a sure method for the construction of every painting, formulated on rational and scientific principles. Along with the other neo-impressionists, Seurat tested all aspects of Chevreul's law of colour contrasts and evolved the rigorous technique of the juxtaposition of small dots of primary colours, which is the hallmark of pointillism. Seurat, like Fuller, attempted to remove all trace of the personality of the artist from the work. Seurat and Fuller represented a much wider trend among artists in the late nineteenth century to employ the discoveries and utilise the developments of science and technology.

The development of the portable camera and the snapshot coincided with the rise of impressionism. Photography was in danger of taking over the traditional pictorial art of portraiture. Consequently, painters were forced to explore other regions and methods outside the reaches of photography. They drew on the unfamiliar angles and perspectives that were representative features of Japanese prints that were flooding the market at the time. At the same time, they learnt from photography that the camera could capture a subject from an unexpected view or angle. Degas, perhaps more than any other painter of the period, made use of photographic effects. In his ballet paintings, for example, the dancers on the stage are viewed from below in the stalls, from above in a box, or from the wings. Often the full view of the stage is partially obscured by the heads of the audience in front, by one end of the box, or by the figures standing in the wings. The snapshot often captured people in full motion and the photographer could not always fit in the total view, with the result that people or objects were cut off by the edge of the photographic plate. Degas made use of this 'cropping' effect in his paintings of outdoor subjects and ballet rehearsal scenes.

Similarly, the development of lithography made possible the bold spare composition, the strong line and the sharp colour contrasts of poster art, to which artists such as Cheret, Bernard and Lautrec contributed so much. The new poster art, much influenced by Japanese prints, heralded the beginning of a new relationship between living art and the public. In other words, as Lautrec noted at the time, the museum began 'to move to the streets' (Mathey 1966).

In 1896, Fuller returned to America to appear in a New York music hall and was given the highest salary to date in vaudeville. Morinni has noted that the kind of transformation of the audience that had occurred in the Folies Bergère in the 1890s had also occurred in New York:

> the newspapers suggested Saturday matinees for ladies, an unheard-of innovation, in order that the feminine portion of New York society might watch Loïe in her four dances, 'La Nuit', 'Le Feu', 'Le Firmament', 'Le Lys du Nile', without the 'protection' of male escorts.
>
> (Morinni 1978: 212)

Fuller did not remain long in America and her subsequent visits were also of short duration. Most of her American engagements were in vaudeville but in 1909 Fuller made a bid for the artistic recognition she received in France by performing in the opera houses in Boston and New York.

The transformation of the American audiences for Fuller's concerts that Morinni described above, was representative of the changes that were taking place within variety theatre in general in America in the 1880s and 1890s, which, as Kendall (1979: 37) has shown, 'were part of the impetus that would eventually make dance into an art'. The American variety theatre was cleaning up its hitherto dubious image in order to attract a wider and more respectable audience, including women and children, who had never been to the music hall before. The American variety theatre, following the lead of the French and English music halls, was giving way to the more sophisticated and luxurious atmosphere of vaudeville, yet another manifestation of the maturing modern industrial city (Barth 1980). The name vaudeville was used by some promoters to point to the new respectable image and to separate it from the old-type variety shows with their lewd jokes and seedy atmospheres which were hardly deemed fit for respectable men, let alone women and children. The new vaudeville audiences, 'cooler, more polite, and actually seated further away from the stage, demanded more than an actor's skill, they wanted an aura' (Kendall 1979: 37).

Prior to the 1890s, the solo speciality acts in variety theatre were performed mostly by men. Given the reputation of this kind of show and its mostly male audiences, it was unthinkable for a woman to expose herself alone on the variety stage, except, perhaps, as part of a double act with a brother or some other suitable male relative. From around the 1890s when variety was giving way to vaudeville, increasing numbers of women began to perform solo on the stage, usually in the skirt dance genre, which, since Fuller's original *Serpentine*, had become a very popular mode of entertainment. It was around this time that the first American 'art' dancers, like Gertrude Hoffman, began to appear on the vaudeville stage. This new generation of dancers, as indicated above, had little prior knowledge of the theatre and were mostly from poor but genteel backgrounds (see Kendall 1979, Chapters 2 and 4 for a fuller discussion of these first 'art' dancers on the vaudeville stage). The shift in variety theatre to the more respectable atmosphere of vaudeville, in part, provided a space for these middle-class women to enter the arena of theatrical dancing. It was also becoming more acceptable for young middle-class girls to participate in some formal dance training, which included social and character dancing, basic ballet steps and perhaps some form of Delsarte-type training.

The female performers who appeared in large numbers on the vaudeville stage stood for a new type of woman, the woman who was responding to the desire to make her way in those areas of the city which were opening up to her. Determined to succeed in their chosen career and to overcome the old stereotype of the chorus girl, they served as an inspiration for the women in the audience (Barth 1980).

At the same time as Fuller was creating the illusion of fire, a butterfly or a moth, through the play of light and colour on moving drapery, an anti-formalist movement was developing in art and design, called 'art nouveau'. Art nouveau began to emerge in the 1890s as a reaction to the persistent copying of classical styles of design, in favour of a new decorative style based on natural forms such as the butterfly or the lily. The creators of art nouveau, such as the architect Horta and the furniture designer Majorelle, unlike the Pre-Raphaelite art and reform movement in England, believed that they should make use of the machinery and new materials that industrialism had made possible. The proponents of art nouveau, like other artists of the time, were heavily influenced by Japanese design. They considered that the interiors and exteriors of buildings should form an organic unity. Fuller's work influenced the creators of art nouveau and, in turn, they influenced her.

Fuller was more influential in Europe than in America and, perhaps, it is for this reason she has often been subsumed under Duncan and St Denis. It is clear that Fuller captured the spirit of the times in Europe, but it is also evident that she was much in advance of the times because many of the innovations in dance that are normally accredited to Duncan were pioneered by Fuller (Kermode 1983, Mazo 1977). Fuller preceded Duncan in using the works of the great classical composers for her performances, in dancing solo and in training a group of dancers in her style. Although Duncan is normally credited with abandoning the corset, Fuller preceded her in this also (Mazo 1977). Fuller, like Duncan after her, eschewed the *danse d'école*, believing that emotion was best expressed through natural movement (Fuller 1913). However, unlike Duncan, Fuller believed that the personality of the dancer should be transcended into an image of abstract form. Although Duncan promoted the cult of the personality through her dance, she also pushed the feminist reformist movement much further than Fuller by proclaiming that the woman's body in dance should not be transformed into a decorative object but, through expressive movement, should proclaim its living presence to the world in its natural sensuous form.

ISADORA DUNCAN

Isadora Duncan (1878–1927) and Ruth St Denis are believed to have been born within a year or so of each other (both women obfuscated their age over the years). In many respects they shared similar ideals which they carried through in very different directions into their respective dance careers. Like Fuller before them, Duncan and St Denis won acclaim for their dance art in Europe, and Germany in particular. Duncan was extremely popular in Russia, and Fokine – the ballet choreographer for the Ballets Russes, whose collaborative works had a profound effect on the development of ballet – was probably inspired by her work (Jowitt 1988). St Denis, of course, worked primarily in America while Duncan, as did Fuller, made Europe her base and only occasionally performed in her native country. It appears that Duncan offended puritanical America's sensibilities, not only by her 'half-naked', 'barefoot dancing' (Mazo 1977) which she unashamedly pronounced as 'art' but also by her unconventional and highly publicised lifestyle. Towards the end of her career, particularly as a result of her last concert in Boston in 1922, Duncan was despised by the American public because she preached communism at them from the stage at a time when America was becoming obsessed with the threat to democracy posed by the 'Red menace'.

In Europe, Duncan and Fuller were renowned for their unconventional behaviour as well as their dance. Fuller was a lesbian who surrounded herself with adoring young women and even the free-spirited Isadora was shocked by the 'extreme attitude of affection' that her young companions showed towards Fuller (Duncan 1955). Duncan openly had affairs with men and her children were born out of wedlock. Duncan even performed in America when she was pregnant and it was quite evident to a number of people in the audience that she was carrying a child. In Europe, despite their unconventional lifestyle, Duncan's and Fuller's art was treated with great respect, but it was partly because of their lifestyle that neither achieved the same adoration from the American public. St Denis, on the other hand, embodied the ideals of Americans and this, in part, enabled her to capture the public's imagination.

Nevertheless, Duncan, both on and off the stage, had an enormous influence on American life (see Loewenthal (1993) for a recent re-appraisal of Duncan's legacy and influence in the fields of dance and culture). Like Fuller she had many imitators. Her beliefs about art, education and women's rights found acceptance in progressive education circles, in the artistic avant-garde and in the Bohemian quarters of Greenwich Village. In dance, as indicated before, she influenced classical ballet and she laid the foundation for many of the principles of modern dance (Ruyter 1979).

In both her dance and her life Duncan rallied against the strictures placed upon women. In both a physical and metaphorical sense, she shed the corset in dance and life and attempted to achieve a unity of experience, dance as life and life as dance. She danced in loose draperies, barefoot, barelegged, barearmed and often with her hair flowing. Fuller, as discussed above, probably shed the corset and tights first, but even she was shocked by the sparsity of Duncan's dance attire which made her appear nude (Fuller 1913).

Although Fuller emphasised the notion of natural movement in dance before Duncan, the movement of the body was transformed through light and drapery into a different object. Duncan, perhaps following the older dancer's lead, took up the notion of natural body movement, but developed it in terms of the natural expression that comes from the body itself and is expressive of that body in nature, not of something else. It is also possible, as Kendall (1979) has argued, that Duncan's concern with loose clothing and natural expression stemmed from her childhood experiences in California where dress reform was almost a uniform for the artistic set of San Francisco in the 1890s and the Duncan family saw themselves in that light. In California, dress reform was informed more by Pre-Raphaelite notions of the aesthetic of the natural than by the health and hygiene tradition to which St Denis was exposed through her mother (Kendall 1979).

Duncan, unlike Fuller, did not simply stumble upon dancing but had studied it systematically as a child. As a baby she learnt Irish jigs and reels from her grandparents; later she studied character dancing with her sister who was a professional dance teacher and in time became her sister's most skilful pupil and assistant. There is also some evidence to suggest that she studied ballet with Katti Lanner in London and with Marie Bonfanti in New York (see Lloyd 1974: 5, Ruyter 1979: 34) although Duncan (1955) maintained the she abandoned ballet after just three lessons. As her own dance developed, Duncan came to reject ballet totally. In an essay written in 1902 or 1903 Duncan had this to say of the *danse d'école*:

> The school of ballet today, vainly striving against the natural laws of gravitation or the natural will of the individual, and working in discord in its form and movement with the form and movement of nature, produces sterile movement which gives no birth to future movements, but dies as it is made.
>
> (Duncan 1983: 263)

This statement resonates with Fuller's (1913) notion that 'Nature is truth and art is artificial', although Duncan's tone is more evangelical and more in line with the conjoining of beauty with Nature which was central to the aesthetic dress reform movement. Ballet in America, and in most of Europe at the end of the century, was in a state of ossification and Duncan's tirade against it embodied the views of many artists and intellectuals of the time. The heirs of Petipa, in the form of the Ballets Russes, who put a bolt through the ballet world and brought it sharply into the twentieth century by 'defying all known genres', had yet to emerge out of Russia and into the opera houses of Europe (Sorell 1981). By rejecting the illusion of anti–gravitation in ballet, Duncan affirmed the dancer's relation to the ground, an area that dancers such as Graham and Humphrey would reaffirm and explore in great depth.

Duncan believed that ballet movement and ballet dress deprecated the female body and, in so doing, contained the seeds of its own destruction. The concern with costume, again, brings Duncan in line with the dress reformers:

> – look – under the skirts, under the tricots are dancing deformed muscles. Look still farther – underneath the muscles are deformed bones. A deformed skeleton is dancing before you. This deformation through incorrect dress and incorrect movement is a result of the training necessary for ballet. The ballet condemns itself by enforcing the deformation of the beautiful woman's body! No historical, no choreographic reasons can prevail against that.
>
> (Duncan 1983: 262)

Before she found herself, Duncan, like St Denis, trod the boards in vaudeville doing 'something with skirts and frills and kicks' and worked in the conventional American theatre (Duncan 1955). Unlike St Denis, Duncan was brought up in the urban environment of San Francisco which had a thriving legitimate theatre and a host of variety shows, and her family were enamoured by theatrical entertainment. From 1895 to 1897 Duncan worked in Augustin Daly's company in New York and on tour.

Among other minor roles in his pantomimes, she played a dancing fairy in Daly's production of *A Midsummer Night's Dream*. However, she found this work unsatisfactory and determined to compose and perform her own dances. Like Stebbins and Russell, Duncan became a salon performer.

It appears that her solo performances bore a close resemblance to the favoured forms advocated by the American Delsarte manuals of the day, gestural representations of a poem recited by her brother and short dances to music (Kendall 1979). Delsartism was filtering into the theatre at this time and there is evidence to suggest that Duncan did have some direct contact with this form of expression (see Shawn 1974: 80). Moreover, as Ruyter (1979) has shown, there are several parallels between Duncan's beliefs and those of the leading American Delsartians. For example, Duncan, like Stebbins, believed that the art of ancient Greece represented the highest ideals of artistic achievement and that movement was a means for the promotion of spiritual ends. For Duncan, however, the spiritual is rooted in the body, not in some other-worldly being. Duncan was also aware that she was not dancing as the Greeks had done but, rather, with the spirit of 'Nature' that she had perceived in their art forms (Duncan 1955).

From a very early age the Duncan children were exposed to a staple diet of nineteenth-century 'culture' through their mother, who was a pianist and music teacher. Mrs Duncan, a lapsed Catholic and a passionate follower of Robert Ingersoll (who was known as the 'great agnostic' and attracted capacity audiences across America for his anti-orthodox speeches which proclaimed the values of practical humanism) also exposed her children to agnosticism. The Duncan family were devoted to art and consequently, when they went to Europe, they visited museums and art galleries. Their particular interests centred on the art of Greek antiquity and the renaissance.

The American stage at the turn of the century was an inappropriate setting for someone with Duncan's ambitions and romantic pretensions to art (Kendall 1979, Ruyter 1979). Nor could she see any future as a salon performer to New York or Newport society, because she firmly believed that wealthy Americans had absolutely no artistic sense. Like Fuller before her, Duncan considered that her art would flourish and find appreciation in Europe, and in 1899 the family set sail on a cattle boat for England.

It was in Europe that Duncan's dance emerged. In London and, shortly afterwards, in Paris she immersed herself in art and literature, gave concerts to small but enthusiastic audiences and was taken up by the cultural élite of both cities. The musicians she met through Charles Hallé, the painter and director of the *New Gallery* in London, encouraged Duncan to direct her attention towards dancing to serious art music, such as the waltzes of Chopin. Within a few years Duncan came to rely on music as a source of inspiration for her dancing, particularly the works of the great romantics.

Duncan considered that the function of dance was to celebrate and reveal, through body movement, the inner emotional life which stems from the soul. She believed that the starting point to release this inner spiritual impulse was to be found in the solar plexus. The solar plexus is that area of the body, between the lower ribs and above the stomach, that corsets restricted and the dress reformers tried to free (Kendall 1979). But at this time, despite the fact that the attempts of the dress reformers and the advocates of physical culture to free women from restrictive clothing were beginning to gain ground, the majority of middle-class women were still encased in corsets and weighed down by long heavy undergarments (see Roberts 1977 for a discussion of women's fashions in the nineteenth century). For Duncan, movement should spring from the centre of the body and flow through to the other body parts; the arms and legs should not move as separate entities. This concept of whole body movement was clearly antithetical to the codified system of ballet. Duncan had observed that, in ballet, the pupils were taught that movements were centred in the lower part of the spinal column and that from there, the trunk, legs and arms must move freely to create peripheral designs in space. This method, according to Duncan (1955), resulted in 'mechanical movement' which was not worthy of the human spirit.

Duncan's discovery of the centre, as Martin (1967) has indicated, was well known in the field of psychology as the 'automatic system', but it was entirely new to the practice of dance. Movement that springs from the solar plexus releases the upper regions of the body into and through the surrounding space, with the lower body following through. Duncan's discovery of the upper body's expressivity corresponded to the expressive gestures most favoured by Delsarte's anti-formalist aesthetic. Martin (1967) considered that Duncan's concept of expressive movement emerging from the centre had enormous ramifications for the art of dance.

> It was, in fact, the principles of expressional movement upon which all modern dance has been built. Fundamentally it consisted of the realization that movements did not originate in the moving member, but appeared there only as a part of the total reaction of the individual to the situation. Arms and legs ceased to be objective entities to be arranged in pleasant designs or trained to perform independent feats; they now began to be moved only as a result of the central impulse arising from the emotional necessity.
>
> (Martin 1967: 132)

In order to reveal the movement, Duncan performed in a Greek tunic, representative of those worn by the goddesses and nymphs in the paintings of Botticelli and Titian; her dancing was set against a background of blue velvet drapes. Although Duncan paid attention to lighting (Jowitt 1988), it was never as dominant a feature of the performance as it was for Fuller. With the emergence of art nouveau, with its ornamental style of soft curves, spirals and flowing movement, drapery became a dominant artistic theme. Like Fuller before her, when Duncan danced her drapery was always close at hand and, thus, her performance also embraced an elemental feature of this new decorative style. However, while Fuller used light and drapery as essential components of her dance images, Duncan employed them as accessories so that they might not detract from the substance of the dance, the revelation of the soul through movement. With the emergence of American modern dance in the late 1920s, every conventional theatrical device became subordinate to the primacy of movement. Dancers such as Graham and Humphrey, like Duncan before them, removed the smile from the face, shoes from the feet and, in order to emphasise the torso, designed stark costumes around the basic leotard garment, while theatrical settings were reduced to a dramatic backdrop of dark drapes. Graham and Humphrey, however, were not only rebelling against ballet, but also, as I shall go on to discuss, against the lavish exotica of the Denishawn production format.

Duncan chose the recital as the means of presenting her communion with inner nature. In principle, she remained a recital artist although in later years she also danced with members of her school. St Denis, on the other hand, almost from the beginning planned her dances to include others. The concept of the recital, as indicated earlier, was not Duncan's invention; rather, its impetus was given through Delsartism and the vogue for amateur salon performances during the latter half of the nineteenth century. Prior to that time, solo dances had been extremely unusual outside the field of ballet. Although dancers such as Fuller preceded Duncan in solo dances, the latter's success in the field 'finally established the recital as possibly the best presentation for the "modern" dancer' (Sorell 1981: 324). In 1905, Fokine created *The Dying Swan* as a recital piece for Pavlova at the moment when 'the expressive solo' began to come into fashion. However, the recital work did not feature in the subsequent development of ballet and the arena of the solo was left to the modern dancers (Sorell 1981).

After discovering the 'central spring of movement', Duncan sought to develop a 'first movement form' that would emerge naturally from a series of movements, as a result of a reaction of 'a primary movement' to a specific emotion, such as sorrow, fear or joy (Duncan 1955: 58–9) – that is, she was searching for 'first movements' that would contain a natural affinity between the mover and the movement or between form and function. She attempted to develop the first principles of movement in a series of dance studies without music. Although these studies, in their original forms, were never performed in public, nor were the 'first movements' codified into a technique, it is yet another indication of Duncan's greatness that she was the first to raise the issue as a problem for dance (Martin 1967). Since Duncan, the concern to go back to the origins of dance (the body), to rediscover the sources and develop first principles of movement, has been a continuing feature of non-academic dance in America.

Between 1915 and 1920 Gertrude Colby, Margaret H'Doubler, and Bird Larson were seeking first principles of movement for educational dance. In the late 1920s Doris Humphrey, Charles Weidman and Martha Graham were seeking to discover dance and specifically American dance. And as late as 1967 Anna Halprin, a leader of the avant-garde in American dance, said that what she was really searching for was 'the genesis of movement'.

(Ruyter 1979: 51)

The return to the sources of art, the negation of tradition and the desire for constant renewal, are features of one aspect of modernity as defined by Baudelaire, 'the transient, the fleeting, the contingent' (the other side being 'the eternal and the immutable') (Harvy 1989: 10). Duncan's searchings, therefore, embodied key elements of this new aesthetic. Modernism is concerned to uncover the substance of art by peeling off the layers of all past traditions, and to work afresh from and through the primary substance of the art form, which, in dance, is movement. Duncan's practice, however, did not fully embrace modernism. By taking the art of ancient Greece as the dance model, and by relying on music as the emotional stimulus to release the substance of dance, her work also embodied elements of romanticism. Ultimately she stood on the cusp between modernism and romanticism.

From the very beginning of its development, as indicated above, American modern dance has been characterised by individuality, diversity and anti-authoritarianism (Martin 1967). Just as modern painting has encompassed a number of 'isms' such as primitivism, expressionism, surrealism, constructivism, etc., so too has American modern dance. As Louis Horst has pointed out, 'There are as many physical techniques as there are performer/teachers' (Horst and Russell 1977: 18). Movement, for Graham, is based on the principles of 'contraction and release'; for Humphrey on 'fall and recovery'; and for Holm (following Wigman), on 'tension and relaxation'. Herein lies an important distinction between Duncan and the first American modern dancers. Duncan's work did not give rise to a definite technique, like that of Graham for example, although she believed in disseminating her ideas and to this end, in 1904, founded her first school in Germany. If Irma Duncan's *The Technique of Isadora Duncan* (1970) is a valid representation of what Duncan taught, then the majority of her classes were devoted to very simple movements such as walking, running, jumping, rising and sinking.

Duncan instructed her pupils to listen to the music with their soul in the belief that, from there, dance would emerge that would be at one with nature.

I never taught my pupils any steps. I never taught myself technique. I told them to appeal to the spirit as I did to mine. Art is nothing else.

(Rosemont 1981: 58)

By implying that great art relies on intuition and that dance should be expressive of the soul, Duncan unwittingly unleashed a wave of self-expression in dance. Like Fuller before her, she had many imitators in Europe and America, but again, like those of the older dancer, they were mere shadows of the original. Although she did not succeed in codifying her 'first movements' into a technique, Duncan developed the practice of it in her own work to a high degree, especially in her tragic dances. So much so, according to Martin (1967: 137), that dances which were reportedly improvised in response to particular events contained 'vital substance and form'. It is here that the gap between Duncan the dancer and her imitators becomes visible. Duncan was in such command of her work that her performances, unlike those of her imitators, did not descend into a flurry of self-expression (Jowitt 1988).

Duncan used dance to make political and social statements and, in so doing, foreshadowed yet another aspect of dance in America in the 1930s. She was not concerned solely with art for art's sake. Rather, she maintained that she sought to find and express 'a new form of life' through her dancing (Duncan 1955). Politics and art, for Duncan, were not separate entities. Above all else, she considered that her dance was symbolic of women's freedom and her concern with political freedom often found its way into the content of her work. In her first performance in Budapest in 1902, she dressed in a red tunic and, to the music of the *Rakowsky March*, danced to the glory of the Hungarian revolutionaries. In America, during the First World War, she wrapped herself in the French flag and danced the *Marseillaise* in order to arouse the support of her countrymen/women for the allies. On her last two visits to America in 1917 and 1922, again dressed in her red tunic, she performed *La Marche Slav* in celebration of the Russian Revolution and in an attempt to dispel the growing American opposition to the new political order in Russia.

From contemporary reviews of these works, Duncan's movement style appears to have been pantomimic, emotive and with much emphasis on facial expression (Martin 1967), factors which the first American modern dancers would reject in favour of non-literal movement forms. In theory, Duncan eschewed pantomimic gesture, viewing it as nothing more than a substitute for words, but in practice, according to Martin (1967), she used it with 'great frequency'. Nevertheless, the political content and intention of these dances, if not their actual movement forms, were consistent with those of the radical dance activists in America during the 1930s. With the onslaught of the Depression at home and the rise of fascism in Europe, many American artists came to believe that art should speak to the masses, not just to the few, and that its content should reflect the social problems of the day in an unambiguous manner. This view was given further impetus with the introduction of the New Deal Federal Relief projects for the arts in 1935. Under the auspices of *The*

Workers' Dance League, groups which included the *Red Dancers* and *Rebel Dancers*, performed works on topics like eviction, poverty, unemployment and hunger, to large audiences in trade union halls and workers' centres (see Prickett 1992 for a detailed analysis of the leftist dance movement in America in the 1930s). As Margaret Lloyd (1974) has pointed out, these politically motivated dancers were perhaps the first to question the existing order of modern dance that was beginning to be established. Although Graham was vehemently anti-fascist and created several works on that theme, and Humphrey was sympathetic to the aims of the left-of-centre *Federal Dance Theatre*, they also stated that dance should not be used for propaganda purposes (see Chapter 6 for a fuller discussion of the relation between politics and art). Humphrey and, in particular, Graham were concerned to establish dance as an independent art form. The dancers who came under the banner of *The Workers' Dance League*, however, like Duncan before them, believed that dance should not only be a vehicle for themselves as performers, but also for the masses (see Wheeler 1990).

Duncan, then, prefigured numerous aspects of American modern dance. With her work, according to Martin (1967), there emerged the first American dance of any significance. He considered that she was the first dancer to embody those characteristics of anti-authoritarianism, functionalism and individualism which American Puritanism and the frontier spirit had promoted, and which later became essential features of American modern dance. Although Duncan's ideas and 'vision of America dancing' were clearly a spiritual source of inspiration to the development of modern dance (Ruyter 1979), it is difficult to assess how much direct influence her *work* had on the next generation of dancers. St Denis recalled Duncan's influence on her own work, and in 'music visualisation' (Terry 1960: 26–8), which, in turn is evident in Humphrey's early works, such as *Air for the G String* (1928) (see Jordan (1986) on the development of music visualisation tradition). The Russian–American ballet dancer, Alexandra Danicova, also remarked that certain aspects of Hanya Holm's class work reminded her of Duncan (Terry 1960:6).

Although Duncan had a strong commitment to teaching, no one dancer of distinction emerged from her school and none of the leaders of the first generation of American modern dance was trained in her method. There are several possible reasons for this. First, as indicated above, Duncan seldom performed in America after she had established herself in Europe. Therefore, few, if any, of the first generation of American modern dancers would have had the opportunity to see her perform. Second, Duncan did not manage to establish a school in her native country, despite repeated pleas to her American audiences for money towards that end. Even if she had succeeded in this, it is probable that her stated 'vision of America dancing' could not have been realised under her auspices because she failed to formulate her theory into a set of procedures that could be taught systematically beyond a certain rudimentary point (Ruyter 1979). Further-more, although Duncan emphasised the importance of individuality in dance, the tendency for followers to reify and imitate her resulted in her movement style being crystallised into an academic mode. Thus, according to Ruyter (1979), Duncan's anti-formalist aesthetic suffered the same fate of that of Delsarte; it became a formalism in itself.

Duncan's lifestyle and attitudes towards America made it difficult for her to be acceptable to the American public. She made no secret of the fact that she hated many aspects of American life, such as the pursuit of the dollar, and the attitudes that had been promoted by the negative side of Puritanism (Duncan 1955). She maintained that the puritanical distrust of the body, which had pervaded American life, made it virtually impossible for the majority of the people to treat her Dionysian celebration of the body in dance (and life) as anything more than smut. On several occasions she chastised her American audiences for their puritanical outlook, ironically, with a self-righteous ferocity characteristic of that very force which she so despised. Duncan boldly proclaimed her dance as 'Art', 'and then as now', as Marcia Siegel has stated, 'Americans hated to have art thrust at them'. (Siegel 1979: 9).

Duncan further alienated the American public by marrying a Russian and by proclaiming the good of Bolshevism and the evils of capitalism. In the years immediately following the end of the First World War, public opinion in America moved sharply to the right and resulted in a wave of anti-black, anti-union and anti-Bolshevik feeling. When Duncan and her Russian husband arrived in America in 1922, they were detained on Ellis Island and there she was interrogated on her political views. Front-page headlines in the daily newspapers across the country branded her as 'an agent of Moscow' and many 'patriotic' groups joined in and pronounced her a Bolshevik (Rosemont 1981). Newspapers were more interested in her personal life than in her dance. Many of her performances were cancelled. Duncan returned to Europe in January 1923, but not without first voicing her indignation, from the stage and in the press, at the treatment she had received at the hands of the press and in places like Boston. In an article published in Hearst's *American Weekly* in January 1923 Duncan vowed never to return to America and kept her word (Rosemont 1981). Her death (she died accidently, strangled by her scarf which got caught up in the wheel of her car) in 1928 was almost as famous and dramatic as her life.

It is clear that Duncan's views were incompatible with those of the American public and ultimately, like Fuller, she belonged to Europe. St Denis, however, the last of these several American art dancers to go to Europe, belonged firmly to America. Some years after returning home, she and Ted Shawn founded the institution which subsequently provided a significant influence on American modern dance in terms of personnel: Denishawn. Duncan, in effect, as Lloyd has pointed out (1974), became the spiritual leader of American modern dance after it had been established (see also Terry 1960: 28, 37).

RUTH ST DENIS

The parallels between the life of Ruth St Denis (1879–1968) and that of Isadora Duncan extend further than those already indicated. Both were brought up in the margins of society in poor but educated households, where the mother was the most dominant influence (Kendall 1979). Neither of them came from a theatrical background, unlike Fuller, whose father was a fiddler in variety theatre. St Denis, like Duncan, was a product of American Delsartism. She also studied ballet with Marie Bonfanti in New York. Like Fuller and Duncan, St Denis worked in vaudeville and the conventional theatre. She, too, became dissatisfied with this work and determined to create her own dance images. Before travelling to Europe to establish herself as a dancer, St Denis, like Duncan, danced for the social élite in New York. It was in Germany that, first, Duncan and, later, St Denis, found their most appreciative audiences. Apart from a brief period in the eighteenth century, ballet did not take root in Germany and as a result the country was not so ballet-minded as Paris or London. Therefore, the Germans were more receptive to new non-academic dance forms such as those offered by Duncan and St Denis (Ruyter 1979).

Duncan's success in Germany enabled her to found her first school in Grünewald in 1904. In 1908 admirers of St Denis offered to build a theatre especially for her in Weimar if she would sign a contract to remain in Germany for five years. She declined, however, because, unlike Duncan, she missed America and the American theatre and wished to return home.

In 1900 St Denis and Duncan encountered Fuller and Sada Yacco at the Paris Exposition. At that time St Denis was in Paris with David Belasco's company and Duncan had already left the American theatre and was being taken up by the artistic set of London and Paris. Both were impressed by Fuller's work and that of the Japanese actor–dancer. It is evident that both Duncan and St Denis drew inspiration from Fuller's dance, although, as Kendall (1979) has pointed out, each took separate elements and developed them in a different direction.

Furthermore, St Denis, no less than Duncan, showed a strong sense of mission throughout her career. However, although both founded schools to carry on their work, St Denis did not share Duncan's commitment to teaching. Rather, of the two founders of Denishawn, it was Shawn who demonstrated greater dedication in that direction.

Despite the parallels in the details of their lives, St Denis and Duncan were utterly different as women and dancers. Like Whitman and Nietzsche, Duncan sought to return to the body, to celebrate its living sensuous presence in the world. St Denis, on the other hand, wished to become a vehicle through which the spiritual is revealed (Kendall 1979). For Duncan, the spirit was firmly rooted in the body, not in some transcendental being. By contrast, St Denis sought to use the body as a means to escape the physical realm into that of the spiritual. Duncan viewed sexuality, art and the spiritual as corporeal, whereas St Denis placed them in order of hierarchy, with the spiritual first and sexuality last (Kendall 1979, Ruyter 1979).

Whereas Duncan was brought up in an urban area on the West Coast, St Denis grew up on a farm in New Jersey. Unlike Duncan, she was not exposed to nineteenth-century European 'culture' or the kind of aesthetic of the natural favoured by West Coast bohemians. St Denis's mother, a strict Methodist by religion and a doctor by profession who had to give up practising through ill-health, determined to bring up her daughter to be healthy in body and mind (Shelton 1981). The youngster's spiritual well-being was taken care of by the practice of bible reading. Mrs Denis's views on health were closely affiliated to those of the women reformers stemming from the water cure tradition and, therefore, she allowed her daughter to run free on the farm, unfettered by conventional restrictive clothing or traditional strictures on female mobility.

St Denis's childhood training in dance appears to have been more haphazard than Duncan's. Her first movement lessons were in Delsarte, given by her mother who read the exercises out of an instruction manual. In 1892, St Denis saw Stebbins perform both statue-posing and an interpretive dance. She was deeply impressed by the expressive potential and 'the dignity and truth of the human body' in movement and stillness and Stebbins' unique conjoining of 'spirituality and spectacle' became the model for her own dance career (Shelton 1981: 19). It is clear that St Denis valued the Delsartian contribution to dance as she and Shawn engaged a teacher to give lessons in Delsartism to the students at Denishawn. However, St Denis was more inclined towards the theoretical framework of Delsarte himself rather than that of American Delsartism (Ruyter 1979). American Delsartism found its most significant inspiration in ancient Greece while St Denis turned towards the Orient for her inspiration. She sought to transcend the body through dance into the realm of the spiritual with 'yogic' as opposed to' humanistic' endeavours (Ruyter 1979). American Delsartism, on the other hand, was not intent on transcending physicality and its use of yoga was treated as yet another, albeit exotic, method of physical culture.

In addition to lessons in Delsartism, St Denis took classes in social dance at a local dancing school run by Maud Davenport, and she auditioned for Karl Marwig, a fashionable Swiss dancing master in New York who was also a booking agent for New York showgirls. Instruction in social dancing as a means of teaching comportment and manners had a long history in America. Marwig represented the utmost in refinement. He also offered

the most advanced tuition in the field of the day; social dancing embell-
ished with some basic ballet steps from the French or Italian schools and
a few gestures from Delsarte (Kendall 1979). Marwig recognised a talent
in St Denis and offered to give her free tuition. She was unable to take
advantage of this, however, because her parents could seldom afford the
fare from New Jersey to New York. In the early 1890s St Denis moved
to New York to embark on her stage career as a solo show dancer in
vaudeville. In the mid-1890s she took ballet lessons from Marie Bonfanti
around the same time as Duncan.

Unlike Duncan, St Denis gained extensive experience of the American
theatre before she launched her independent career as an art dancer. From
1883 to 1889 she performed in vaudeville engagements whenever the
opportunity arose. From 1898 to 1905 she worked in the conventional
theatre as an actor–dancer. In 1898 she worked briefly for the same
Augustin Daly who had employed Duncan several years before. From
1889 to 1905 she was a member of David Belasco's company. Belasco
was a leading theatrical producer of the day and his lavish productions
were a combination of the romantic with the realistic. The plots of the
plays he chose to produce were not representative of everyday life but,
rather, were magnifications of melodrama in the musical theatre tradition.
They centred on unusual incidents such as rescue, murder and betrayal.
He set these events in realistic settings, creating the illusion of reality
with vast and detailed sets, huge crowd scenes and extravagant costumes
and props. St Denis absorbed much from her experience with Belasco
in particular and the American theatre in general, which she carried
through into her own dance career (Kendall 1979, Shelton 1981).

The contrast between a St Denis production and a Duncan production
is striking. St Denis's own productions and those of Denishawn were
clearly in line with the Belasco tradition, the earlier ballet spectaculars
and the glitter and pace of vaudeville (Ruyter 1979). St Denis, according
to Martin (1967), was largely a character dancer. In her Oriental cycle
she personified either a specific individual, a deity or a 'symbol of spiritual
qualities' and did not seek to reveal the self, but, rather, to objectify
more impersonal concepts. The theatre as a creator of illusions was a
perfect vehicle for this.

Duncan not only became dissatisfied with the possibilities that were open
to her in the popular theatre much earlier than they were for St Denis, but
she also came to reject totally the glitter of theatricality. Where St Denis
was lavish, Duncan was stark, performing mostly solo, in simple garments,
against a dramatic backdrop of plain blue velvet drapes. Moreover, Duncan
refused to work in the music halls or vaudeville houses, maintaining a strict
distinction between her art and popular culture, while St Denis, who also
wished her work to be viewed as art, performed on both the concert and
vaudeville stage. Although St Denis performed on the vaudeville stage, she
was none the less seen as an 'exotic', and not a genuine vaudeville performer

like Eva Tanguary (Barth 1980). It is unlikely that Duncan would have been successful on the popular stage even if she had agreed to perform in vaudeville, precisely because she was so austere. In the late 1920s and early 1930s, when American modern dance was in its infancy, dancers such as Graham and Humphrey, following Duncan, sought to reinstate the distinction between dance as art and popular culture.

When St Denis decided to create her own dance images, a predilection for spectacle and her belief in Christian Science led her to look to the religious myths and legends of the East for her source material. Like Duncan, she spent months in libraries and museums researching her chosen topic. Initially she wanted to create a ballet to be entitled *Egypta* in which she would play the goddess Isis, but she changed her focus temporarily towards the East and the legend of Radha, the mortal maiden who was loved by Krishna. In 1906, in a vaudeville house in New York, St Denis launched her independent career as an art dancer with *Radha*, and two other shorter pieces, *Incense* ('Art Nouveau in Dance', Shelton 1981), and *The Cobras*.

For her first matinee performance of *Radha* to society ladies in New York that same year, St Denis attempted to create an 'Oriental' atmosphere before the concert began by placing genuine Hindus inside the foyer of the theatre and having the air heavy with the scent of incense. In order to create the illusion of being 'Radha' she wore a gauze skirt trimmed with gilt, her midriff was bare and her bodice covered in jewels. She had jewels on her head, bangles on her arms and bells on her ankles and, to complete the picture, she stained her skin brown. However, there was no attempt to make authentic ethnic dance movements, rather the gestures were intended to be suggestive of the spirit of Indian temple dances.

Exotic dancing, in the form of belly dancing or the kootch, was not new to the American stage. The hootchy-kootchy had been popularised by an Egyptian dancer called Little Egypt in the early 1890s. However, St Denis's *Radha* was something new and distinct from the hootchy-kootchy activities of other 'Oriental' dancers of the day, as the reviews of her first performances seem to indicate. 'In their self-embarrassment', according to Walter Terry (1956: 52), 'the reporters tried to review her on the basis of comparisons with other performers while admitting the novelty of her offerings'. On the one hand, they compared her with the 'Persian dancers of the Midway' and found her to be more exotic, and, on the other, they reported that 'none of her dances are open to vulgarity' (Terry 1956: 52).

The dance began with St Denis as Radha sitting on a pedestal with her worshippers bowed before her. The figure came to life, bowed to her followers, and danced for them with objects symbolic of the five senses – among others, a cup of wine from which she drank and a garland of flowers which she pressed to her breast. The movement built up to an ecstatic frenzy with high kicks, back-bends and whirling and ended with a symbolic swoon to the floor.

The confusion arose because there were no real standards by which to judge her work. The changes that had taken place within variety theatre in the 1890s had created a space for the emergence of female solo performers in vaudeville, where previously women had been restricted to the chorus lines. By 1906, America was used to skirt dancers, clog dancers, acrobatic dancers and 'stunt toe dancing', but not to serious dance. The Russian dancers who provided American audiences with their first glimpse of 'proper' ballet since the days of the earlier ballet extravaganzas, had yet to make their appearance. Dance, at this time, represented a small part of all theatrical productions in vaudeville, musical comedy or opera, and there were no permanent dance companies to tour and perform in a full-length dance performance. St Denis was the first American to employ the themes of the Orient in a profound manner. She planned her dances to the last detail and costumed herself in accordance with the demands of the dance and not to the fashion of the period (Kendall 1979). Moreover, her dancing was sensual, her backbends and slow highkicks were regarded as 'truly sensational' but she was not regarded as vulgar (Terry 1956). In short, she embodied many aspects of the popular American stage of the day but she had something else besides, an 'aura', a sense of mystery, and the new audiences were looking for this added dimension (Kendall 1979).

St Denis, like Duncan, became something of a cult figure in New York society circles, but she too sought greater recognition for her art. In 1906, following in the footsteps of Fuller, Duncan and Allan, she left for Europe and success.

Around the same time as St Denis was launching her career in dance, significant social changes were taking place in America. The rapid industrial expansion begun in the nineteenth century continued through to the 1900s at a steady pace, despite the financial panics of 1873 and 1893. The process of industrialisation was aided considerably by the manufacturing north's success over the south in the civil war, the growth of the Pacific railway, and the ending of the frontier. As manufacturing increased, so too did urbanisation and the growing modern cities began to take on their present shape as manufacturing centres. The demand for labour drew a flood of immigrants to the cities. People of different nationalities had emigrated to America since the colonies were founded. However, in the late nineteenth century the numbers increased sharply and the composition of nationalities varied significantly. Prior to the 1880s, the majority of immigrants had come from northern or western Europe, but by the 1890s these were superseded by an influx of immigrants from southern and eastern Europe. While these new immigrants breathed energy and diversity into American life, there were difficulties of assimilation, not only in terms of cultural differences; but because they were in competition for jobs with the native urban poor, they were regarded with suspicion. The newer immigrants tended to congregate by nationality in the slum areas of the cities, creating foreign enclaves, and this further exacerbated the tensions between them and the native urban poor.

By the 1880s vast fortunes had been made. Corporations had emerged which could control market prices and exercise the power of life and death over communities, despite attempts by Congress to regulate the freedom of the trusts and the corporations. The conflicts and inequalities that resulted from rapid capitalisation led to industrial and agrarian unrest and the emergence of organised labour and populism in the 1890s. However, a deep-rooted devotion to *laissez-faire*, the divisions between the working class on grounds of race, and the interests of 'big business', contributed to the postponement of the emergence of a powerful unionised labour force. The cause of populism was defeated temporarily by McKinley's Republican victory in 1896. With the succession of Theodore Roosevelt in 1901, however, an era of 'progressive' reform was ushered in which continued until America entered the First World War.

The progressive era witnessed the emergence of modern American society, the development of which was accelerated by the contemporary revolution in transportation and communication: mass production of the automobile, the telegraph system, the telephone network, electrical power, the gramophone, the wireless and moving pictures. These new means of communication directly affected production and consumption. By breaking down distances and differences between isolated communities across America, they helped to draw the American people closer together than ever before. The nationalistic fervour which resulted from the Spanish–American War in 1898 also contributed to this process. Americans were beginning to become conscious of themselves as a people and it was around this time that the other arts, which hitherto had lagged behind American literature, began to develop.

> In Theodore Roosevelt's second term of office a new spirit of insurgence seized the American imagination, as national interest was focused on reform. Writers and artists suddenly came out into the open to take up the cause of the common man against organised corporate power and abuses of privilege.
> (Hunter 1972: 29)

The period was characterised by a new style of 'exposé' or 'muck-raking' journalism and the reforming zeal of a new generation of naturalist writers like Theodore Dreiser and Stephen Crane (Hunter 1972). It also witnessed the emergence of the first organised attempt by a group of American artists to establish an 'American' style of painting.

This group of young painters, whose leader and spokesman was Robert Henri, were mostly trained in Philadelphia, but they soon became known as the 'New York Realists'. In 1908, because of a rebuttal by the National Academy, The Eight staged their first independent exhibition of American artists in New York. The title of the 'ash can school' was later given to The Eight, their followers and pupils because they dwelt on themes that spoke to the less seemly side of American culture. They were not dedicated to creating art for art's sake. Rather, 'The Eight treated themes new to American art – the shabby neighbourhoods and the seamy side of the lower urban classes' (Rose 1967: 12). However, unlike the naturalist writers of the day, or the later social realist painters of the 1930s, The Eight did not seek to cast judgement on such matters but instead attempted to describe what they saw, often using the skills they had learnt as artist-reporters. In their revolt against the strictures of the academy, 'They were willing to forsake the precincts of high art for the more immediate vitality of popular culture' (Rose 1967: 12).

In rebelling against the official academy, The Eight were not reacting against the dominant pictorial tradition of western art, as the French avant-garde had done. There was no such tradition in America to rebel against. Rather, The Eight challenged the stuffiness and privilege of the academy and its rules and regulations. Like reformers in other areas of American life during the progressive era, they championed the cause of democracy and individualism (Rose 1967).

At the same time as The Eight were emphasising life over art, an aesthetic revolt that marks the beginning of American modernism was taking place under the auspices of art for art's sake. In New York in 1905 the photographer Alfred Stieglitz opened the little Gallery of the Photo-Secession in the attic of 291 Fifth Avenue to show photographs. In calling his gallery Photo-Secession Stieglitz was appealing to the spirit of modernists in Europe who named themselves secessionists. Photo-secession means to break with the conventional idea of what comprises a photograph. Within two years Stieglitz expanded his operation to exhibit painting and sculpture as well as photography. During the following decade the '291', as it came to be called, became the centre of the avant-garde in America (Rose 1967).

Stieglitz was an innovator who changed the history of photography, and the painting and sculpture he exhibited at the 291 also seceded from conventional views of what constituted art. The 291 gave the first American exhibitions of European modernists like Matisse, Toulouse-Lautrec, Rousseau, Picasso and Brancusi. Stieglitz also encouraged the emerging American avant-garde. American modernists exiled in Europe found a forum for their work in America through Stieglitz. For example, he published Gertrude Stein's articles on Matisse and Picasso in his avant-garde magazine *Camera Work*. In 1910, at the same time as the Society of Independent Artists (which included Henri and The Eight) held their first show, Stieglitz presented the first group exhibition of American modernists which included the work of Max Weber, John Marin and Alfred Maurer.

While Henri, The Eight and the Independents emphasised democrati-sation in art, Stieglitz and the modernists spoke to the few. Although both factions were rebelling against the National Academy, their viewpoints were radically opposed to each other. The first group extolled the virtues of life over art, while the second, in agreement with Oscar Wilde's view that 'life limits art', believed in art for art's sake and that works of art should speak for themselves, and should not be translated into words.

> Thus, the polarisation of non academic painters in America into two groups, a socially oriented faction and an avant-garde faction – which has endured more or less until the present – was already an accomplished fact early in the twentieth century.
>
> (Rose 1967: 39)

The first decade of the twentieth century also witnessed the beginnings of a shift in attitudes towards theatrical dance in America. During St Denis's two and a half years' absence, a wave of art dancing, in the form of a plethora of Salomés, took hold of America. Clearly this interest in aesthetic dancing was just discernible before St Denis left for Europe and she and Duncan were part of it.

The most famous of these new aesthetic dancers was Gertrude Hoffman, who, like Duncan and St Denis, emerged from the margins of middle-class society. However, unlike her predecessors, Hoffman did not go to Europe but, instead, took her Salomé on a national tour. The other Salomés did the same and thus, as Kendall (1979) has shown, they brought a level of sophistication to even the smallest towns in America.

By 1909, when St Denis returned from Europe, the American public were beginning to be aware that a dancer was more than a pretty face or a good pair of legs; she was someone special who could magically offer her audience a sense of far-away places or distant times. St Denis, unlike Duncan, had an unfailing ability to perceive what the American public desired and the good commercial sense to respond to it. For her first concert in New York since her return from Europe, St Denis provided the audience with her interpretation of Salomé, in addition to her *East Indian Suite* which comprised five dances (*Yogi* and *Nautch Girl* had been added to the original three). The reviews proclaimed that St Denis's Salomé outdid all the other versions and that she had 'dazzled' the audience. From that point on, she was treated seriously as an artist. Clearly her success in Europe played a significant role in this because, at that time, America still looked to Europe for the assessment of artistic merit. Notwithstanding, St Denis had other attributes which also contributed to her success in America. Not only did she 'dazzle' her audience with theatricality, she was beautiful and, more importantly, she was not overtly sexual: factors which moved at least one music critic (there were no dance critics) to compare her with Duncan:

> In comparison with the dancing of Ruth St Denis, the posturing, the prancing, the loping, the bounding of Isadora Duncan seem common and material. It is true that Miss St Denis has natural advantages over the majority of her

sisters in art. She is tall and of entrancing proportions. . . . The ensemble of her body is as a flawless lyric.

And yet there is this to be said that to some might be paradoxical: although her body is of a woman divinely planned, there is no atmosphere of sex about her whether she is immovable upon the alter – a picture of beauty never to be forgotten – or dancing the sense of touch.

(Terry 1956: 61–2)

In order for dance to become a part of American cultural life, notable changes were essential. To begin with, dance had to engage the attention of the American public and the moral prejudices against it had to be counterbalanced. In other words, as Ruyter (1979) has argued, dance had to become both 'attractive and nice'. Thereafter, a process had to be set into action to enable more people to see and enjoy dance, more to study it, and more to take up a career in dancing. This, in turn, by creating more performers, would enable yet more people to be introduced to dance, and thus continue the reproductive process necessary for the development of dance in the culture.

St Denis made a significant contribution to this process. She helped to break down the barriers against dance by giving it different (spiritual) ends, but, at the same time, she put on a good show. That is, she was different; she had the aura of an exotic about her but she was also recognisable to her American audiences as their 'New Jersey Hindu' (Kendall 1979, Shelton 1981). Although Duncan also attempted to give dancing different ends, her notion of the spiritual was not acceptable to the majority of Americans and she eschewed the trappings of theatricality and the popular theatre.

By contrast, St Denis never strayed far from middle-class American values. Her inclination towards Christian Science and her interest in yoga were in line with part of the New Thought Movement or the 'Boston Craze', the followers of which proclaimed that the bases of a good life were founded on moderation, self-improvement, chastity and virtue. Their ultimate goal was to attain harmony with the infinite universe. By aligning herself with such a creed, St Denis remained in line with the most tolerable American middle-class aspirations and principles (Ruyter 1979).

Furthermore, St Denis's interest in the East placed her in line with a respected American philosophical and literary tradition which began with the transcendentalism of Emerson and Thoreau in the middle of the nineteenth century and continued through to the twentieth century. The interest in the Orient, however, was not restricted to such scholarly writers, nor was it new. It could be traced back through to colonial trade and shipping (Shelton 1981). But this interest was being surmounted as the frontier was closing at the end of the century, and there was growing contact between the East and West through trade expansion, travel and the development of mass communications and transport systems. It was given further impetus by the Chicago Columbian Exposition of 1893.

The Exposition was to have its panoramic and theatrical displays, its continental cafés, and a staggering abundance of devices and appliances for instruction, comfort, and amusement. . . . Those who had been dazzled by the Rue de Caire at the Paris Exposition of 1889 would find it surpassed by the Chicago version of a street in Cairo, complete with the wrigglings of Little Egypt. The living representatives of savage, civilized, and semi-civilized nations were to occupy models of their native villages – Dahoman, Indian, Chinese, Turkish, German. Here there would be an ice railway, a Moorish palace, a Japanese bazaar, a Bohemian glass factory, and an exhibition of Irish lacemaking.

(Ziff 1967: 3)

In the late nineteenth century, many popular writers were also drawn to Oriental themes, and translations of eastern literature were available in both academic and popular editions. 'While scholars, spurred by the first translations into English of the *Sacred Books of the East*, pondered the *Bhagavad-Gita* and the *Qur'ān*, laymen bought copies of such popularizations as a Delsartist's *Hindu Philosophy in a Nutshell'* (Shelton 1981: 55).

Interest in exotica was not confined to literature. By 1909, when St Denis was at the peak of her solo career, Oriental style furnishings, in the form of Turkish-like tassled cushions, large vases containing ostrich feathers, parlour palms and so forth, were to be seen in the corner of the living room in many middle-class homes in America (Kendall 1979). This 'Turkish corner' decor, like St Denis's movement, costumes and stage settings, was not intended to be authentic; rather, the aim was to create an atmosphere of Orientalism. The new 'polite' cosmopolitans in the 1900s bought kimonos and Japanese prints; society balls took on Indian, Japanese and Chinese themes; and Japanese prints could be found decorating the walls of even quite ordinary households (Shelton 1981). Society women were particularly enamoured of Orientalism. The society hostesses wore caftans and kimonos in preference to being laced up in tight corsets and heavy garments and could be found lounging elegantly on cushions while discussing poetry and philosophy. Suzanne Shelton (1981) has suggested that it was the love of the Orient that bonded St Denis with the social élite who supported her, which, in turn, helped her to make the successful transformation from Ruthie, 'a mere variety dancer', to that of the artistic exotic dancer Ruth St Denis. Her supporters saw in her a 'serious attempt to translate oriental principles into American art' (Shelton 1981: 56). As Kendall (1979) has pointed out, it was to St Denis's advantage that she was a 'New Jersey Hindu' rather than a genuine East Indian because, in her approach, American audiences could recognise their own home-grown version of Orientalia. Thus, St Denis was in line with both a distinguished American intellectual tradition and the new found popular taste for the exotic.

From 1909 to 1911 St Denis toured extensively throughout the United States, performing in smaller towns in addition to the larger cities and prominent cultural centres, thereby bringing her vision of dance art to a large section of the American public. In 1911 Ted Shawn saw her perform and was so stirred by the experience that he determined to work towards his own vision of American dance. It is significant that, from this time onward, American dancers began to draw inspiration from the field of American dance itself where previously they had relied totally upon other sources (Ruyter 1979). This helped to set in motion the process of the cultural reproduction which was necessary for the development of dance in America.

In 1914 Shawn became St Denis's partner and husband and in 1915 they created Denishawn and the first company school in Los Angeles. From 1914 to 1931 St Denis and Shawn (sometimes together and sometimes separately) and members of the company toured extensively at home and abroad, bringing Denishawn's distinctive brand of exotic dance theatre to highly appreciative audiences. As well as attracting the subsequent leaders of American modern dance, Denishawn provided dancers for the theatre and for the newest form of entertainment, films. They also had a large number of imitators who attempted to bring the lavish Denishawn style of theatricality to a wide range of audiences across the country.

By 1911, 'aesthetic' dance was beginning to develop at a pace that would have been inconceivable when first Fuller, then Duncan and then St Denis had started out. When Duncan and St Denis first dared to expose their bodies to the American public, middle-class women were still firmly encased in their corsets, despite the craze for cycling and physical culture in the 1890s, and the activities of the women dress reformers. By discarding the stereotypical image of the ballet-girl dancer and demonstrating the expressive potential of the female body moving freely in space and time, Duncan and St Denis contributed further to the process of breaking down traditional attitudes towards the female body which was first given impetus by the health and hygiene reform movement and American Delsartism (Kendall 1979).

In the years between 1911 and 1930, something of a transformation had taken place with regard to performance dance. Across America by the 1920s, 'absolutely ordinary middle-class girls became performers in theatre, movies, and dance' (Kendall 1979: 155). The aesthetic dancers of Duncan's and St Denis's generation, for the most part, emerged from the margins of middle-class society with little prior knowledge of the theatre. The earlier ballet-girl dancers were either drawn from the working classes or, like Fuller, were born into the theatre, and they had little opportunity to advance up the social scale because of the social stigmas attached to theatrical dancing. However, the young women who entered dancing as a profession in the 1920s did not do so for economic reasons as, in part, Duncan and St Denis had done earlier. Neither did they seek to challenge the established norms of society. On the contrary, 'dancing was there; they simply took the imaginative leap from lessons to a career' (Kendall 1979: 155). That it was there, where heretofore it had been absent, can be attributed to the pioneering efforts of dancers such as St Denis and Shawn, the influence of Duncan and to a certain extent Fuller, developments in the theatre and in progressive education in America.

Ted Shawn brought a number of valuable points to the partnership with St Denis. To begin with, he brought a religious commitment as strong as St Denis's in terms of missionary zeal, although he was 'less mystical and otherworldly' (Ruyter 1979). He also brought a wide knowledge of the range of dance styles available in America at that time, experience in performing and teaching dance and an ability to organise dance programmes.

Shawn first studied dance in Denver with Hazel Wallack, a former dancer with the Metropolitan Opera Ballet. He made his first appearance with his teacher in a club in Denver in 1910, at the height of the dancing Salomés. It appears that they performed a mixture of ballet, ballroom and the aesthetic Salomé styles. Shawn moved on to Los Angeles to gain further dance experience and there, with Norma Gould, he performed exhibition ballroom dancing at the time when ragtime and 'thés dansants' were in vogue. Shawn also presented and arranged several programmes of classic and interpretive dancing, as the new 'free-style' dancing was called. He and Gould formed a small touring company and in 1913 they appeared in an early Edison film entitled *Dance through the Ages*, which Shawn directed. They came east, touring as entertainers for the Santa Fe Railroad. Shawn studied Delsarte for a short period at Mary Perry King's Uni-Trinitarian School of Personal Harmonizing in Connecticut. In New York in 1914, he studied different styles of ballet, French, Russian and Italian, Spanish dancing and the latest ballroom steps. There he began to teach and on occasion perform with Gould and in the autumn of 1914 he joined St Denis prior to her tour of the south.

Shawn also brought to Denishawn a commitment to teaching and the desire to create a school of dance, the breadth of tuition of which would surpass anything hitherto available in America. From the outset, the form and organisation of Denishawn were of his making, while St Denis, who was more concerned with her own personal development, provided the atmosphere. The students at Denishawn were exposed to a wide variety of dance forms, including: basic ballet technique (in bare feet), Delsarte expression, Greek dancing, Oriental technique, music visualisations and creative dancing. This eclectic non-academic approach was advanced by Shawn who maintained that a well-trained dancer should know all forms of dance. In order to widen the students' dance experience, Shawn brought in guest teachers of Delsarte, Dalcroze, Japanese sword dancing, the Hula, or of anything else that caught his imagination. In many respects Denishawn embodied the ideals of progressive education. It mirrored the progressive theories of John Dewey who described modern education as a process of individual growth and development. As well as dance classes, the students were offered piano lessons, French lessons and classes in stagecraft. The intention was to promote individuality and to produce well-rounded individuals who could perform a range of dance styles.

Shawn added a wider variety of ethnic dance themes to St Denis's original Oriental programme, including Spanish, Amer-Indian and Christian themes and exhibition ballroom dancing. Like St Denis, Shawn had a predilection for spectacle and a gift for extrapolating elements of popular culture and incorporating them into a Denishawn programme.

From the beginning of its development until the present day, serious American dance has drawn on popular culture. It took the American public many years to realise that ballet was more than theatrical entertainment, that it constituted an aesthetic mode, and that it required many years of rigorous training to perfect the technique. When Anna Pavlova and Mikhail Mordkin performed at the Metropolitan Opera House in 1910, the audience had no conception that their dancing had evolved out of a sustained tradition. Most of the public considered that Pavlova was like their own American classic dancers because, like Duncan, Allan and many other interpretive dancers, she wore the familiar Greek tunic and danced to the music of Chopin. Moreover, ballet was not restricted to the opera houses but was just as likely to be performed as a speciality act in vaudeville. Even the great Pavlova appeared alongside 'circus acts, drill teams and an ice show' (Siegel 1979: 2). In the 1930s, when the demarcation lines between dance as art and commercialism were heavily drawn, choreographers such as Graham and Humphrey drew on native themes and the resources of the American character to create their own, defiantly modern, dance images. But the advocates of modern dance were not alone in this. For example, although Lincoln Kirstein was intent upon establishing ballet as a high art in America, he emphasised that an 'American style of ballet' should be developed. Similarly, pioneering American classical choreographers created ballets on native themes using popular musical idioms, such as Ruth Page's *Frankie and Johnny* (1938). As Siegel (1979) has argued, throughout the brief history of serious dance in America, both ballet and modern choreographers have been influenced by their work in the legitimate theatre, films and television.

> The early modern dancers often created serious works to be performed as part of Broadway or nightclub shows. Jazz dancing fed directly into the vocabularies of ballet and modern dancers, and ballroom-exhibition styles have been used very successfully by stage choreographers. This constant stream of vernacular and popular material flowing into our art dance, sometimes by design and sometimes inadvertently, is one of the major sources of the creativity of American dance.
>
> (Siegel 1979: 3)

The continuous flow from the commercial to high art is not restricted to dance, but is also evidenced in the development of other artistic fields in America, such as painting and music. In the case of the painting, as Rose (1967) has stressed, there are no clear-cut boundaries between fine art and commercial or applied art in America, as there are in Europe. Many American artists supported themselves as illustrators, sign writers or commercial artists before they turned to art and eventually used these vocational techniques in their art works. Indeed, illustration has often been seen as a fine art in America. This, according to Rose (1967: 8), was a result of 'the egalitarian nature of American society with its lack of fixed traditions and its constant demand for an art that can be understood by the majority'. The American public has only recently begun to identify high art with fine art. Before photography became adapted to the needs of newspaper publications, artist–journalists served as newspaper photographers do now. During the civil war, the painter Winslow Homer sketched battles for the newspapers. Early twentieth-century artists – such as John Sloan, William Glackens, Everett Shinn and George Luks, who became members of The Eight – started out as artist–journalists for the Philadelphia Press sketching pictures of fires, strikes, industrial disasters and similar events. They were encouraged by Henri to use their artist-reporting skills, 'rapid execution and spontaneous style', for their paintings of humble subjects (Rose 1967).

The process of dance renewal, which began with St Denis, continued and was strengthened by her partnership with Shawn and the resultant Denishawn organisation. By accentuating the spiritual side of dance, by leading extremely 'proper' lives and by insisting that the Denishawn students and performers did the same, St Denis and Shawn helped to persuade the American public of the moral value of dance. Unlike Duncan, they remained firmly within the bounds of American middle-class morality. They did not patronise their public, as Duncan did in later years; on the contrary, being so close to the values of that public, St Denis and Shawn knew what the audience wanted and they had the ability to produce it. If money was required to stage a new production or to maintain the school, they would actively compromise their ideals by adapting the programme to the demands of vaudeville. For example, when ragtime was in vogue they injected a ragtime number into their programme, despite the fact that St Denis reportedly despised that form of dancing. Duncan, on the other hand, who also hated ragtime, would never have compromised her artistic ideals in this way. The fact that Denishawn continued in the St Denis–Belascoesque style to produce attractive fast-moving programmes which left no one in the audience bored, contributed to its appeal and ensuing success.

In addition, the extensive touring of Denishawn between 1914 and 1931 enabled a considerable portion of the American public to become acquainted with dance as a serious art (Shelton 1981). By producing a type of dance travelogue, Denishawn often provided Americans with their first glimpse of the dances of different cultures. Moreover, by establishing a dance company and school, St Denis and Shawn provided an invaluable training ground for the next generation of American dancers. Three of the four dancers who became known as the 'Big Four' of American modern dance in the 1930s emerged from Denishawn: Martha Graham, Doris Humphrey and Charles Weidman. The fourth, Hanya Holm, was trained in the technique of the German modern dancer, Mary Wigman. Two non-dance figures who contributed much to the development of American modern dance also emerged from Denishawn: Pauline Lawrence, the dress designer for the Humphrey–Weidman company, took classes in dance and costuming and was an accompanist at Denishawn from 1917 to 1928; Louis Horst, Graham's first musical director, was Denishawn's musical director from 1915 to 1925. A number of the leaders of the second generation of American modern dance emanated from these two major strands. Thus, Denishawn played a significant role in the process of cultural reproduction of dance in America.

5 ICONOCLASTS FROM DENISHAWN

One of Denishawn's most important contributions to the development of American modern dance lay in the fact that St Denis and Shawn believed in cultivating their students' natural talents and powers of movement expression. By not subjugating their students to the demands of a single system, according to Ruyter (1979) Denishawn helped to set non-academic dance in America in a direction of diversity and individuality of form, which it has continued to maintain. Although Martha Graham, Doris Humphrey and Charles Weidman were trained in what might be called the Denishawn style or look, they were, nevertheless, very different from each other: Humphrey was lyrical, Graham displayed a dramatic intensity and Weidman had a flair for comedy. These differences were promoted by either St Denis or Shawn, although, as Shelton (1981) has pointed out, the dancers often complained that they always appeared as someone other than themselves.

Non-academic dance in America has its roots in individualism and anti-authoritarianism. It was partly as a result of this that what finally came to be called American modern dance entailed 'a dance that fulfilled the needs of its leaders' (Siegel 1979: 17).

> Martha Graham's early company were a group of women with muscular legs, powerful feet, arms and pelvises, and little subtlety in the upper body. The early Humphrey–Weidman dancers had exceptional fluidity in their arms and legs, rhythmic sensitivity, a feeling for the pulse and the swing of their own weight.
>
> (Siegel 1979: 17)

Individualism and anti-authoritarianism have not only been features of non-academic dance in America, but also of twentieth-century American art. For example, the paintings of the first group of insurgent realists were also characterised by difference, despite the artists' stated concern to develop a native style. The exhibition of The Eight in 1908, as Rose (1967: 25) has noted, was criticised for 'its clashing dissonances of eight differently tuned orchestras', as well as the subject matter of the paintings.

The works of the group (The Eight) were indeed heterogeneous: they included realistic cityscapes and genre paintings by Henri, Glackens, Sloan, Shinn, and Luks; the quiet Impressionist landscapes by Lawson; the idyllic fantasies of Davies; and the strictly patterned landscapes by Prendergast. This so-called dissonance was to set the pattern for later groups of American artists who showed together under no other banner save nonconformity.

(Rose 1967: 25)

Anti-authoritarianism and individualism were integral features of the Protestant ethic and the frontier spirit, which, according to Martin (1967), had impinged themselves on the fabric of the American character. Therefore, in major features of their foundation, American modern dance and fine art in America can be seen to reflect important aspects of prevalent notions of American character.

Although American modern dance was soon defined by the various styles and individual concerns of its leaders, the early modern dancers shared many ideas in common. Paramount among these was the belief that dance mirrors its own social environment, and that it comes out of the life and the circumstances of its immediate time and space. If the purpose of dance is communication, the modern dancers argued, then American dance should develop forms that would reflect and speak to the contemporary American experience. In other words, American dance should be functional for the society. Functionalism, according to Martin (1967), was another central aspect of the Puritan ethic and the pioneer experience that had helped to form the American character. Hence, American modern dance's emphasis on functionality can be treated as yet another expression of the legacy of Puritanism and frontierism on American culture.

Ruth St Denis began her concert career in the era of progressivism in America when almost everything conspired to make anything seem possible. The next generation of American dancers, such as Graham, Humphrey and Weidman, inherited a very different world. Modern dance emerged in the 'jazz era' in the wake of the aftermath of the First World War and its initial growth took place during the Depression.

America entered the First World War in 1917 in a wave of fervent nationalism (McCoy 1977: 21–3). The country's involvement in the war led to a dispute between political isolationism and internationalism. During the war, the American public felt the full weight of the Federal government as never before. Industry, fuel, housing and the press came under the Federal boards, and Congress afforded President Wilson unprecedented powers of authority. The war also provided the context for the most sweeping attempt to legislate social reform through the Eighteenth Amendment to the Constitution, prohibition, which was passed in 1919. The surge of nationalism, voiced in the terms of fears for national security, resulted in the curbing of civil liberties with the introduction of the Espionage Act in 1917, and the Sedition Act of 1918. In conjunction with the state laws against subversion, these acts had far-reaching effects for American society (Nye and Morpurgo 1970b). The 'hate the enemy' campaign fostered by war propaganda resulted in the Federal authorities using their new powers to arrest and imprison over a thousand people, including Eugene Debs, the Socialist candidate for President in 1912 who had polled a million votes. The tide of nationalism did not cease with the end of the war in 1918 and a campaign was waged against Communists or Bolsheviks. In America, that meant anyone who had any 'leftist' leanings. Foreigners, blacks and religious groups – even Catholics or Jews – were discriminated against and suspected of anti-American activities. The Ku Klux Klan, silent for almost twenty years, claimed four million members by 1924. The age of progressivism had turned to an age of reaction (Nye and Morpurgo 1970b).

The recession that followed the war gave rise to a sharp increase in unemployment. The Wilson administration appeared to have no coherent policy to deal with the postwar economic problems. Ultimately, Wilson's concept of 'the war to end all wars' with the express aim of making the 'world free for democracy', turned sour (McCoy 1977: 22). The high cost of the war in terms of capital and lives led Americans to question why they became involved in the first place. Increasingly, the First World War became known in America as 'Wilson's War' (Nye and Morpurgo 1970b). America's refusal to take up membership of the League of Nations Covenant which was created by the Treaty of Versailles in 1919, meant that the country was turning its back on international politics in favour of political isolationism. Wilson submitted the treaty to the Senate in 1919, but it received a stormy passage. In March 1920, the Senate voted to end the war with Germany but would not ratify the treaty. Wilson vetoed the Senate's resolution and the war with Germany did not end officially until the resolution was passed later that year with the change of administration to the Republicans.

The new administration under President Hardy, and after his death in 1923, President Coolidge, advocated 'a return to normalcy' (McCoy 1977, Nye and Morpurgo 1970b). The powers given to the President were revoked. The Republican standpoint was characterised by Harding's neo-liberal statement that there should be 'less government in business and more business in government' (McCoy 1977: 68). Under the Republicans the corporations grew bigger than they had done in the McKinley era. By 1930, 50 per cent of the country's wealth was controlled by a mere two hundred companies. As the 1920s moved on, America entered a period of economic boom.

> The overwhelming fact about the twenties – was that they rolled in money. Presidential addresses to Congress . . . sounded like the chairman of the board's report to stockholders. Except for agriculture, mining and textiles, the national economy reached the highest level of profit yet recorded in American history.
> (Nye and Morpurgo 1970b: 672)

The mood of the 1920s vacillated between confidence and doubt (Carroll and Noble 1977, McCoy 1977). Optimism was expressed not only by a booming economy but also in cultural terms, by the growth of progressive education, which advocated growth and change. The era witnessed the founding of America's best-known music schools and the opening of some sixty new art museums. However, the postwar era produced a certain amount of scepticism about many aspects of American cultural life. Family ties had been loosened with the war and the dominant Victorian values had been considerably weakened. The divorce rate increased and church attendance dropped dramatically. The disillusionment that resulted from the war gave rise to a calling into question of the traditional values attached to liberal democracy. There emerged a new generation of writers such as Scott-Fitzgerald, Lewis, Hemingway and O'Neill, who became known as the 'lost generation' with their cynical novels and plays which emphasised the meaninglessness of life and disillusion with contemporary society. In this era of cultural isolationism and disillusion with Europe, American historians began to look for what was unique about American history and the specifically American character. Social critics like Henry Mencken began to reinforce the view that America was a cultural desert, provincial in outlook and a commercial jungle. Puritanism was blamed for almost all the negative factors of American culture. One of the reactions to this was the desire to be free of moral constraints. Among other things, it was characterised by the image of the new woman of the 1920s, with her bobbed hair, short waistless dresses (the dress reformers ultimately had time on their side) and frank talk about sex.

The era that witnessed the emergence of American modern dance, then, was very different from that in which St Denis embarked on her concert career. The change in the socio-economic climate coincided with emergent shifts in performance dance and in the other arts.

> The climate was right for a rebellion against a dance that was too decorative for postwar tastes. Change was essential for those artists who wanted to speak for their times.
>
> (Terry 1956: 48)

The modern dancers rejected the formalism of ballet and the exoticism of Denishawn as the basis for their American dance because both drew their inspiration from former epochs and foreign places. Instead, they sought to return to basics, to their own bodies, to experiment with movement, and to analyse its cause and effect. Although Duncan and St Denis had rejected ballet as the basis for their dance, and they too had begun by working outwards from their own bodies, they had relied respectively on the art of classical Greece and the Orient for their source of inspiration. The modern dancers, by contrast, wanted to discover how they, as Americans, moved. In order to create a 'new' dance that would respond to contemporary America, they sought to return to the source of the dance itself which they found to lie in 'significant' body movement. In so doing, they were putting into practice one of the principles of modernism which, according to Greenberg (1961), is to uncover the nature of the artistic medium and to work in terms of its specificity. Like St Denis and Duncan before them, the modern dancers wanted dance to be viewed as an art form. Indeed, Duncan and St Denis had imparted an idealistic vision of an American dance to their followers. 'But', as Ernestine Stodelle has noted, 'its technique and choreographic form would have to be forged by the next generation of dancers' (Stodelle 1984: 49). Moreover, the modern dancers did not believe that music should serve as the inspiration to release the stuff of dance, as Duncan had advocated; nor did they consider that the dance should be a visual representation of the musical structures as with St Denis's 'Music Visualizations'. Rather, in order to establish dance's independence, the modern dancers sought to emphasise the primacy of movement over the music and all other aspects of performance.

Although the dance metaphors that emerged in the name of American dance were highly individualistic, the above concerns constituted a central core of the movement in general. In this chapter and in the two chapters that follow the development of Martha Graham's work through to the 1940s is used to exemplify the development of American modern dance during its first two decades. Major areas of difference between Graham and the other acknowledged leaders in the field are examined as they emerge in the discussion. This is not to say that Graham or the 'Big Four' constituted all that American modern dance had to offer during that period. Rather, as with the discussion on Fuller, Duncan and St Denis, the concern is to take Graham as a starting point to make wider connections with the social and cultural world.

The name of Martha Graham (1894–1991) has been closely associated with the name of American modern dance itself. She was the first of the modern dancers to leave Denishawn. Her own dancing career spanned some fifty years and she made a significant contribution to the concept of dance theatre. Her repertoire, as one commentator has emphasised, is the largest and most diverse body of work to have been produced by a single choreographer to date (Stodelle 1984). In the course of creating her dances and in preparing other dancers to perform in them, she developed a system of movement that has become almost as firmly established a system of dance training as that of ballet. Moreover, a number of the dominant figures of the next generation of American modern dance, such as Erick Hawkins, Merce Cunningham and Paul Taylor, were members of her company.

There was nothing in Graham's background to indicate that she would achieve such heights in the dance. She did not emerge from the margins of middle-class society, as Duncan and St Denis had done. Rather, like many of the young women who embarked on a career in dancing in the latter part of the 'teens and early 1920s, Graham came from an upper-middle-class Protestant background. She grew up in a near suburb of Pittsburg, Pennsylvania, where her parents were pillars of the establishment. Her mother was a direct descendant of the Puritan, Miles Standish. Her father was a practising physician and 'alienist', a specialist in the treatment of nervous diseases. As a child Graham did not experience the kind of freedom that either Duncan or St Denis had been afforded. On the contrary, her parents were staunch Presbyterians, and with the father as an authority figure, a strict and orderly household was maintained, while obedience and moral rectitude were demanded of the offspring.

When Graham was fourteen years old the family moved from the east to Santa Barbara in California. In Los Angeles in 1911, Graham saw a performance of St Denis, after which, like Shawn, she determined to become a dancer. However, it was almost unthinkable for someone from Graham's background to pursue such a career. True to their Puritan heritage, her parents believed that the theatre was a worldly indulgence and, as such, sinful. Her father in particular insisted that she continue her education in the hope that she might go on to Vassar college after finishing high school. Graham, as a conventionally dutiful daughter, continued her high school studies but after graduating in 1913, instead of going to Vassar, she enrolled at the Cumnock School of Expression, an arts institution that offered instruction in acting and stagecraft to young people who wanted to go on to the stage. By going to such a college Graham was one step nearer her ambition, although it conflicted with her father's plans for her future. In the doctrine of Puritanism, however, the issue of conscience is somewhat ambiguous, which provides an escape clause for individuals who stand up against authority. The Puritan code demands of the individual obedience to the Will of God, and within the family, to the father as the head of the household. At the same time, however, inherent in Puritanism is the principle of individual conscience as the final arbiter of what is right and just. It is this aspect of the 'Puritan conscience' that provides a rationale for going against certain established beliefs or views. For example, when Milton said, 'though I may be sent to Hell for it, such a God will never command my respect' (Weber 1976: 101), it is almost certain that his Puritan conscience was close at hand. Emerson's impassioned speech against the enactment of the Fugitive Slave Law in which he said 'I will not obey it, by God' (Schlatter 1962: 41), can be viewed in the same vein. Similarly, Graham (1973), in later years, was to say that she had been 'called' to the dance. In other words she had been 'elected' and (in accordance with the Puritan code) she could do no other except pursue it to the end, despite the fact that the end itself could be objected to by that very same code and by her father.

Immediately after graduating from the Cumnock School of Expression in 1916, Graham enrolled in the Denishawn summer school in Los Angeles. Even at Denishawn, at least for some time, there was little indication of her potential as a dancer. Graham's prior dance training had been restricted to a few classes in interpretive or aesthetic dancing at Cumnock. Despite the fact that the demands made of a Denishawn dancer, in contrast to those of a ballet dancer, did not depend on rigorous childhood training, at 22 years of age, Graham was considered rather old to begin to train as a dancer. Furthermore, compared to many of the other students, and to St Denis in particular, she was short, dark and inclined to be overweight. St Denis decided that she did not want Graham in her class and handed her over to Shawn to teach. It was he who recognised and encouraged Graham's potential for dramatic dance. Towards the end of the summer session St Denis used Graham as a demonstrator in some of her classes. When America entered the First World War in 1917, Shawn immediately volunteered for the ambulance corps and St Denis went on a Liberty Bond tour. In order to keep the summer school going in their absence, Shawn asked Graham and certain other students to teach classes.

In 1917, Doris Humphrey, who was slightly younger than Graham, enrolled in the Denishawn summer school. Although Humphrey came from a middle-class Protestant background, whose line of descent can be traced back to the Puritan, William Brewster, and to Ralph Waldo Emerson, her parents loved the theatre arts and encouraged their daughter to do the same. Humphrey's mother, who came from a musical family, could play the piano well and her father was an amateur musician. They managed a theatrical hotel in Chicago. Unlike Graham, Humphrey had been trained in almost every form of dance that Chicago had to offer at the turn of the century. Moreover, she had been taught by an excellent teacher, Miss Hinman, which was extremely rare in America at that time.

By the time Humphrey arrived at Denishawn, she was not only an accomplished dancer, but was also experienced in performing and teaching. In 1913, shortly after leaving high school, she appeared on a concert tour for the Santa Fe Railroad, and in 1914 she established her own dancing school in Chicago. Humphrey was taller, slimmer and more lithe than Graham, as well as being a lyrical dancer. St Denis noticed her immediately and invited her to return to Denishawn the following year as a teacher and a member of the company. During her long association with Denishawn, Humphrey worked mostly with 'Miss Ruth', performing, teaching and composing dances, while Graham worked mostly with Shawn. Graham and Humphrey did not appear together in the same work until after they had both broken away from Denishawn.

In 1920 Shawn created an Aztec ballet entitled *Xochitl* in which Graham danced in the title role. It is important to note that Shawn did not simply construct the dance and then place Graham in the role of the princess Xochitl. Rather he designed it to suit his protégée's unique qualities. In the years to come Graham would also create the major roles in her dances with specific members of her company in mind. Shawn considered that

Graham's physical appearance and expressive movement qualities were not suited to an Oriental or Greek style dance. Instead, he turned to American–Indian culture as his source of inspiration. The story of *Xochitl* was based on a Toltec legend and Shawn commissioned the setting and the costumes and an original score based on Mexican–Indian music. According to Margaret Lloyd (1974), this was the first use of an American theme on the American stage. In later years Graham would explore the rites and myths of the south-west American Indians as the basis for her own work, as with *Primitive Mysteries* (1931). *Xochitl*, with its elaborate costumes and settings, can be located within the tradition of the nineteenth-century ballet extravaganzas. It was one of several very popular 'art' dances that Shawn created for vaudeville and its success made Graham a junior star in the company.

From 1920 to 1923, Graham toured in vaudeville and with the Denishawn concert group. For much of the time her partner was Charles Weidman who, along with Graham and Humphrey, was also to play a significant role in the development of American modern dance. Weidman, like Graham, was inspired to become a dancer after seeing a performance of St Denis and Shawn in 1914 in his native town of Lincoln, Nebraska.

Graham left Denishawn in 1923 to become a solo dancer in the Greenwich Village Follies. She became dissatisfied with the work and after two successful seasons she left the Follies and 'show business' to embark on a career as an independent concert artist, as St Denis and Duncan had done a generation before. She took up a teaching appointment at the Eastman School of Music and a part-time performing/teaching position at the Anderson–Milton School, both of which had been recently established. The year at Eastman provided Graham with the opportunity to develop some of her ideas by working on herself and with several very good students. Among other works that she staged for the Eastman theatre, Graham choreographed *The Flute of Krishna* (1926). In terms of its thematic content, costuming and much of the movement style, which is predominantly sensuous in quality, the dance can be clearly located within the Denishawn tradition, as a film of the stage production shows. At the same time, however, as some of the movements were performed with a certain un-Denishawn angularity, the work can also be seen as having trace elements of the sharp-percussive style that Graham was to develop over the next several years.

Graham gave her first performance as a concert or recital artist in New York on 18 April 1926. Appearing with her in some of the dances were three of her students from the Eastman school and the accompanist was Louis Horst, who became her musical director and mentor. Although this date marks the beginning of the first decade of American modern dance, as Stodelle (1962a: 6) has noted, 'it began without a fanfare or slightest indication of the revolution to come'. Although Graham was beginning to develop her movement ideas, the exotic Denishawn genre was clearly visible in her first concert works. It took Graham three years to find herself. The titles of her dances, the costumes and the choice of music in her first two seasons of programmes, indicate her lingering debt to Denishawn. For example: *Maid with the Flaxen Hair* (1926) to music by Debussy; *Dance Languide* (1926) to music by Scriabin; and *Scherza* (1927) to music by Schumann. In *Maid with the Flaxen Hair*, Graham wore a blonde wig with long braids. A writer in the *New York Morning Telegraph* described her appearance in this dance as 'a maiden after Rosetti, slender, slim, and exotically graceful'. The writer went on to say that her graceful appearance compensated for her 'lack of power and virtuosity' (Martin 1967: 181). This description not only indicates that, at this point, Graham had not yet found her own direction, but also it demonstrates that, despite many critics' adverse comments to the contrary in later years, she did have the ability to be graceful (Martin 1967).

Graham's October dance programme in New York in 1927 gave an indication of the direction that she and American modern dance would take over the next several years. Amidst the majority of Denishawnesque titles and choice of musical accompaniment in that programme, *Revolt* to music by Honegger stood out in sharp relief. It was Graham's first dance of social protest and others soon followed. Her focus of attention was beginning to move 'from the past to the present, to find contemporary subject matter for dance' (McDonagh 1974: 58). The symbolism of the title did not go unnoticed, at least in the popular theatre that Graham had abandoned two years before, because Fanny Brice satirised both the dance and Graham in a burlesque number for the Ziegfeld Follies called *Rewolt*.

Although *Revolt*, and Brice's response to it, gave an indication as to how Graham and a serious American dance might develop, and the reception it might expect to receive, Graham's first definite break with her Denishawn heritage, according to Stodelle, came the following season.

> With the Program that included 'Immigrant' and 'Poems of 1917' along with 'Fragments', there emerged a tautness of style and considerable strength and originality.
>
> (Stodelle 1962a: 6)

Horst composed the music specifically for *Fragments: Tragedy, Comedy*. Although this was not a new practice in itself, it was the first time that the music had been composed after the dance had been completed (see Chapter 8 for a more detailed discussion of the relation between modern dance and music). With the *Fragments* suite, Graham displayed a gift for both drama and humour. However, from this point on, according to Martin (1967: 191), it became more commonplace to speak of Graham's 'starkness of style', her 'ugliness', 'technical virtuosity' and 'seriousness', as opposed to her 'pictorial gracefulness'.

Further indications of the rumblings of revolt in the dance were to be found elsewhere. Less than a month before Graham's important 1928 recital, Humphrey and Weidman, who were still members of Denishawn, gave their first independent concert. Included in their programme was a dance by Humphrey entitled *Color Harmony*, the design of which, like *Fragments*, had been completed before the composer, Clifford Vaughan, had created the score. Although Humphrey and Weidman wanted to develop their own work, they had hoped to do so within the confines of the Denishawn organisation. Humphrey, like Graham, was becoming increasingly aware that there was a need to create a form of dance that did not derive from foreign and/or ancient cultures but from 'young people of the twentieth century living in the United States' (Cohen 1977b: 61). Moreover, and again like Graham, she did not wish to compromise her new found artistic ideals to the demands of vaudeville as she had seen 'Miss Ruth' do sometime before. Humphrey was shocked to see that for their appearance in the Follies, St Denis and Shawn had altered the tempo of their dances to fit in with the fast pace of the vaudeville stage and St Denis had pulled her skirts up 'four or five inches higher than they should have been' (Cohen 1977b: 63). This was compounded by the fact that Shawn, in particular, who had become quite dogmatic, viewed the Denishawn format as *the* American dance. Humphrey had been told that it was not necessary to experiment because Denishawn had 'thought of everything' (Cohen 1977b). The rupture came finally when Humphrey was voted off Denishawn because she refused to go into the Ziegfeld Follies for a season to earn money for the new Greater Denishawn building in New York. That would have entailed a sacrifice of both her experiments with movement and her aesthetic ideals, and Humphrey, above all else, like Graham, saw herself as 'an artist first' (Cohen 1977b). Weidman and Pauline Lawrence left Denishawn with Humphrey and, following in Graham's footsteps, they set up their own studio to carve out a dance space for themselves.

Humphrey and Weidman's early dances, like those of Graham, contained strong elements of their Denishawn heritage, but they also gave advance warning of what was to come. Thus, as Martin (1967: 230–1) has observed, although Weidman's Oriental dances such as *Japanese Actor* (1928) and *Singalese Drum Dance* (1928), were hangovers from the past, works like *Minstrels* (1928) and *Scherzo* (1928), contained facets of what was to become known as the special 'Weidmanesque quality' for 'character dances in a comedy vein'. Weidman helped to raise the position of the male in dance by developing a method of training specifically for men. However, his most significant contribution to American dance lay in his fusion of 'pantomime and pure movement' into the 'creation of a genuinely unique dance-theatre material' (Martin 1967: 230).

Similarly, Humphrey's *Air for the G String* which was first performed along with *Color Harmony* in 1928, contained elements of the top layer of the later Denishawn period (Siegel 1977). This was particularly evident in the attention given to drapery as an integral feature of the dance.

Drapery was a central aspect of St Denis's work that she, in turn, had derived from Fuller. The dance is clearly derived from the tradition of music visualisation (see Jordan 1986). A sound film of Humphrey's dance was made in 1934 by Westinghouse, which shows Humphrey dancing in the central role. The most striking thing about the dance is its extraordinary sensuous quality, which is unexpected in the early work of a 'modern dancer'. The film possesses an upmarket Hollywood lustre and the sound track describes the dance as a 'musical accompaniment'. To the producers, who were promoting sound film, the dance was of secondary importance. *Air for the G String* is a dance for five women. The dancers are costumed in floor-length unwaisted straight dresses, with long flowing trains attached at the shoulders. The movement consists mostly of processional patterns in which 'the women are continuously sculpting the space with precise lines and flowing curves' (Siegel 1977. 25). The decor consists of a series of columns reminiscent of a Greek temple, around and between which the dancers travel. As with Graham's *The Flute of Krishna*, *Air for the G String* incorporates traces of what came to be regarded as particular to Humphrey's dance (see Jordan 1986). It has definite tendencies 'toward the compositional originality that became Humphrey's distinction' because, for example, the dancers are not simply modelled 'in beautiful arrangements of draperies', but with flowing movement that never stops to freeze in the form of a tableau, the dance takes on the qualities of a moving sculpture (Siegel 1977: 25–6).

By the end of 1929, with dances like *Adolescence*, *Heretic* and one called simply *Dance*, all trace of Denishawn had disappeared from Graham's work and in its place there emerged a dance form that was based on an economy of movement which was concentrated, asymmetrical and percussive.

> In complete revolt against the languorousness, the even flow, the softness, of the more sentimental approach, . . . she [Graham] turned to a kind of movement which could be based on an initial beat like that of a percussion instrument. Instead of maintaining a constant dynamic progress, each movement was attacked with a sharp accent.
>
> (Martin 1967: 193)

With the programme that included *Heretic*, Graham introduced her extended all-female company, or 'Group'. In Graham's early work, the Group was used 'sparingly, and always as elements of pure design' (Stodelle 1962a: 7). The dancers were employed somewhat like the traditional *corps de ballet*, in that they were never used as individual personalities. At times the group seemed to symbolise Graham's collective self; at other times they functioned as an obstructive oppositional force as in *Heretic*.

It appears that Graham was more concerned with creating dances as an experimental vehicle with which to demonstrate her own individuality (Siegel 1979). She made many more solos than group dances during this early period. By contrast, Humphrey, from the beginning of her independent career, was interested in the possibilities of group choreography as an expressive medium of dance.

According to most commentators, *Heretic* was the first outstanding work of Graham's career and it also represented a landmark of American modern dance. A dance in three parts, to the accompaniment of repeated bars of an old Breton folk-song, *Heretic* symbolised the struggle of the individual against an intolerant society. The characterisation was suggestive rather than representational, indicating an important departure from the dance scenes of Denishawn in favour of non-literal dance images that were to become a hallmark of the emerging American modern dance. Graham cast herself in the role of the outsider who stood apart from a solid formation of antagonists, danced by the Group. The efforts of the advancing individual to break through the 'wall' were repelled by the Group with movements which, according to Martin (1967: 194) were 'potential rather than actual' and with postures and a collective demeanour of antagonism and intolerance.

On several occasions the outsider managed to break through the line but the antagonists reformed to prevent further entry. In thematic content, *Heretic* foreshadowed later larger scale works like *American Provincials* (1934) and *American Document* (1938), which explored America's Puritan heritage.

The 'look' of Graham and her Group was as stark and uncompromising as her new movement style. The face was masked out with whitening, dark shadows were drawn under the eyes, the mouth was a slash of bright red, and the hair was drawn severely back. The dancer's costume was a neck-high, floor-length, tubular-shaped dress made of stretchable material. Moreover, as early photographs (see Helpern 1991/2) and films displaying the early technique (performed by Bonnie Bird and Dorothy Bird and housed in the Dance Collection in New York Public Library), the dancers of the Group were not built like the 'sylphs' of ballet or the Graham company today, nor were they tall and willowy like many of the Denishawn dancers. Rather, they were solidly built, with the appearance of being firmly rooted in the ground. Where ballet emphasised the turn-out of the legs and thighs at a ninety-degree angle for greater freedom of movement, Graham and her dancers kept the legs in parallel (Helpern, 1991/2), further accentuating the solidity of their appearance. Where ballet strove to defy gravity, Graham celebrated it. The ground, as Graham came to view it, is not dead matter, rather it symbolises life, and from it energy is derived. She used the ground as a definite direction and the dancers would thrust into it on the down-beat, and rebound from it. Where ballet contrived to conceal energy, Graham revealed it. In the process of experimenting with her own body and teaching her findings to her dancers and other students, Graham evolved her own system of training. In addition to using the floor as a direction, Graham came to view the back as the most important part of the dancer's equipment, 'the tree of life from which 'everything branches out' (Terry 1975: 54).

> In her own classes at Eastman and in the years that followed she [Graham] invented exercises that would make the students more conscious of the floor, aware of the power of the back, certain that the most intense feelings were revealed not simply in the gestures of the hands but in the powerful contractions, releases, stretchings, pullings and spasms of the muscles of the torso.
>
> (Terry 1975: 54)

Almost echoing Delsarte, Graham (1968b: 99) began with the proposition that 'movement is the one speech that cannot lie', that it is an external manifestation of an inner-emotional state or feeling and that dance gesture should give voice to 'the hidden but common emotions'. Therefore, she took as her starting point for dance, the ordinary 'natural' everyday movements of the body. The focus of attention was directed towards the whole body, and the torso in particular, in contrast to ballet. Graham sought to 'reveal on the "outside" what was happening on the "inside" ' (Terry 1975: 53).

In order to reveal the 'inside' on the 'outside' Graham generated a technique based on a movement principle which she termed 'contraction and release'. The action of contraction, initiated by a squeezing out of the breath, begins sharply in the pelvis and goes through the whole body. Like 'a clenched fist', it is a concentration of the body's energy. If carried out with sufficient force it can pull the body off balance, carrying it from one plane or position to another. With the intake of the breath, the action of release is initiated in the base of the spine and continues through the back, returning the body to 'a normal state, not floppy in complete relaxation' (Terry 1975: 53–61). Duncan, true to her dress reforming heritage, had maintained that movement springs from the solar plexus and St Denis, likewise, had exposed the midriff, giving visibility and considerable freedom of movement to the area around the waist (Kendall 1979), one of the important areas of women's bodies that the dress reformers sought to free from the tyranny of the corset. Although Graham did not emerge from a world of clothing or feminist reformers, she went one step further than her predecessors in that she used the female anatomy as a central feature of her technique. Graham came to the view that the impulses of movement through breathing do not begin in the diaphragm but in the pelvic region, the area which houses the vagina and the womb. She was aware of the relationship of the pelvis to sex and childbirth and she taught her dancers to be aware of it also (Bird 1984). Although Graham (1991) stated in her autobiography that she did not consider herself to be a feminist, this attention to the female body as a source of inspiration for movement, echoes some of Duncan's feminist affirmations. Moreover, as Garafola (1993: 171) has argued, from the late 1930s sex and power became explicit themes in Graham's dances. It is also important to note that the technique emerged from her choreographic needs and intentions and not vice versa (Bird 1984). As her dancing changed and developed, so too did the technique (see Helpern 1991/2 and Horosko 1991 for detailed discussions of the development of Graham's technique over the years). When Graham was first developing her technique, she gave names to the exercises such as, 'the sob', 'the laugh', 'pleading' and so forth. Emphasis was placed upon performance and movement symbolism, not simply technique for its own sake (Bird 1984).

> Graham worked from inner feelings, making connections between breath and intensities of emotion that took physical shape in movements initiated by contraction and release. Graham explored sounds and words, sobs and laughs, in terms of their dynamic range and spatial tension. Her classes were highly experimental, exploring endless movement possibilities around an idea before establishing a form.
>
> (Helpern 1991/2: 11)

Humphrey's technique of 'fall and recovery', like Graham's principle of contraction and release, emanated from her experiments with movement and the desire to create a 'new' choreographic form. In contrast to ballet, she too came to recognise the power of gravity as a dramatic element in the dance and the special body rhythms that were created by using the breath. Just as Graham could contract and release any part of the body – a shoulder, or a foot for example – so Humphrey came to consider that a dancer could 'breathe' with the various parts, or the whole, of the body. *In Water Study* (1927), a dance with no musical accompaniment, Humphrey used the breath motif to create the rhythm and forms in the dance. The theory of fall and recovery was based on what Humphrey (Cohen 1977b: 118) termed 'the arc between two deaths': the 'static death' of the vertical plane and 'the dynamic death' of the horizontal plane. Humphrey drew on Nietzsche's concepts of the polar opposition between the Apollonian and Dionysian drives in the human being; the first impels the individual to achieve rest, peace, stability and balance; while the second drive leads him or her towards excitement, danger and ecstatic abandon. Humphrey came to consider that these mental drives have their equivalent in states of the body. Falling away from and returning to a state of equilibrium, for Humphrey, is the continuous flow that is at work in every human body, and dance lies in the drama of motion between these two polarities.

> Fall and recovery, climaxed by that moment of suspension when the person asserted his freedom from the powers of nature. The dancer and space. Man and his environment.
>
> (Cohen 1977b: 119)

Humphrey observed that in the process of fall and recovery the body creates new shapes in space or 'design', and new accents or 'rhythm', and that these vary with the degree of 'dynamics' or tension supplied, with 'drama' as the end product. The potential for dance was to be found in these elements and they formed the theoretical basis of her book, *The Art of Making Dances* (1959).

In their own individual ways, Graham and Humphrey developed their choreography out of the 'natural' or ordinary movement impulses of human beings. In this respect, as Lloyd (1974) has argued, they differed significantly from the choreography that consists of formal designs of steps and patterns. However, with Graham and Humphrey, the ordinary movement impulses were not used literally but were transformed into formalised movement, thus creating a new kind of formalism.

> We may move in natural rhythm; we do not move naturally in rhythmic form. Nor do we go about with arms held high or out at chest level, distorting our locomotion with partial falls or sudden sideways bends. If we tried moving the modern dance way on the sidewalk we would no doubt be looked upon as sorely afflicted or locked up for disorderly conduct. If the modern dancers moved in a perfectly natural way upon the stage, it would not be dance.
>
> (Lloyd 1974: 85)

The first modern dancers' insistence on transforming the 'raw materials' of ordinary movement into dance movement through form or an idea would be rejected in the 1960s by the emergent avant-garde of American dance, the postmodernists.

6 DANCE, MODERNITY AND CULTURE

In their pursuit of a serious American dance under the auspices of art for art's sake, Graham, Humphrey and Weidman banished themselves to the cultural margins. They abandoned the financial security that popular organisations like the Follies and Denishawn offered. Art, for the dissenters from Denishawn, was not for sale to the highest bidder. In a metaphorical sense they became the pioneers of dance, hacking out a space for their art from an inhospitable terrain. To the American public, dancing, above all else, was supposed to be pretty and entertaining. The iconoclasts from Denishawn did not seek to be decorative or to pander to the audience. Rather, they sought to engage their audience, to make people think, to be thoroughly modern and direct in their approach.

> 'Modernism' in the American dance means unswerving and unsentimental directness of idea presented in a style wholly dictated by that idea, with everything ruthlessly whittled away that is non-essential to the main structural lines. . . . Be the idea great or small, beautiful or ugly, it stands 'forth naked and unashamed. In other words its style of presentation is absorbed by the idea and becomes transparent.
>
> (Gage 1930: 230)

The general public and the majority of critics were shocked and baffled by what the 'morbid moderns' presented in the name of dance (Martin 1968). Graham, for example, whose dancing was viewed as the most ascetic of the moderns, seemed to defy all the commonly accepted notions of dance, particularly the locomotion element. As Lloyd (1974: 50) has pointed out, 'in her attempt to simplify movement to its core', Graham 'scarcely moved at all'. Moreover, Martin (1968: 8), writing in 1937, declared that 'Graham does the unforgivable thing for a dancer to do . . . she makes you think'. Duncan, too, had dared to confront the American public, to make people think, with her dance and her polemics, and she had been repudiated and all but banished to Europe for daring to question the moral and political order. Graham, Humphrey and Weidman, however, did not feel impelled to leave America for the more conducive artistic climate of Europe as St Denis and Duncan had done a generation before. There are several possible interconnected factors involved here. First, through the process of dance reproduction, American dancers began to find inspiration and source material for their work in their own culture (Ruyter 1979). At the same time, it also gave them something to rebel against. Second, the modern dancers were not isolated in their aesthetic revolt because artists in different fields were also calling into question their dominant aesthetic traditions (see Sayler 1930). Third, unlike their predecessors, the modern dancers found a platform for their work in the colleges and progressive schools which, in turn, furthered the process of dance reproduction and legitimation (Ruyter 1979, Kriegsman 1981). This chapter will focus on these three interrelated aspects in more detail.

In the 1920s, dancing was no longer such an isolated phenomenon in America as it had been at the turn of the century because of the reproductive dance cycle that performers such as St Denis had set in action, and other related contemporary cultural developments outlined in the previous chapter. On the contrary, the following comments on dance made in 1926 by the critic Carl Van Vechten (Padgette 1974) give an indication of the variety and quantity of dance to be found in the American theatre, and in popular culture at the time when Graham and the other dance iconoclasts were starting out on their own.

> I am sick of Greek tunics and bare legs, satiated with oriental dancing, Persian, Javanese, Chinese and Polovstian, surfeited with turkey trots and bunny hugs and fox trots, bored with tangos and maxixes, boleros and seguidillas. Argentine and Spanish dances of whatever nature. I have had my fill of ballroom dancing, cakewalks, pigeon-wings, clogs, jazz and hoe-downs. Terpsichore has been such a favorite of late, literary, pictorial, musical and even social, that the muse has become inflatedly self-conscious, afflicted with a bad case of megalomania.
> (Padgette 1974: 171)

Thus, although emergent dance modernists like Graham, Humphrey and Weidman did not agree with the dollar-oriented character of dance in America and its embeddedness in popular culture, at least dancing was now 'there' to be confronted.

Moreover, the position of theatrical dance in Europe had strengthened considerably since St Denis's return to America in 1908. The ballet had been revitalised through the agency of the Ballets Russes which Diaghilev first brought out of Imperial Russia's Maryinsky Theatre in 1909 to perform in Paris. At the beginning the company was conceived of as a showcase for Russian dancers rather than a permanent institution and included in the first season such stars as Pavlova and Mordkin (Anderson 1974, Haskell 1968). As Diaghilev's Ballets Russes gained success in Europe, however, it became more independent from the Imperial theatres of Russia and ultimately achieved total independence. Kermode (1983) has argued that it was largely as a result of the Ballets Russes' success in

Paris that Duncan was never able to establish herself in France as she had done in Germany. Diaghilev's choreographers, Fokine, Nijinsky, Massine, Nijinska and Balanchine, worked to modernise and regenerate ballet from within the technical system itself. For the productions, Diaghilev brought together a number of the leading European modern artists and musicians to collaborate with the choreographers in order to create a 'total theatrical spectacle' (Anderson 1974).

The 1920s also witnessed the emergence of German modern dance. It grew almost simultaneously with American modern dance and was another important agency in the process of dance reproduction in Europe in the 1920s and early 1930s (see Manning 1993).

In Zurich, during the First World War, Mary Wigman, an assistant of Rudolf Laban and a former Dalcroze student, set out to discover a 'new' language of dance gesture formulated on the idea of 'movement for movement's sake' (Sorell 1981). She founded her dance technique on the principle of 'tension and relaxation'. Wigman also maintained that music for the dance should function as a rhythmic support for the movement. It should be integral to the dance but it should not interfere with the primacy of the movement. She created dances without musical accompaniment and pioneered the use of percussion accompaniment. Her first group dance, *The Dances of Life*, completed in 1918 (and recorded in a system of notation invented by Laban), marked the beginning of her public career. According to Sorell, 'All her dance creations emerged from her awareness that her body was a visible manifestation of a being that exists only as a truthful mirror of humanity' (Sorell 1981: 382). In 1926, the same year as Graham's debut as an independent concert artist, Wigman formed her first dance group and founded two schools in central Europe. Harald Kreutzberg and Hanya Holm, both of whom played a role in the development of American dance, emerged from Wigman's studios.

Although Wigman did not perform in America until 1931, her reputation preceded her and the American modern dancers would have been familiar with Wigman's ideas (see Garafola 1993 for a discussion of competing perspectives principally between Agnes de Mille and Graham on this issue with regards to Graham). Given that the American dancers could not hope to compete with the Europeans for an audience in America, it seems unlikely that they would have been prepared to compete with them in Europe. However, one of the American modern dancers, Helen Tamiris, did go to Europe in 1928 for a short time. Tamiris was invited to take part in the Salzburg festival, and was the first American dancer to appear there since Duncan. Although her performance was a success, she, like Duncan, did not have enough money and her expenses were paid by a philanthropist named Otto Kahn. Financial problems and the belief that she could not create an American dance on foreign soil, led Tamiris to return to America.

The other leading modern dancers did not go to Europe until after they had established themselves in America. In 1936 Graham was invited by the German government to perform in Germany for the Olympic games. It would have brought her dance to the attention of an international audience but Graham declined on the grounds of her opposition to the Nazi government's anti-Semitic policy.

Another contingent feature which enabled Graham and the other dance iconoclasts to remain in America to develop their work lies in the fact that the aesthetic revolt in America was not restricted to dance. On the contrary, as Oliver Sayler's (1930) survey of the arts in America in 1930 clearly demonstrates, a condition of chaos was prevalent or at least looming throughout the arts. The revolt against commercialism and a movement towards art for art's sake in the legitimate theatre in America, for example, took place between 1915 and 1920 at the time when the rapid growth of the motion picture industry was beginning to be perceived by some commentators as a real threat to the survival of the theatre. At the start of the century, by contrast, it had been treated as a 'frivolous novelty' (McDonagh 1974). Theatrical commercialism was at a peak in the beginning of the second decade of the century and a movement away from the 'big business' of Broadway was evidenced by the establishment of the 'little theatres' such as The Neighborhood Playhouse in New York's Lower East Side and the Provincetown Players which was founded in Massachusetts but settled in New York's Greenwich Village (McDonagh 1974). The Neighborhood Playhouse grew out of the community drama project of the Henry Street Settlement and was run by the Lewisohn sisters. It offered a variety of legitimate dramatic productions, dance festivals, music and revues. It was reorganised in 1927 with Irene Lewisohn as the director. She had studied Delsarte with Stebbins and had been responsible for many dance productions and after the reorganisation she began her 'orchestral dramas' (McDonagh 1974). Graham and Horst, among others, taught there and Humphrey, Weidman, Graham and a number of other dancers of the time performed in these dramas.

The Provincetown Players was an organisation of artists and writers whose policy was dedicated towards the production of new plays. Importantly, the emphasis was placed on quality, not box office receipts, and the organisation attracted a number of talented actors, designers and writers, with its greatest achievement being the discovery and promotion of Eugene O'Neill. In 1916 a quarterly magazine called *Theatre Arts* was launched. Like Stieglitz's *Camera Work*, *Theatre Arts* was an ardent promoter and interpreter of modern aesthetic movements. It also provided a forum for the development of standards of criticism (McDonagh 1974).

The first concerted aesthetic revolt in American art music took place in the 1920s. Several young American composers, such as Roger Sessions, Aaron Copland, Carl Ruggles and Wallingford Riegger, reacted strongly against the stuffiness of the Conservatoire and began to compose music drawing on jazz and modernist developments in music in Europe, such as the work of Stravinsky, the French group *Les Six*, and Schoenberg (Copland 1968). With their stark, percussive, polytonal, dissonant works, this so-called 'band of young Turks' created shock waves throughout the academy and in the concert halls (Tawa 1984). In taking up the banner of modernism, the composers alienated the mainstream of concert hall audiences (Tawa 1984). Nevertheless, these young composers were given a considerable amount of support and platform for their work by sympathetic conductors like Leopold Stokowski, the *enfant terrible* of music who was the conductor for the Philadelphia Orchestra, and Serge Koussevitsky, the director of the Boston Symphony. Like Stieglitz who championed modernism in art in America, these two conductors championed the cause of the musical avant-garde. In 1930, under the auspices of the *League of Composers*, Stokowski gave the first American staged production of Stravinsky's *The Rite of Spring*. To choreograph the work he chose Leonide Massine who had created a revival of the work for Diaghilev in Paris in 1920. Further confirmation of Stokowski's commitment to modernism can be demonstrated by the fact that he persuaded Massine to use a little known American modern dancer, called Martha Graham, to dance the role of the sacrificial Chosen Maiden, and not a trained ballet dancer (see Daniel 1982 for a fuller discussion). Presented on the programme with *The Rite of Spring* was Schoenberg's *Die glückliche Han*, directed by Rouben Mamoulian. Humphrey was chosen to choreograph and perform the part of The Woman in the Mamoulian production, thus indicating that her abilities as a choreographer were evident even at such an early point in her career. According to Daniel (1982), Graham said that she was asked to choreograph the work but she refused on the grounds of lack of experience.

The aesthetic revolt in fine art that saw the beginnings of American modernism took place at the 291 gallery in New York during the first decade of the century. However, the size of the audience for the exhibitions that Stieglitz mounted was minuscule and mostly confined to like-minded artists. By far the most significant event in the history of American modernism was the International Exhibition of Modern Art that was held at the 69th New York Regiment Armory in 1913, or the *Armory Show* as it was called.

> The [Armory] Show is customarily described in such terms as 'bombshell', 'explosion', 'assault', 'shock', 'miracle'. It was one of those upheavals about which it is said that after it 'nothing was ever the same again'. It supplied the 'mandate' from which succeeding generations of vanguard critics, museum directors and art educators have continued to derive their authority.
>
> (Rosenberg 1982: 187)

This exhibition was sponsored by the Society of American Artists and Sculptors who were wholly innocent of 'radical intentions' (Rosenberg

1982). Their aim was to exhibit work that was largely ignored by the main galleries. Principally, this meant the work of American and European modernists who had hitherto exhibited only at the 291. Stress was placed on the word 'international' and one-third of the show was given over to foreign works representing the various modernist movements in Europe, and included Duchamp's *Nude Descending a Staircase* and Matisse's *Blue Nude*. The organisers hoped to be able to show that American art had reached a point in its development where it could stand alone and compete with the most advanced art that Europe had to offer (Rose 1967, Hunter 1972).

The art-going American public was used to the notion of international because it was almost obligatory for young American artists to complete their training in Europe, just as young American composers were expected to be 'finished off' in Europe. The problem, according to Rose (1967), lay with the word 'modern'. Some American modernists – Max Weber, T.S. Eliot and Gertrude Stein for example – remained in Europe because they found the climate there more conducive to their type of work. America was not prepared for the one-third modernist works of the exhibition and it was that third which spread shock waves throughout the art world and the American public (Rose 1967, Rosenberg 1982). The largely uninformed American art public who came to see the Armory Show were confronted with an enormous amount of images that were foreign, unfamiliar and non-representational. Worse still, they were reputed to stand for the best art works of the era. Although the content of The Eight's and the Independents' paintings had shocked the public, people could at least recognise what the paintings were meant to portray because the images remained within the bounds of representational art, with their illusion of three-dimensional space (Rose 1967). With modernism, however, the third dimension disappears giving way to literal space or, as with cubism, pictorial space is distorted for the sake of the formal structure of the work itself.

The Armory Show received an enormous amount of publicity, a great deal of which was unfavourable (see Rosenberg 1982: 189-91). The press declared an all-out attack on modern art. Cubism was the subject of numerous jokes, and the *American Art News* launched a competition to find the 'nude' in Duchamp's painting. Ex-president Roosevelt said that Duchamp's composition reminded him of 'a Navajo rug', and the 'primitive' aspect of Matisse's work was also the object of derision. Arguments for and against the case of modernism were couched in terms of either radical politics or moral or cultural values, as well as artistic merit (Rose 1967). For the artists, the spirit of modernism stood for a re-awakening of the spirit of the American Revolution. In contrast, for the critics of the show, that very same artistic spirit represented political anarchy and social unrest. At the same time, however, because the political climate, for the most part, was still progressive and liberal, unrest in art was sometimes viewed as a reflection of political unrest, which in turn was considered as a condition for growth and political reform (Rose 1967).

Some artists, for example Henri and Stieglitz, believed that the values expressed by contemporary art reflected the basic American values of individualism and growth. However, critics of the Armory Show injected a puritanical edge into the discussion and urged the public to dismiss modern art on the moral grounds that it was decadent and opposed to the American character (Hunter 1972, Rose 1967). In this view, modern art, which shelters under the name of individualism, stands for nothing more than unchecked licence and experimentation and a denial of the moral order of society, which can only lead to chaos and anarchy. In contrast, other writers argued that provincialism and prudishness placed restrictions on American culture, inhibiting growth and experimentation (Hunter 1972, Rose 1967).

The political, moral and cultural issues that the Armory Show provoked, were the subjects of discussion throughout America at that time when 'the old clashed with the new in every sphere' (Rose 1967: 77). The fact that 'the shock of the new' (Rosenberg 1982) did not come from within the culture itself but from Europe, in part, could explain the American people's unfavourable reaction to it. The introduction of modern art into America occurred at the same time as thirteen million immigrants were being assimilated into the country and fears were being expressed that America was becoming swamped by foreigners. These fears were frequently given voice through a rejection of Europeanism and a celebration of Americanism and often resulted in 'political chauvinism' and 'cultural isolationism' (Rose 1967). The artist was forced to 'Americanise' European art in the same way as the immigrant was assimilated into the dominant culture. 'Consequently', as Rose has demonstrated 'the new painting and sculpture proved an admirable target for the various kinds of insecurities and aggressions thus released' (Rose 1967: 77).

Nevertheless, as Rose and Rosenberg have pointed out, the Armory Show succeeded in making the American public aware of the developments in art and in providing a forum for young American painters. It also marked the beginning of modern art collections in America. Although the organisers intended to show that American artists had nothing to fear from exhibiting alongside the Europeans, the American contributions looked underdeveloped in comparison with the polish of the European works and European art continued to dominate the artistic scene for another thirty years. The radicalism of modern art was not easily assimilated into American culture and the modern artists remained in the shadows of the American art world for several decades. However, after the Second World War, New York emerged as the centre for avant-garde art with such painters as Jackson Pollock, Willelm De Kooning and Robert Motherwell coming to the fore (Rose 1967).

The Armory Show's success by scandal was matched in Paris in the same year by Diaghilev's ballet production of Stravinsky's *The Rite of Spring*, choreographed by Nijinsky. The rhythm and colour of the score marked a new departure in the field of music. For Diaghilev, it was nothing less than 'le moment de la musique moderne' (Haskell 1968: 82). The score was based on the story of an ancient pagan rite celebrating the birth of human activity. Stravinsky said that he envisioned 'a solemn pagan rite' in which the elders 'seated in a circle, watched a young girl dance herself to death' (Sorell 1981: 370). The chosen maiden was being sacrificed 'to propitiate the god of spring' (Sorell 1981: 370). The music called for a dance that would realise its complex rhythms and 'stark primitivism' and, according to Levinson (Kirstein 1969), Nijinsky responded to the challenge by standing the normal ballet positions on their heads by turning the gestures and steps inward. With simple isolated movements, the dancers 'bent at the knees, straightened up', lowered and raised their heads and stamped their feet to the accented rhythm of the score, while the 'jerks' and 'leaps' of the Chosen Maiden were described as 'the ultra-modern version of pirouettes and entrechats' of ballet (Kirstein 1969: 289).

> The opening night on May 29, 1913, turned into a chaotic scandal. In the ensuing tumult the dancers could not even hear the music. The audience was outraged; it felt fooled and insulted by what it took to be bewildering dissonant sounds and a monotonous repetition of movements. It could not yet sense the wild pathos of death and birth in it, the convulsion of sophisticated naïveté.
>
> (Sorell 1981: 370)

The Armory Show in America, like *The Rite of Spring*, symbolised the revolt against the institutionalisation of artistic value. It set into motion the era of 'surprise me' in art, or the principle of newness for its own sake, which Rosenberg (1962) has termed 'the tradition of the new'.

Although the revolt in the arts in America was limited to a small number of artists in different fields, the modern dancers were not completely isolated in their aesthetic rebellion. New York was the centre of this aesthetic revolt and like-minded artists gravitated towards Greenwich Village which, echoing the Left Bank of Paris in the 1890s, had become a nucleus for the emerging avant-garde painters, musicians, writers and dancers. Although Graham, Humphrey and Weidman, like 'the young Turks' of music, restricted their potential audience size when they took up the banner of modern art, they found an appreciative audience for their work in like-minded artists and in left-wing political activists who equated the artistic rebellion with their own radical politics. In the 1930s 'Red Decade', *The New Masses* sponsored works by modern dancers, composers and so forth (see Prickett 1992 for a detailed discussion). The dancers also performed in trade union halls. Graham and Humphrey, however, although sympathetic to those who fought against social injustice, maintained that art and politics should not be mixed. In this respect, as I indicated earlier, they differed from their predecessor, Duncan, and several groups of the younger dancers in the 1930s (see Graff 1994). In an interview in 1936, Graham stated that, despite opinions to the contrary, there was no intention on her part to make dances of social or political protest. She stated: 'If I had something of great social importance to say, I would say it from a lecture platform' (Terry 1978: 6). Here, Graham seems to be negating her own former practice because a number of the themes of her early works, such as *Immigrant: Steerage, Strike* (1928) and *Poems of 1917: Song Behind the Lines, Dance of Death* (1928), dealt with important issues of the day, as did several dances in the 1930s (see Prickett 1994). For Graham, however, the dance should not be tied to narrative, the movement should be suggestive of feelings or ideas, not a direct reflection of them. That is, form should not be subjugated to content. Humphrey, like Graham, believed that dance would suffer if the movement were subordinated to the social or political dogma; it would lose its specificity and thus its independence as an art form.

> The idea of social reform, class struggle or whatever it is, can overwhelm the dance when nothing counts so much as the message. This is usually better from a speaker's platform or in a book, because we have strayed into the world of fact. A statistic is not a good subject for a dance, no matter how emotional the composer might feel about it.
>
> (Humphrey 1959: 36)

For Humphrey and Graham, then, dance is, or should be, a transformation of reality through the medium of formed movement, which itself is a transformation of everyday, 'natural' movement.

In the late 1920s and early 1930s, the modern dancers were overshadowed by the popularity of Denishawn and a long stream of foreign imports who commanded more publicity and better venues. Although each modern dance company had a dedicated following, the audiences were minimal in comparison with those for Wigman or Kreutzberg, for example. The cost of hiring a theatre was prohibitive and beyond the means of the independent concert artists. Consequently, the modern dancers were restricted to hiring a theatre when it was not in demand, which, for the most part, entailed that they performed on a Sunday. However, because of the existence of the Sabbath Law prohibiting dance events, they ran the risk of being closed down by the authorities (mounting pressure from dancers contributed to this law being revoked in 1932). In order to remedy this situation, Tamiris conceived of and organised the ill-fated Dance Repertory Theatre. By bringing the leading exponents of American modern dance together under one roof, Tamiris envisaged that a wider and less specialised audience could develop – one that would come to see the diversity of modern dance and not, as often was the case, the individual personalities involved.

Graham, Humphrey and Weidman agreed to participate in the venture with Tamiris and the first season of the Dance Repertory Theatre was given at Maxine Elliott's Theatre in New York in January 1930. The three companies shared the cost of theatre rental, publicity and the hire of musicians. Rivalries in the modern dance field at the time were fierce, with each company considering that its approach constituted the only valid one. The intense competition worked all the way along the line from performers, to audience and to students. It was almost an act of high treason for a student at Graham's studio to take a class at the Humphrey–Weidman studio, and vice versa. This remained the case several years later when modern dance found a home at the Bennington School of the Dance. The egocentrism of the dancers did not lend itself easily to such a cooperative venture as the Dance Repertory Theatre. Agnes De Mille joined in the second season and the project required several distinguished patrons, but it did not continue to a third season. Given the rivalries between the major factions, it is hardly surprising that such an enterprise did not succeed (Lloyd 1974). However, as Lloyd (1974: 37–139) has shown, the Dance Repertory Theatre did achieve a measure of success in terms of criticism and box-office takings. If it had continued, according to Lloyd, it could have provided a much needed platform for the movement and the possibility of a dance subsidy, and the leaders of the movement could have spared themselves years of living on the brink of financial ruin and anonymity. After the second season they were offered a tour by Messrs Schubert, but only Tamiris was inclined to accept and the offer was thus rejected. Consequently, although the modern dancers received little support from the world of entertainment, they did not take advantage of what that world was prepared to offer.

The modern dancers received a considerable amount of support from such sympathetic critics as John Martin of the *New York Times* and Mary Watkins of the *New York Herald Tribune*. Martin was appointed as a space writer for dance in 1927, and in 1928 he became the first permanent newspaper dance critic in America. The *Tribune* hired Watkins as a dance writer in 1927. Previously, newspapers had sent their music critic or their drama critic to cover dance concerts, and it was only pressure from Denishawn that led to the emergence of professional newspaper dance critics.

St Denis and Shawn pointed out to publishers and editors that a minor musician would be given the courtesy of a review by a trained music critic whereas they, the great Denishawn company, could play to record breaking engagements at, say, Carnegie Hall in New York and barely get a mention.

(Terry 1975: 69)

It is somewhat ironic that Martin, who had moved from theatre reviewing, turned his eyes favourably towards the modern dance scene in New York which was anti-ballet and anti-Denishawn, and not to Denishawn in California. He became an ardent advocate of American modern dance and its exponents' concern to develop a serious American dance. In 1933 he wrote the first theoretical book on the subject, *The Modern Dance* (1972). More books and magazine articles followed, in addition to his weekly column in the *New York Times*.

From 1931 to 1938, at the New School of Social Research, Martin conducted a series of lecture–demonstrations in order to clarify the subject of modern dance for the attendant audience and make it more available to a wider public. The lecture–demonstrations took the form of an introduction to a given artist by Martin who would explain the particular technique, after which the dancer and/or group would demonstrate it (Church 1937a, Lloyd 1974). Most of the leading modern dancers, and others who were less well known, took part in these demonstrations (see Church 1937a for details). Martin was concerned to explain that modern dance was not a unified system but a 'point of view'. It was through such demonstrations that many students, teachers and other interested parties became acquainted with the differences and similarities between the various modern techniques and styles. During the 1930s, Martin lectured on modern dance in numerous colleges, towns and cities across the country, bringing the form to the attention of many people who hitherto were not aware of it or could not understand it.

Although the dancers failed to receive much support from the field of entertainment, as Lloyd (1974: 316–23) has demonstrated, their cause was advanced and the process of dance reproduction expanded by the support they received from the academic world. Martin, Horst and the leading modern dancers gave lecture–demonstrations and classes to physical education students and to students in progressive schools, such as the Cornish School in Seattle and the Neighborhood Playhouse School in New York. Many of the dance-oriented gym teachers in the colleges studied at the Humphrey–Weidman and the Graham studios. These gym teachers were not trained dancers. Their basic training included some Delsarte, Dalcroze, modified ballet steps and some form of interpretive dancing. When modern dance first made its entry into these colleges of physical education, it was used by the teachers as an aid to gymnastics rather than as a creative tool.

> They appropriated it as an advanced calisthenics, as a logical successor to the interpretive dance, and because it was much more assimilable and practicable for educational purposes than ballet, modified or classic. In the early days . . . the point of view was preponderantly that of evolved gymnastics, and the choreography was mainly a combination of movement techniques with little or no imagination in the use of space.
>
> (Lloyd 1974: 317)

The emergence of American modern dance coincided with the revolution in American education. Through the philosophy of education of thinkers like John Dewey, the principle of individual creativity and the idea of 'unity in diversity' came into fashion (Ruyter 1979). Denishawn, as discussed in Chapter 4, was loosely founded on this kind of approach. At the University of Wisconsin, interpretive dance had been brought into the curriculum by Margaret H'Doubler in the early 1920s. In 1926, Wisconsin offered the first dance major in America and many dance teachers received their initial dance training from H'Doubler, whose approach was philosophical, analytical and creative (see H'Doubler 1977). One such student who was destined to have an enormous influence in the field of dance education was Martha Hill. Hill also studied with Graham and was an early member of the Group from 1929 to 1931. In 1930 she took up a post in the physical education department at New York University where she introduced dance into the curriculum.

In the depth of the Depression in 1932, a new women's college opened in Vermont: Bennington College. This college came to provide the burgeoning American modern dance field with a centre for developing its ideas, a body of students who would eventually promote the cause of modern dance in educational establishments across the country, and a much needed source of income in a very difficult economic period (this discussion on Bennington is drawn primarily from Kriegsman 1981: 5–32). The educational philosophy behind Bennington College encapsulated that of Dewey and progressive education in general. The arts at Bennington were viewed in the same light as other academic subjects. Dance constituted a significant element within the Arts and Music section and in 1936 dance became an autonomous division.

Hill became the head of the dance programme at Bennington but she also maintained her lectureship at New York University. In order to make use of the campus facilities in the summer and thereby earn extra income for the college, the president of Bennington, Robert Leigh, charged Hill with setting up a summer school devoted entirely to the study of the emerging art of modern dance. This was to be the first of its kind in America. Hill was made director of the project and Mary Jo Shelly, a physical education instructor at New College, Columbia, was appointed to the post of administrative director. Hill and Shelly invited four leaders in the field to teach on the project: Graham, Humphrey, Weidman and Holm. It was through their participation at Bennington that they became known as the Big Four. Horst and Martin were also recruited as visiting faculty to lecture on composition and dance history.

Unlike the other three dancers, Holm was not known as a concert artist in her own right. Indeed, it was not until she created *Trend* in 1937 that she gained critical acclaim as a choreographer. None the less, she was a representative of a major school of modern dance which was gaining converts in America and a number of Americans had gone to Germany to study with Wigman. Moreover, and perhaps more importantly, Holm was known on the college circuits for her considerable skills as a teacher and demonstrator, and the Bennington project was principally an educational experiment.

In July 1934 the Bennington School of the Dance was opened with the express aim of bringing together 'leaders and students interested in an impartial analysis of the important contemporary trends in the dance' (Kriegsman 1981: 11). The heterogeneous character of modern dance was stressed by 'providing students with contrasting approaches to technique and composition' (ibid.). Related aspects of the dance such as music and setting were addressed in order to make available to students 'an integrated analysis of the whole movement' (ibid.).

The experiment was so successful that the Bennington School of the Dance continued for nine years, eight at Bennington and one on the campus of Mills College in California. It helped to establish the supremacy of the East Coast in the American dance scene. The negative side of this supremacy is that the work of other choreographers, such as Lester Horton, who were working in the West Coast at the same time, went virtually unnoticed (Lloyd 1974).

Although Bennington was conceived as a training place for dancers and teachers it became a meeting point for leading artists of the period and a workshop for experimental work in choreography and its interrelation with the other arts. Dancers could show their work there before taking it onto the New York stage (Kriegsman 1981).

One leading American modern dancer was conspicuous by her absence from Bennington in that first year: Tamiris. Neither was she invited to participate in the following years. Tamiris's background was very different from that of Graham, Humphrey or Weidman. Her parents were Russian–Jewish immigrants who lived in a poor district of New York and they were an artistic family. As a child she studied interpretive dancing with Irene Lewisohn at the Henry Street Settlement (before it evolved into The Neighborhood Playhouse) and later gained a scholarship to study ballet at the Metropolitan Opera Ballet School. For two years she was a member of the *corps de ballet* at the Metropolitan Opera, after which she toured South America as a ballerina with the Bracale Opera Company. She studied with Fokine, took classes in Duncan technique and became a speciality dancer in musical revues and nightclubs. In 1927 she gave her first solo concert called *Dance Moods* and according to Lloyd (1974) the programme contained the seeds of many later developments in modern dance. To begin with, Tamiris danced to the works of three American composers, including Gershwin. The other modern dancers also began to draw on the resources of American composers. Moreover, one dance was without musical accompaniment, which, except for one Humphrey–Denishawn composition, was the first silent dance in America (see Lloyd 1974). Another dance was notable for its earnest treatment of jazz rhythms (Lloyd 1974). Tamiris, like the other major leaders in the field, wanted to create an American dance that would reflect the contemporary American experience. In order to achieve this, Tamiris believed, the American dancer should draw on native sources as much as possible. Very early in her career Tamiris began to choreograph Negro spirituals.

Perhaps Tamiris was not treated very seriously because she continued to embrace the world of concert dance and that of Broadway, while others such as Humphrey and Graham were renouncing the entertainment side of dance in their efforts to achieve for it the status of an art. Gershwin suffered a similar fate because he engulfed the world of serious and popular music at a time when composers such as Copland were trying to generate a 'serious' American music. Tamiris, unlike Graham for example, wanted to make dances for the public: 'the validity of modern dance', according to Tamiris, 'is rooted in its ability to express social problems' (Lloyd 1974: 141). Her dances dealt with contemporary social issues using popular musical idioms such as jazz and Negro songs. Unlike Graham and Humphrey, then, Tamiris considered that propaganda is compatible with art and that art and entertainment need not be mutually exclusive.

The Big Four gained much from their involvement in the Bennington project. For six weeks of the year they could explore new ideas, work with large numbers of groups and collaborate with musicians and stage designers to create new works on a scale hitherto impossible and, at the same time, earn some money. Holm, for example, created *Trend* (1937) at Bennington and it was there that she began a long association with the stage designer, Arch Lauterer. Weidman composed two major works at Bennington, *Quest* (1936) and *Opus 51* (1938). Moreover, he offered a balance to the otherwise all-female preserve at Bennington. Humphrey premiered some of her most renowned works at Bennington, such as *New Dance* (1935) (this is not strictly a Bennington premiere because, as Kriegsman (1981) points out, it was performed under a different title at Burlington prior to the Bennington festival), *With My Red Fires* (1936) and *Passacaglia in C Minor* (1938). But it was Graham who gained the most from the Bennington experiment. The administration favoured her more than the others although she also gave a great deal to it.

It was not only the individual artists who gained from the Bennington project, but the cause of American modern dance itself. Bennington provided modern dance with its first subsidy, and other colleges followed its lead. By inviting leading choreographers to teach college students, Bennington helped to establish a fruitful relationship between professional and non-professional dance in America that has continued to the present day. Furthermore, it aided the dance legitimation process in American society.

> Bennington gave the modern dance an aura of academic respectability and a shelter and conferred cultural and intellectual status upon it. In return the summer school gave Bennington College an international reputation and enlarged constituency and influence beyond a small, elite class of undergraduate women.
> (Kriegsman 1981: 28)

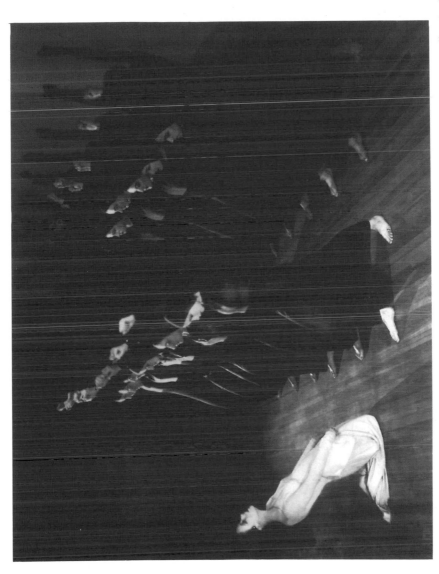

Plate 5 Martha Graham in *Heretic* (reproduced courtesy of the New York Public Library Dance Collection).

Plate 6 Martha Graham in *Lamentation* (© Barbara Morgan (1980) *Martha Graham: Sixteen Dances in Photographs*).

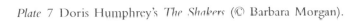
Plate 7 Doris Humphrey's *The Shakers* (© Barbara Morgan).

Plate 8 Martha Graham in *Frontier* (© Barbara Morgan (1980) *Martha Graham: Sixteen Dances in Photographs*).

7 SHIFTING HORIZONS

Heterogeneity was not only a salient characteristic of the modern dance movement, but also of the work of the individual artists. Graham, for example, as Martin (1967) pointed out, was always a 'constant surprise', and the 'tradition of the new' (Rosenberg 1962), as discussed above, requires just such an effect. Once Graham had removed 'all extraneous substances' from her movement, Martin (1933b) reported in his weekly column that she continued in a vein of 'incessant and almost restless variation of manner and method'. The scope of her dancing ranged from the psychological expressionism of such works as *Lamentation* (1930) to works of pure dance movement such as *Celebration* (1934) and to the primitivism of dances such as *Primitive Mysteries* (1931), inspired by the ritual practices of the south west Amer-Indian Christian sects. In addition to these, Graham went through a Greek period in which she created works such as *Bacchanale* (1931) and *Ekstasis* (1933), which explored the notion of ecstasy inherent in Greek religion. It is important to note, however, that these dances had little in common with Duncan's Greek inspired dancing. Graham's asymmetrical, angular percussive style would have been anathema to Duncan. Although Graham was viewed as the most morbid of the morbid moderns, she also created humorous works like *Harlequinade* (1930), and *Satyric Festival Song* (1932) which, according to dance critic Mary Watkins (1932), 'really brought the house down'.

Around the mid-1930s, Graham's work began to enter into yet another new phase of development, her Americana period in which she explicitly drew on the American cultural heritage. It began with *American Provincials* in 1934 and culminated in 1944 with *Appalachian Spring*. During this time she created such Americanist works as: *Frontier* (1935), *Panorama* (1935), *Horizons* (1936), *American Document* (1938), *El Penitente* (1940), *Letter to the World* (1940), and *Salem Shore* (1942). However, the works of this period were not devoted solely to Americana, just as all the works of the early 1930s were not of a serious nature. In addition to the Americana pieces, Graham also created several works that were given impetus by the issues surrounding the Spanish Civil War: *Chronicles* (1936), *Immediate Tragedy* (1937) and *Deep Song* (1937), thus contradicting her own dictum on the separation of dance and politics (see Graff 1994). *Deaths and Entrances* (1942) explored the relationships of three sisters (the Brontës) who live together in relative isolation in a large house filled with their memories. In 1939, she made a satirical work entitled *Every Soul is a Circus*, the uncharacteristic humour of which prompted the reviewer of the *New York Herald Tribune* to call Graham 'the Beatrice Lillie of the dance' (Terry 1978: 54). None the less, the dominant thematic strand running through this phase of her work constituted an exploration of America's cultural heritage and, in particular, the Puritan element of Graham's own biography. It can be viewed as an attempt to develop further a dance form that has its roots in American culture as opposed to the Europeanism of classical ballet or the Oriental exotica of the Denishawn heritage.

As Graham moved out of her period of introspection to explore the outside environment, her dance form also changed. The staccato and percussive style of her 'long woollens' period, with the minimum of theatricality in terms of costume and setting, gave way to a certain softening of movement form and the development of dance as a theatre piece. Graham's development from the recital format towards an integrated dance theatre was indicative of the modern dance movement in general in the mid-1930s.

> The sharp percussive outcries of the early experiments in modern dance began to give way in the Bennington years to a fluid, even lyrical movement. The modern dance was evolving from the darkly austere 'abstract' style of the 1920s and early 1930s to a more consciously programmatic theatre dance that attempted to integrate costumes, stage design, music, spoken word, and poetry with movement. Elaborate program notes accompanied dances to explicate the choreographer's intent and help audiences 'understand' the modern dance. Longer dances lasting half a program or more replaced recital pieces, large groups of dancers flooded the stage.
>
> (Kriegsman 1981: 31)

This transition can be indicated by considering briefly two of Graham's dances: the minimalist, introspective, *Lamentation* (1930), and the positive, outward-going *Frontier* (1935). Although the diverse character of Graham's work has been emphasised above, because of certain core elements in these works, *Lamentation* can be used to exemplify the 'long woollens' concert dance period, and *Frontier* to point to the beginnings of Graham's development towards an integrated dance theatre.

Lamentation, a dance of grief or sorrow to piano music by Kodaly, was remarkable for its time on several levels. It disrupted artistic and commonsense assumptions of dance in terms of its movement and costume and the starkness of its approach. It is one of the few early works that Graham kept in the repertoire. Two films of the dance, made in 193? and 1943 show Graham performing. The later film, which is in colour, is not a record of the complete dance but is a series of poses with movement in between (Leatherman 1967). In western aesthetic conventions and in commonsense thinking, stepping and travelling are viewed as constitutive features of dance, '*Lamentation*' by contrast 'is dancing sitting down' (Siegel 1979: 39). When I screen a range of Graham's works for students, there are two dances that they articulate as still being very 'modern'; the first is *Lamentation* and the second is *Cave of the Heart* (1946) (1976 filmed versions). Although *Cave of the Heart* is much more theatrical and technically and choreographically sophisticated in orchestration, both dances reveal through the surface of the outer body's projection in time and space, the idea of a woman whose inner body is being consumed by emotion; the grief in *Lamentation* is replaced by greed and envy in *Cave of the Heart*. In *Lamentation* the solitary figure was seated on a low bench and she never took a step away from it. Moreover, the dancer's body was encased in a triangular tube of purple jersey, with only the feet, hands and part of the face visible, further confounding ordinary and artistic assumptions of what a dancer should look like. The movement was taut and angular and ceaseless. At the beginning of the dance the verticality of the torso contrasted sharply with the wide stance of the feet, which were firmly rooted to the floor. The top half of the body rocked, twisted and stretched at acute angles to the point of imbalance and was pulled back into the centre.

Frontier was Graham's second direct exploration of the American theme. Horst wrote the score especially for the dance. Like the earlier *Lamentation*, it has remained in the repertoire. There is also a film, made in the 1930s, of Graham performing the solo. (The following discussion is largely based on reviews and the 1976 filmed version performed by Janet Eilber.) Where *Lamentation* made use of constricted space, *Frontier* used space expansively. The solo figure in the earlier work, shrouded in the jersey tube, did not connote the idea of any particular type of person's attitude towards grief. Rather, the concept of grief was treated in an abstract manner. By contrast, the solo figure in *Frontier* evoked the idea of a particular type of person, the nineteenth-century pioneer woman, through her movement which was still non-representational, and her costume. Graham wore a stylised version of a nineteenth-century sleeveless homespun dress with a blouse underneath with long dolmen sleeves. The focus of *Lamentation* was inner-directed in that the movement was constantly pulled back to the narrow confines of the centre of the torso. In *Frontier*, the movement returned to the centre only to expand out again through the whole body and into the surrounding space. Its focus was outward-directed.

Although she had previously used a low platform, such as the bench in *Lamentation*, *Frontier* marks Graham's first use of actual stage design. The setting was designed by the sculptor Isamu Noguchi who went on to create more than twenty sets for Graham. Like Graham's dance, the setting was evocative of the frontier, rather than representational. The frontier post or fence was indicated by a short barrier of two horizontal bars at the centre-back of the stage, in front of which stood Graham. Two cables of ropes, joined together at a point immediately behind the barrier on the floor, stretched diagonally outwards and upwards to the left and right. The V-shape of the ropes created an illusion of expansive space beyond and to the sides of the fence. The setting evoked the vastness of the American landscape before it was fully tamed by the settlers. The sense of space that *Frontier* celebrated as an important feature of the American experience, can also be found in the structurally horizontal landscapes of nineteenth-century American luminist painters such as Martin Johnson Heade and John F. Kensett (see Wilmerding 1980).

Graham, like other dancers in the 1930s and early 1940s, was interested in American history and culture and with *American Document* (1938) she created a condensed history of the United States in the form of the theatrical minstrel show tradition (see McDonagh 1974: 133–4). This was perhaps the first time that Graham drew so heavily on the resources of popular entertainment for her art dance. It was a dance in six episodes: 'Entrance', 'Declaration', 'Occupation', 'The Puritan', 'Emancipation', and 'Hold Your Own'. The work witnessed the integration of costume, music, drama and dance. In it, Graham used the spoken word much more than in any previous work. The Interlocutor recited passages from American history, such as the Declaration of Independence. In the Puritan episode, the Interlocutor spoke alternate lines from the tongue-lashing sermons of the New England Puritan preacher, Jonathan Edwards, and from the sensuous 'Song of Songs'. The dialectical opposition of Puritanism and sensuality became a recurrent theme in Graham's work over the next few years, as in *Letter to the World* (1940) which was based on the life of New England poet, Emily Dickinson, and in *Appalachian Spring* (1944).

America is a heterogeneous culture, and the concern to promote, understand and differentiate America's cultural specificity from the other cultural heritages out of which it was forged – particularly the Anglo–Saxon element – led to an exploration of American themes such as pioneerism, non–conformism, individualism and democracy, in many of the arts in the 1930s and early 1940s. During the period of isolationism after the First World War, many American artists were acutely aware that indigenous work was not taken as seriously as that of artists from the other side of the Atlantic. In dance, for example, as discussed above, a dancer with a foreign sounding name, particularly a Russian one, had more opportunity of performing in the right places than an American dancer. In 1933, Martin complained about this in one of his regular Sunday columns.

> American dance has made the greatest contribution to the art that has been made since the eighteenth century. . . . It was necessary for both Isadora and Ruth St Denis to go to Europe for recognition, and it would sometimes seem even today that without an assumption of a few syllables as –ova or –itska it is difficult for a dancer of American origin to be fairly received at home.
>
> (Martin 1933a)

A similar complaint was made by the composers. Copland and other young American composers had little opportunity to perform their works in concert because the mainstream of music circles, in terms of conductors, audience and academia, held European composers in much higher regard. Part of the problem was that music in America was in the control of the Europeans, as dance had been in the nineteenth century.

> One can understand the complete frustration of so many American composers and their exasperation with the American cultural establishment when one considers that whatever they composed, whether in an up-to-date European style or in a native idiom, and however skillfully they structured their compositions, the most honored conductors, orchestras and opera companies were arrayed against them. The people in America possessing the authority to pass judgement on their music were, more often than not, European born or wealthy and unadventurous members of the board of trustees.
>
> (Tawa 1984: 57)

In the early 1930s America was in the grip of the Great Depression following the Wall Street Crash of 1929. Initially it was the wealthy, the owners of stocks and bonds and the financial brokers who felt the effects of the Crash. By 1933 the impact of the Crash had spread from the top to the poorest unskilled workers, although the owners of vast American fortunes were able to maintain their wealth. Businesses failed, factories reduced production and manpower, or ceased to exist altogether, shops closed and employees took reductions in their wages in order to prevent further redundancies. At the close of 1931 seven million people were out of work. By 1932, when Franklin D. Roosevelt was elected President, the figure had risen to above fifteen million. The plight of the poor was made worse because there was no employment insurance or public relief programme. President Hoover, Roosevelt's predecessor, believed that private philanthropy should attend to the needs of the unemployed. When circumstances forced him to form a committee to consider the matter, its verdict was that the country should tighten its belt. Individual states, cities and counties were either not prepared to set up relief programmes or could not afford to do so.

Even before the Depression most artists lived in a precarious economic state, apart from the few who had made it to the top of their profession. Graham's dancers, for example, when they were not rehearsing, worked as waitresses or shop assistants in order to get enough money to survive, as the concerts seldom paid their way (Graham 1991, McDonagh 1974). Graham taught movement to actors in such institutions as the Anderson–Milton School in order to supplement the almost non-existent income from her dance recitals. The members of the other modern dance companies did the same.

American painters had difficulty making money from their art long before the Depression (Hunter 1972, Rose 1967). Often they took jobs related to their skills, such as illustrating, sign writing, advertising, teaching and so on. John Sloan, who was one of The Eight, supported his family for some fifteen years by writing puzzles for a Philadelphia newspaper (Rose 1967).

Musicians had also been living on hard times before the onslaught of the Depression. Technological innovations in the gramophone and radio had reduced the demand for live music. The introduction of the sound film in 1928 led to thousands of musicians losing their jobs (Copland 1968, Meltzer 1976). With the Depression other areas of employment for musicians became extinct, such as opera, hotels, lessons and so forth. By 1933, according to Milton Meltzer (1976), almost two-thirds of the membership of the American Federation of Musicians were unemployed. The introduction of the radio and sound film also affected the theatrical profession. By their very nature, theatrical productions require a great deal of capital in terms of theatre hire, cast, equipment, etc., and as Harold Clurman (1983) has shown, the economic climate of the Depression made potential investors of theatre productions extremely wary of putting their money into such a risky venture.

Many Americans felt that the attitudes and attributes of their forefathers, which had fostered the growth of a liberal democracy and had enabled America to emerge as the industrial giant of the twentieth century, were again required to pull the country out of this period of economic gloom. Therefore, it is not surprising that themes which evoked some of the lost innocence and strengths of the culture should find their way into the thematic material of the arts. The Red Decade witnessed an enormous growth in the labour movement and the emergence of the powerful American trade unions. A number of artists and intellectuals turned towards communism or became radical liberals and themes of social protest permeated their work. As the decade wore on, the rise of fascism in Europe became a source of growing concern and artists arranged benefit concerts for the victims of the Spanish Civil War.

Roosevelt's New Deal policies, which eventually led to the establishment of the Works Progress Administration (WPA) in 1935, took the unprecedented step of making Federal government economically responsible for the plight of the nation's citizens. Relief funds were pumped into the states and the construction industry was boosted by a Federal public works programme. Direct relief was also given through such agencies as the Civil Conservation Corps (CCC). The Civil Works Administration (CWA), the forerunner to the WPA, was set up by Roosevelt in 1933 as a temporary measure to provide employment during the winter months.

Roosevelt put forward a five billion dollar relief programme in April 1935, and the WPA was established, replacing the previous emergency relief programmes. Roosevelt appointed Harry Hopkins as director, but as Hopkins believed that it was better to provide work relief than cash relief, the system of direct relief involved a very stringent means test and many people felt ashamed or unable to ask for it. The idea behind the WPA was that if a worker could not find a job in the private sector he or she could apply to the WPA, the aim being that not only would people be able to survive economically, but they would also be employed in tasks that suited their training and thus would be useful to the country.

Hopkins maintained that artists should also be employed on the WPA (see Meltzer 1976: 18-22). However, as Hopkins believed that it would be of little value to the community to employ them in spheres to which they were unsuited, he recommended that artists should be employed in their own field and that they should bring the arts to the American people. Thus, he set into motion a unique and far-reaching experiment in the history of American art: Federal funding of the arts on a scale hitherto unknown, or to be repeated. Before the establishment of the WPA, the CWA had given funds to the Treasury Department to employ artists and actors in the Public Works of Art Project (PWAP). The Treasury Department also administered a second fine arts programme that became known as the Section of Fine Arts, a project inaugurated in 1934 and continued until 1943. In 1935, what was termed Federal Project Number One came into existence. The original areas included in the WPA arts relief programme were: the Federal Art Project, the Federal Theatre Project, the Federal Writers Project and the Federal Music Project, with the Historical Records Survey added at a later date. Hopkins appointed a national director for each of the projects. Holger Cahill headed the art project, Hallie Flanagan, theatre; Harry Alsberg, writers; and Nikolai Sokolai, music. By the end of 1935, 40,000 artists were employed on 'Federal One'.

Dance was established as an independent project rather than an aspect of the Federal Theatre Project. It was largely through the sustained efforts of Tamiris that this was accomplished (see Schlundt 1972: 38-40). Tamiris formed and chaired an organisation called the Dance Association, through which she contacted Hallie Flanagan and persuaded the head of the Federal Theatre to set up a separate Dance Project. Don Oscar Becque, a minor producer, was chosen as the director. He declared that the two main aims of the project were: the development of a 'common denominator technique' and the extension of American dance in terms of content and form into the creation of full-length theatrical dance works (see O'Connor and Brown 1980: 214–15). The New York executive committee included Humphrey, Weidman, Tamiris, Felicia Sorel and Gluck-Sandor. Donald Pond became musical director, with Genevieve Pitot and Wallingford Reigger as assistants. They were given a budget of 155,000 dollars over six months to employ 185 dancers and to mount eight productions. Humphrey planned to restage *Suite in F*, Weidman worked on a new version of *Candide*, Tamiris proposed to extend her *Walt Whitman Suite* into *Salut Du Monde*, Gluck-Sandor planned a revival of *The Prodigal Son*, Becque worked on *Young Tramps* and Sorel on *Til Eulenspiegel*.

The Dance Project was beset with problems from a very early stage, largely because of the impossible aims that it set out to achieve (see the *Dance Observer* 1936, 3: 87–8 for a discussion of these issues). By the end of June the quota had not been filled, and only three matinee performances had been given: Weidman's *Candide* and Humphrey's three dances, *Prelude, Parade* and *Celebration*. Tamiris's *Salut Du Monde* was not staged until later that summer, with Becque's *Young Tramps* following shortly afterwards. These performances were given 'out of town', as Martin called it (Code 1939a), because no Broadway theatre had been allocated to the Dance Project. The Dance Project made its first Broadway showing in December 1936, almost a year after its inception, with Gluck-Sandor's *Eternal Prodigal*.

According to some commentators, 'Impossibly high aims, red tape, changes in personnel, and inadequate budgets, not to speak of artistic jealousies and rivalries, all contributed to the delays and postponements' (O'Connor and Brown 1980: 214). At a public hearing in November 1936, Becque was blamed for all the shortcomings of the project (Gilfond 1936). His concern to develop a unified technique attracted much criticism and cries of artistic interference from staff choreographers like Tamiris, who had spent years perfecting their own individual techniques. Becque resigned in December under pressure and was succeeded briefly by Lincoln Kirstein. After Kirstein departed, no other director was appointed and the Dance Project merged with other small units of the New York Theatre Project under the leadership of Stephen Karnot (Schlundt 1972).

In May 1937, Tamiris produced her major work, *How Long Brethren?*, on Broadway, in a joint bill with Weidman's *Candide*. Tamiris's dance in particular brought modern dance choreography to a general audience:

> How Long Brethren?' . . . ran to standing-room-only houses for an unheard of forty-two performances. Its success gave the Federal Dance Project in New York respect both with the audience and administration; ironically it also gave Tamiris Dance Magazine's first award for outstanding group choreography. . . . The conjunction of Tamiris the artist with her theme of the suffering Negro was the high tide of historic time for the Federal Dance Theatre.
>
> (Schlundt 1972: 42)

In spite of the critical and box-office success of works like *How Long Brethren?* and *Candide*, the Dance Project was criticised increasingly from within the ranks of dance itself, through the auspices of the National Dance League (Schlundt 1972). This organisation argued that the Dance Project was dominated by a small but vociferous minority of the New York dance world, the 'mad modernistic dancers'. The 'modernistic' dancers were further accused of 'unparalleled unprofessionalism and shameful political agitation' (O'Connor and Brown 1980: 215, Schlundt 1972: 33). The Federal Theatre, generally, had a reputation for being infiltrated and dominated by Reds and other left-wing agitators because of some of their controversial drama–documentary *Living Newspaper* productions and play–operas like *The Cradle Will Rock* (1937) which took an anti-business establishment viewpoint (O'Connor and Brown 1980).

The 1930s, as has already been indicated, was an era of social protest in many sectors of American society. The Congress of Industrial Organisations, formed in 1935 to organise the workers in the mass industries, took on the mighty steel and car industries using mass pickets and sit-ins (Meltzer 1976). In the summer of 1937, Congress voted for cut-backs that entailed a one-third cut in personnel in the Federal Theatre (Schlundt 1972). Weidman led a sit-in demonstration after a performance of *Candide* and *How Long Brethren?* to protest at the proposed cuts in the WPA. He was joined by the cast, members of the audience and artists from the other programmes. It was deemed to be the 'first sit-in strike in the history of the American theatre' (O'Connor and Brown 1980: 215, Schlundt 1972: 43). Two hundred writers staged a sit-in their headquarters to protest against the cuts in their division. Artists held a demonstration in the office of Audrey McMahon, the head of the New York Art Project (Meltzer 1976). Despite the demonstrations, sit-ins, and a number of arrests, the WPA cuts were implemented and the Dance Project was merged into the Federal Theatre in October 1937 (Schlundt 1972: 43–4)). The New York dance units continued to function after they had been merged into the larger project. In 1938, for example, Ballet Caravan contributed a programme of American ballet. The works, however, were not created directly for the Federal Theatre. Humphrey and Weidman contributed to the project with programmes that had been mounted previously for their own company, as with the 1939 performance of Humphrey's *To the Dance*, *With My Red Fires* and *Race for Life*. Tamiris, on the other hand, who had given up her company to devote her services to the project, created a further three works specifically for the Federal Theatre, including *Adelante* (1939), whose theme was the Spanish Civil War.

While the artists took up the challenge to liberal democracy that was being posed by the rise of fascism in Europe, 'In America native fascists were organizing, winning an alarming number of followers' (Meltzer 1976: 137). The Federal Theatre was one of the first casualties of the shift to the right in American politics. It was the first of the arts relief programmes to be closed down by Congress in the summer of 1939 (see Meltzer 1976: 137–41 for a discussion of this process). It had been a major target of the House Committee on Un-American Activities (HUAC) which was formed in 1938 with Martin Dias as chairman. The Dias Committee was convinced that the Depression was caused by a Communist conspiracy, and they managed to convince others that this was the case. It maintained that the 'Communist plays' had been promoted by the Federal Theatre and that there was evidence of Communist sentiments in the state guides compiled by the Federal Writers Project. A further set of hearings under Clifton Woodrum of the House Appropriations Committee (HAC) was conducted in the Spring of 1939 in order 'to get the government out of the theatre business' (Meltzer 1976: 139). After the Woodrum hearings, a relief bill was presented to make drastic cuts in the funds allocated to the WPA. The Federal Theatre was to be closed down and the other three arts programmes could continue only if they received local sponsorship. The bill was carried through in June. The name of the WPA was changed to Works Projects Administration.

There were many supporters of 'Federal One' who came to its defence and attempts were made to save the Federal Theatre, but with no success. By 1939, America was emerging out of the Depression. With the annexing of Austria and Czechoslovakia by Germany, war in Europe seemed inevitable. The demand for war goods helped to strengthen the American economy. As Meltzer (1976) has pointed out, the necessity for relief was made redundant by putting millions of Americans to work to make war materials.

> By the middle of 1940, the arts projects were being hitched to the defense program. The artists, for instance, began building training aids, making posters for military bases, and decorating servicemen's clubs. The WPA community art centers held classes on camouflage for officers and gave craft courses to enlisted men. The creative arts were soon supplanted by the practical arts. Many people on the projects began to find jobs in defense plants, or joined the military.
>
> (Meltzer 1976: 141)

The 1930s was an extraordinary era in the history of the American arts. It witnessed the growth of an indigenous dance art, American modern dance. By the end of the decade, the modern dancers were being faced with the presence of an old rival. European ballet was entering into the American dance scene.

> Having believed that the new modern dance was to be 'the' dance in rough and tumble America, its leaders faced the fact, on the eve of war, that ballet was the dance receiving the support of Americans. Lincoln Kirstein doggedly backed George Balanchine until the choreographer and his style of ballet moved into the centre of the dance world; Lucia Chase poured her wealth into American Ballet Theatre (called by various titles during its life) until its style of ballet, American perhaps, became recognized.
>
> (Schlundt 1972: 61)

The concern here, however, has been to chart the growth of modern dance in America. The Dance Project played a significant role in this development (Schlundt 1972). The success of productions like *How Long Brethren?* and *Candide* demonstrated that modern dance could be appreciated by a wider audience. According to Grant Code (1940a), the Dance

Project made a vital contribution to the entertainment and education of the general public as well as to the development of performance dance (see Code 1939a, b, c and 1940a, b for a history of the Federal Dance Theatre). Code (1940a: 34–5) lists three major points in connection with the WPA Dance Project's record of achievements. First, the choreography, particularly in New York, was of an extremely high calibre. Second, musical composition for the dance grew to a high standard because of WPA sponsorship of American composers and because composers on the programme were able to create music specifically for the dance. Third, worthwhile experiments in group and solo choreography were made, especially with regard to the incorporation of theatrical elements into the framework of the dance. Furthermore, young choreographers were given a platform for their work through the Young Choreographers' Laboratory which was established under the auspices of the WPA. The other divisions in Federal One also had laboratories for their young artists and the Young Composers Laboratory, for example, played an important role in the subsequent development of American music (see Zuck 1980: 168–82). As with the Bennington experiment, the Federal Dance Project owed much of its achievement to a small number of committed individuals, the most important of whom, as Code (1940a) emphasised, was Tamiris.

It was not only dance art that began to flourish in America in the 1930s, but also American music and painting. At the time of the Armory Show America was a backwater in the world of art. After the Second World War the centre of the art world shifted from Paris to New York. In the 1940s, a new kind of American painting called abstract expressionism gained an international reputation and American painters such as Jackson Pollock, Robert Motherwell and Mark Rothko moved into the forefront of the international avant-garde (Rose 1967).

Barbara Rose has argued that the 1930s was the determining era in American art. The two major divergent trends in American art that had been in evidence since the beginning of the century – realism and modernism – were polarised during that era. The conviction grew among artists that because the American experience was different from the European experience, American art should adopt its own specific subject matter and its own forms of expression. Hence, the emergence of American scene painting in the 1930s, which included, for example, urban realists Reginald Marsh and Alexander Brook and regionalists Thomas Hart Benton and Grant Wood. Many artists felt that art should convey some kind of message or point. Often this resulted in a celebration of traditional values and an older way of life, as with the works of the regionalist painters. Alternatively, it could result in works of social protest as with the social realist paintings of Ben Shahn (see Meltzer 1976 for a discussion of the differences between these two genres). Both of these involved a negation of modernism. Non-representational art was treated as a disease that was set to contaminate 'healthy native American art' (Meltzer 1976).

Although most artists in the 1930s were realists of some kind, a small but persistent group of individuals were committed to abstractionism. The most important of these was Stuart Davis (see Hunter 1972: 157–62, Rose 1967: 136–43). Like the romantic realist, Edward Hopper, Davis's work dated from the period of the first group of realists, The Eight. He studied at Henri's school in New York and later worked with Sloan and other realist artists as an illustrator for the old *Masses*. But it was the Armory Show that had the greatest impact on Davis's early development and increasingly he turned away from realism towards abstraction. Benton, as the spokesman and leader of the regionalists, decried modernism and its proponents in America, like Stieglitz, as remnants of the Old World. Davis rejected the narrow provincialism and chauvinism of the American scene painters and instead turned towards European modernism as a means of painting. None the less, he insisted that his paintings were given life by the American scene, despite the fact that they were non-representational. He was one of the first American painters to recognise jazz as an American idiom. He sought to inject the rhythms and tones of jazz into his painting. As Rose (1967: 138) stated: 'Davis was the first American artist to appropriate successfully the means of French art towards the end of making distinctively American pictures.'

Young artists were beginning to turn away from realism towards abstract art, and Davis's commitment to abstraction provided them with a point of reference and support (Rose 1967, Hunter 1972). Like modernists in other artistic fields, the non-representational artists spoke to the few. By taking up the mantle of art for art's sake at a time when art was meant to speak to something outside itself, they were viewed as somehow lacking in moral fibre. They had difficulty showing their work in museums and galleries because many of these institutions were already filled with mediocre imitations of European modernism and the curators felt that American artists should develop their own style. In order to remedy their isolation in the art world and to provide a forum for their work, a group of young artists formed an organisation called 'American Abstract Artists'. Their annual exhibition soon became a forum for young modernists, as the 291 had been thirty years before. The exhibitions mounted by the American abstractionists, like those at the 291, emphasised internationalism and set out to make New York the centre of the avant-garde (Greenberg 1961).

At the same time as the abstract artists were forming their association, the forces of fascism were growing in Europe, and the first trickle of European modernists began to quit Europe for America. During the Second World War the number increased and, according to Greenberg (1961), their presence contributed to the development of the new American modern painting because they gave the young American painters in New York a feeling of living in the centre of the art world. Mondrian, who arrived in America in 1941, is cited as the most influential abstract artist (Greenberg 1961, Rose 1967, Rosenberg 1962). But of even greater importance were the 'surrealists in exile' such as Max Ernst, Dali, André Masson and André Breton (Greenberg 1961). Breton, who wrote the first surrealist manifesto in 1924, became the centre of the movement in New York where he helped to mount exhibitions, produce magazines and hold events which 'scandalised the public' (Greenberg 1961). Ernst's wife, Peggy Guggenheim, put her money behind a number of young American artists such as Pollock and enabled them to survive economically in a world hostile to modern art. She also introduced the young American painters to the modernists in exile. In 1942 she opened a gallery called *Art This Century* which showed abstract and surrealist work. The gallery also exhibited the works of young American painters such as Pollock, Motherwell, Rothko and Sill, alongside the Europeans (Greenberg 1961).

Other influences included Hans Hoffman, who opened an art school in New York in the 1930s where he introduced the emergent American avant-garde to the 'most advanced concepts of European modernism'. Greenberg (1961), who was present at Hoffman's lectures in the 1930s, considered that a student could learn more about Matisse's colour from Hoffman than from Matisse himself.

The revolt of the young New York artists in the late 1930s and early 1940s concerned a rejection of the formalism of abstract art and of the narrow confines of regionalism. Following the lead of the surrealists, they set out to express 'the general, the universal, the elemental' (Rose 1967: 164). The surrealists, however, drew on Freud for their imagery, whereas the emerging American abstract expressionists turned to Jung's theories of archetypes and the collective unconscious as a source for their images. In their view, Freud's theories appeared too culturally specific to be universal. The abstract expressionists were searching for 'symbolic equivalents' for the Freudian interior psyche (Rose 1967). In this respect there is a certain parallel between the work of the abstract expressionists and that of Graham as she developed away from her Americana period into her psycho-mythological cycle. Both were attempting to find a way of gesturing that could reveal the inside on the outside, not in terms of a specific individual, but rather as a universal mythic-psychological force (see Copeland 1983a for a discussion of this relation).

It has been argued (Meltzer 1976, Rose 1967, Rosenberg 1962) that it was not only the presence of exiled European modernists which helped to lay the base for the emergence of abstract expressionism, but the establishment of the WPA Federal Arts Project also facilitated its emergence.

> The WPA is a unique but crucial chapter in American art . . . it radically altered the relationship of the artist to the art audience and to society. By making no formal distinction between abstract and representational art, the

WPA supported the budding avant-garde's contention that both were equally 'American'. By affording artists the opportunity – which most had never had – to paint full time, the WPA gave them a sense of professionalism previously unavailable outside the academic context. By giving artists materials and time, it allowed them to develop their skills and technique to a new level. Throwing artists together in communal enterprises, the WPA experience provided an esprit de corps that carried over into the forties. Not the least of its contributions was the sponsorship of exhibitions and classes which served to arouse the consciousness of art in the far reaches of the country where many people had never before seen an original work of art.

(Rose 1967: 128)

American art music, like the new American painting and modern dance, also reached a point of recognition in the early 1940s that it had not gained before. In the following chapter I shall consider the development of American music in two ways. First, discussion will focus on the relation of music to American modern dance. Second, the development of the work of Aaron Copland from the 1920s to the early 1940s will be used to exemplify the shifts of emphasis in American art music during that period. The reason for using Copland is that his position in the development of American art music is virtually synonymous with that of Graham's in dance. There are many points of overlap between Copland's conceptions of American music and Graham's views on dance and these will be addressed as they emerge in the discussion. The chapter will also include an examination of Copland's music for Graham's dance *Appalachian Spring*.

8 CONCEPTUAL AMERICANISM, MODERNISM AND UNIVERSALISM IN MUSIC AND DANCE

The leaders of American modern dance, such as Graham, Humphrey and Weidman believed that movement was the primary medium of expression of dance. As such, they maintained that the accompaniment should grow out of the movement form and not dominate, as it seemed to do in ballet. Therefore, whenever possible, they commissioned music specifically for their dances. Humphrey had studied music as a child and she composed some of her own scores, such as the arrangement of drum, accordion and wordless soprano voice for *The Shakers* (1931). Graham, unlike Humphrey, did not develop her musicality from childhood, but rather through her long personal and professional association with Louis Horst. From 1926, when Graham began to choreograph and perform on her own, she was encouraged by Horst, her musical director and a composer in his own right, to dance to the music of modern composers and to commission the scores for her works. After 1933, Graham seldom choreographed to a pre-existent score.

Horst was the musical director at Denishawn from 1915 to 1925 and, therefore, was well acquainted with the rebels from Denishawn. He left Denishawn in the spring of 1925 to study musical composition in Vienna. When he returned towards the end of 1925, he resumed his interest in composing for the dance. He accompanied Graham at her first solo performance on 18 April 1926, and for the following twenty-two years was her musical director. Although he recognised a special talent in Graham, Horst was also a continuous source of support for the other major modern dancers and an advocate of the modernist aesthetic. In 1934 Horst published the first issue of the *Dance Observer*. This monthly journal, which continued until Horst's death in 1964, was the first of its kind to give a permanent forum for modern dance and to hail the superiority of that form over ballet. The journal gave prominence to Graham's work. The partisan attitude of the journal can be illustrated by the fact that Lincoln Kirstein resigned from the post as ballet critic when the editorial board refused to publish an article in which he criticised John Martin's views on dance. Martin, as indicated earlier, was a crucial figure in the promotion of modern dance in general and of Graham in particular. Kirstein, however, being a balletomane, was not only critical of what he saw as Martin's blanket acceptance of modern dance, but of the form itself.

Kirstein's first reaction to Graham's dance in the late 1920s was one of total rejection (Kirstein 1968). He found it old-fashioned in comparison to the modernism of the collaborative theatrical productions of the Ballets Russes which he had witnessed in Paris in the early 1920s. Despite his inbuilt resistance to Graham's dance, Kirstein felt compelled to see more of Graham's work.

> This solitary dancer [Graham], not even a girl, with her Spartan band of girls seeming to press themselves into the steel woman she was, appeared either naive or pretentious, which I could never fully decide. But the force of her personality magnetized me continually.
>
> (Kirstein 1968: 26)

Kirstein's gradual appreciation of Graham coincided with his disillusionment with the 'heirs of Diaghilev' and his own concern to promote an 'American classical style' that would 'not be dulled by a veneer of Russian glamour' (Kirstein 1968: 26). It also coincided with Graham's development towards theatricality. Kirstein played an important role in the development of ballet in America. It was he who invited Balanchine to come to America in 1933 to establish the American School of Ballet. The company gave its first performance in 1934. However, because Balanchine showed little interest in creating an American ballet, Kirstein conceived of his touring company Ballet Caravan, as a forum for young American dancers whose interest was in classical ballet choreography directed towards native themes (see Kirstein 1967: 38–48). Like Graham and the other moderns, Kirstein's ballet troupe commissioned the scores for the new ballets. For example, *Filling Station* (1937) was choreographed by Lew Christensen to music by Virgil Thomson, and Eugene Loring choreographed *Billy the Kid* (1938) to music by Aaron Copland. Ballet Caravan gave its first performance in 1936 at the home of the newly emerging modern dance, Bennington College. Other ballet choreographers were also working on ballets with American themes and commissioning the scores from American composers, such as Ruth Page and Bentley Stone who created *Frankie and Johnny* (1938) to music by Jerome Moross, and *American in Paris* to George Gershwin's score.

Like many artists and intellectuals in the 1930s, Kirstein was concerned with establishing an American cultural identity. However, it should be pointed out that, like other liberal-minded Americans of his generation, Kirstein did not consider this search in terms of constructing a nationalistic (racial) identity. Nationalism, in Kirstein's (1968) view, was a negative construct which he associated with the rise of fascist forces in Europe and the subjection of individual freedom to these forces. Consequently, as he came to see something profoundly American in Graham's dance, it was not in terms of 'red, white and blue patriotic exuberance' (Kirstein 1968: 32), but rather, as one that captured the geographical and historical spirit of the culture from a thoroughly modern standpoint. There is a certain ambiguity here: on the one hand, there was a recognition of the dangers of nationalism, while on the other, there was a deep rooted desire to generate a specifically American cultural heritage, on the basis of what Van Wyck Brooks called a 'usable past' (Copland 1953). This latter kind of nationalism, for Kirstein, unlike fascism, was not tainted by ideology. Graham's dance, according to Kirstein, was not that of flag-waving nationalism, nor was it a romantic interpretation of the past, rather it was one which, through the technical mastery of the body coupled with a conscious creative spirit, expressed the spirit of America, both past and present, from a modern and realistic viewpoint (Kirstein 1968).

Kirstein's concept of Graham's Americanism was an affirmation of the dancer's own concern to create an American modern dance. Graham (1930: 253) wrote that: 'It is not to establish something American that we are striving, but to create a dance form and expression that will have for us an integrity and creative force.' Graham considered that American modern dance was not concerned with the establishment of a nationalistic identity. Rather the intention was to create a dance form that would express and communicate the rhythms of American life, which, according to Graham, were sharper and faster than that of the 'Old World'. Rhythm, for Graham is 'the sum total of one's experience' (Graham 1968: 98). Dance forms should stem from the particular life of the culture. To transplant old forms onto different cultures can only lead to a lack in both dance and the culture. The dance loses its creative spirit, and the culture cannot engage its creative force towards a dance form that lacks the expressive and communicative possibilities of the shared experience of the culture. Graham and the other modern dancers considered that to transplant into American culture balletic forms that have their roots in European culture could only retard the creative spirit of the new social order. Hence, Graham and the other dance leaders, as was discussed at greater length in the previous two chapters, had to forge out new ground in dance in order to communicate with the public.

Horst not only created some memorable scores for Graham, such as *Primitive Mysteries* (1931) and Frontier (1935), he was also highy influential as a teacher of choreography. Like Humphrey, who wrote *The Art of Making Dances* (1959), Horst believed that choreography was a craft that could be taught. This was in sharp contrast to the European tradition of ballet, where, for the most part, Horst maintained, choreographers were viewed as unique individuals (usually male) whose artistic ability enabled them to put the set steps and movements together in an aesthetically pleasing manner which would enable the audience to appreciate the technical competence of the performers (Horst and Russell 1977). Horst based his teachings on the 'pre-classic dance forms' of sixteenth- and seventeenth-century European court music such as the sarabande and the pavane, out of which ballet emerged (see Horst 1979 and Stodelle 1964). It is important to note that the concern was not with 'classic forms'. This would have been anathema to Horst and to the other modern dancers. In later years he also developed a course based on 'modern dance forms' (see Horst and Russell 1977).

Although Horst, like the modern dancers, rejected the classical tradition of dance as the basis for modern dance, he did not adhere to the idea of self-expression in choreography. Indeed, one of the reasons he decided to teach choreography was that he believed it was not enough to revolt against ballet and simply do so-called barefoot dancing, but that the new dance had to be given form. In the early stages of modern dance, according to Horst (1969), the dancers reacted in just this manner with the result that there were a number of 'revolting dances'.

Horst considered that the material substance of dance, which is movement, should always be transformed through stylisation or symbolisation. Choreography, according to Horst, was founded on two things: 'a conception of a theme and the manipulation of that theme' (Horst and Russell 1979: 23). However, according to Horst, in order to manipulate that theme and develop it, the dancer must be well acquainted with the basic rules of composition. This is because he considered that all art is founded on the rules of form and a dancer who rejects these in favour of self-expression, considerably weakens the artistic value of the work. Hence, form, for Horst, constituted the basis of dance as art.

As indicated in the previous two chapters, the modern dancers' preoccupation with finding a form that would enable the 'stuff of dance', 'significant movement' (Graham 1968b: 98), to predominate, led them to abandon superfluous movement frills from their choreography, in favour of an economy of gesture and a reduction to the barest essentials of such other theatrical aspects as lighting, costume, setting and music. All extraneous factors, they argued, should be subjugated to the demands of the dance (McDonagh 1974). The use of music as an emotional stimulus for the dance, as in the work of Duncan and St Denis, was rejected in preference to the choreographer making the dance and subsequently requesting the composer to construct a score around the created movement rhythms of the work (Lloyd 1968). This entailed that the composer's own musical concerns should take second place to the choreographer's needs.

Music for the dance, according to Horst, should function as a framing device. It should not exist in its own right outside the dance for which it was composed. 'Music cannot be judged apart from the dance for which it was written, because it is integral to it' (Lloyd 1968: 92). Horst considered that musical accompaniment is important because, through its formal structure, it gives boundaries to the movement. At the same time, it can illuminate the primacy of the movement by going with or countering the movement rhythms (Lloyd 1968). The boundary of the musical structure and the movement compositional form, according to Horst, act together as a check on what he viewed as the dangers of self-expression, the potential diminution of art. The body, for Horst, is 'the most dangerous of instruments' which, without these two elements, 'is likely to run riot into emotional expression' (Lloyd 1968: 92). According to Horst 'Motion is born of emotion . . . and both must be kept under control' (Lloyd 1968: 92). The body, then, for Horst, is the house of emotions, irrational and prelinguistic and must be kept under control by giving it form. Otherwise, it will burst onto the surface of art and reduce its artistic value.

Although Graham experimented with various ways of using music, she seldom danced without it, unlike Humphrey for example. Like Horst, Graham considered that music functioned as a boundary for the movement. In the beginning of her dance career, Graham had been encouraged by Horst to dance to the works of relatively unknown and uncompromisingly modern composers, such as Satie and Schoenberg (see McDonagh 1974: 138 for a discussion of the relation between music and dance in Graham's early work). In order to emphasise dance's independence from music, Horst had then encouraged Graham to make the dance before the composer scored the music, as he had done with *Primitive Mysteries*. From the time of her pivotal work *American Document* in 1938, which saw the introduction of a male dancer into Graham's company and which achieved for her a measure of popularity hitherto unknown, Graham began to develop her own way of working with composers that she would maintain throughout the rest of her career. From that time, instead of making the dance first and then having the composer come into the studio to 'turn out music by the yard' (McDonagh 1974: 138), Graham would prepare an elaborate script to be given to the composer and designer; only after the score had been completed would Graham begin to choreograph the dance.

This view of music and dance as interdependent remained the dominant consideration in the modern dance world until the 1950s, when Merce Cunningham, a former soloist in Graham's company, began to reject and shatter many of the ideas that had become part of the modern dance establishment. Through his collaboration with the composer, John Cage, and artists such as Robert Rauschenberg, Cunningham began to formulate the view that all the different elements of the dance – movement, costumes, decor, lighting and music – are related to each other in terms of coexistence, not interdependence. Each of the elements, according to Cunningham, is entirely separate and not reducible to the others. 'Dancing has nothing in common with music other than the element of time and the division of time' (Cunningham 1968: 86). That is, they coexist, and if they do seem to come together in performance, then according to Cunningham it is a matter of chance, not contrivance.

The experimental use of modern music by American dancers in the 1920s and 1930s helped to promote modern music (Lloyd 1974).

American audiences often received their first introduction to modern music through the performances of the modern dancers. Moreover, by commissioning the scores for their dances, the modern dancers gave young American composers such as William Schuman, Clifford Vaughan, Ray Green, Hunter Johnson and Lehman Engel, a much needed platform for their work (Lloyd 1974). The musical scores for the early modern dancers, however, seldom stood up as compositions in their own right. Copland's music for Graham's dance *Appalachian Spring* (1944), stands as a major exception to this general rule. *Appalachian Spring* won the Music Circle Critics award for the best theatrical production of the year and Copland's score won the 1945 Pulitzer Prize for music. The original score for Graham's dance was for a chamber orchestra of thirteen instruments. Copland subsequently rearranged the music as a concert suite for symphony orchestra, so that it would stand as a musical piece in its own right and this was first performed by the New York Philharmonic–Symphony orchestra in 1945. Stravinsky also had altered his early ballet music so that pieces could be considered as works in their own right, and it is partly because Copland followed in his footsteps that he has been called 'the American Stravinsky' (Zuck 1980). The fact that the original score was for thirteen instruments was entirely in keeping with the modern dancers' view of music for dance. If the sound was too dominant, they argued, it would detract from the importance of the movement. Again, Cunningham would begin to rupture this view in the 1950s by having the music/sound coming at the audience through loud speakers situated in various parts of the auditorium. Initially, some critics – Arlene Croce (1977) for example – considered that this new approach detracted from the dance. But for Cunningham (1968), the music/sound constitutes an autonomous structure with its own specificity and, as such, it is not subservient to the movement.

Copland had composed four other works for ballets before he embarked on *Appalachian Spring*. The first, *Grohg*, which was never performed, was written during his stay in Paris in the early 1920s. *Grohg* was adapted later into *Dance Symphony* (1931). The second, *Hear Ye, Hear Ye*, was composed for Ruth Page and Company in 1934. This little known work was concerned with satirising the American judicial system and Copland drew on jazz for his composition. The other two works which, like *Appalachian Spring*, gained recognition in their own right, were *Billy the Kid* (1938), choreographed by Eugene Loring for Kirstein's Ballet Caravan, and Agnes De Mille's ballet *Rodeo* (1942) for Ballet Russe de Monte Carlo. The significance of Copland's scores for dance standing alone as works in their own right lies in the fact that he was the first American composer to gain both national and international acclaim. Copland made the ballet score of *Billy the Kid* into a symphonic suite in 1941, and from *Rodeo* he orchestrated *Four Dance Episodes* (1943).

The scores for *Appalachian Spring, Billy the Kid* and *Rodeo* make use of American folk music material. The latter two draw extensively on American folk songs and cowboy ballads, while the former is limited to the utilisation of one tune, *Simple Gifts*, a Shaker hymn taken from a collection of Shaker music and dance published by Edward Andrews in *The Gift to be Simple* in 1941. The utilisation of folk material in Copland's work coincided with the composer's (1968: 161) stated 'tendency towards an imposed simplicity'. This tendency towards a simpler musical style began with *El Salon Mexico* in 1936 and ran through to *Appalachian Spring* in 1944 (Chase 1955).

Copland's concern from the middle 1920s, when he began experimenting with jazz rhythms, was to create a musical language that would significantly relate to his experience of being brought up in New York (Copland 1953). He first discovered that this relation was lacking during the three-year period of study with Nadia Boulanger in Paris in the early 1920s. There, he found that French music, unlike his own, was integrally related to the culture.

> The conviction grew inside me that these two things that always seemed to have been so separate in America – music and the life around me – must be made to touch.
>
> (Copland 1953: 99)

This concern would not have been an issue for French or German composers or indeed for most European artists. Because the music of French composers is locatable in terms of a tradition of art, it would be almost nonsensical for a French person to ask how he or she could begin to write French music. However, as demonstrated in the previous three chapters, this was a continuous concern for many American artists in the 1920s and 1930s. The following statement by Graham, written in the late 1930s, regarding her dance development, echoes Copland's retrospective account of his early musical development.

> A clear accent has been placed upon the consciousness of the country. This was a temporary but inevitable isolation necessary to find something akin to a folk condition of truth from which to begin. A necessary part of this development was that we become aware of the ground on which we find ourselves, from which we have been physically and psychically bred.
>
> (Graham 1968b: 96)

At the same time, Graham's view of dance composition in 1931 as 'tending towards an economy of gesture', 'an intensity and integrity of mood' and 'a simplified external means' (Graham 1968: 98), resonates with Copland's development towards a simplicity of musical form in the mid-1930s. Both Graham and Copland recognised that both the emergence of America as an industrial giant and the advent of the First World War had wrought significant changes in American society, and that if art were to communicate with the public it would have to change accordingly. It should be emphasised, however, that neither Copland nor Graham wished to popularise their work in the usual sense of the term. Graham, as I have pointed out, was uncompromising in her pursuit of a dance art, and Copland was also endeavouring to generate a musical language. In many respects Copland and Graham embodied the two sides of Baudelaire's vision of modernity; 'the transient, the fleeting, the contingent' and 'the eternal and the immutable' (Harvy 1989: 10). On the one hand, they were working in terms of 'the tradition of the new' (Rosenberg 1962), emphasising the here and now rhythms of modern industrial America and the idea of constant renewal, but, on the other, they were trying to locate their work in terms of more fundamental, universal principles.

During the 1920s, several young American composers, including Copland, Roy Harris and Virgil Thomson, began to search out past American composers who had 'an interest in the American scene' in order to find a usable past upon which to develop their American music (Copland 1953: 100–6). Interest in the American scene, as indicated previously, was prevalent in many of the arts in the 1920s and 1930s. American writers could draw on a respectable American literary tradition, but this was not the case for dance, art or music. The young composers' search for a usable past had been abandoned by the late 1920s, largely because they felt that there was none of any significance and their agenda was somewhat different.

> Our concern was not with the quotable hymn or spiritual: we wanted to find a music that would speak universal things in a vernacular of American speech rhythms. We wanted to write music on a level that left popular music behind – music with a largeness of utterance, wholly representative of the country that Whitman envisaged.
>
> (Copland 1953: 104)

Copland, like Graham, then, wished to make a strict separation between art and entertainment.

Copland's preoccupation with writing music that would be 'immediately recognized as American in character' (Copland 1968: 158) led him to explore popular musical idioms, and jazz in particular, just as American painters drew on the resources of popular cultural forms like illustration. Copland was particularly interested in exploring the rhythmic elements of jazz. However, Copland (1968) maintained that his jazz–influenced work took a different orientation to that of Gershwin and the difference was founded largely in Copland's concern to transform the popular cultural element of jazz into the framework of the modernist aesthetic.

> Gershwin is serious up to a point. My idea was to intensify it [jazz]. Not what you get in the dance hall but to use it more cubistically – to make it more exciting than ordinary jazz.
>
> (Copland 1968: 59)

Although Copland's words are somewhat dismissive of Gershwin and 'ordinary jazz' (the general devaluing of jazz music will be taken up later in the discussion), they do emphasise the point that he did not see his work moving in the direction of populism, again indicating the tension between art and entertainment.

The experimental use of jazz in such works as *Music for the Theatre* (1925) and *Concerto for Piano and Orchestra* (1927), gained Copland the reputation as a radical in musical circles. By the beginning of the 1930s, Copland had left jazz behind. He then became more interested 'in writing music of a more austere character, intellectual in conception and expression' (Chase 1955: 496). The works that belong to this austere period include *Piano Variations* (1930), *Short Symphony* (1933) and *Statements for Orchestra* (1934), with *Symphonic Ode* composed between 1928 and 1929 marking a transition from the jazz-oriented period to the more austere style. Although Copland (1968) has stated that *Concerto for Piano and Orchestra* was effectively the last of his experiments with jazz, his biographer Arthur Berger (1953) has argued that analysis can reveal that jazz is still an 'inspiring agent' in the later *Symphonic Ode*.

With the emergence of *Piano Variations,* Copland's change of style emerged 'completely crystallized' (Berger 1953). This work helped to establish Copland as a composer of significance in modern music circles. However, within the wider serious music going audience, it was considered rather 'freakish and inaccessible' and 'austere' (Berger 1953: 25). As a work it is sparse and full of broken rhythms that seemingly go nowhere. As Chase has argued, 'The *Piano Variations* is a work of masterly construction, forceful in utterance, modern not only in manner but in essence' (Chase 1955: 497). Like Graham in dance, Copland was sifting out all extraneous elements to get to the core of the music. He was operating on the modernist principle of the reduction of the artistic medium to the thing itself (Greenberg 1961).

In 1931 Graham choreographed *Dithyrambic* to Copland's *Piano Variations.* Like Copland's score, the dance required total concentration from both the performer and the audience (Martin 1967). Graham at this time was stripping movement to the bones and the economical style she was developing suited the broken rhythms of Copland's music. The composition was linear in form with sharp touches of segmental movements that seemingly bore no relationship to each other. The dance built up to a climax with a series of slow falls. According to Bonnie Bird (1984), in order to perform these falls in a particular manner, Graham had to turn her feet out instead of maintaining them strictly parallel. The dance also witnessed the introduction of spiral movement into Graham's work (Bird 1984).

> The dance was spare, uncompromising, fearsomely difficult to perform, and, from the audience's standpoint, difficult to follow . . . 'Dithyrambic' relentlessly moved ahead with flicks and touches of movement, each of which bore no

relationship to the one that came before. This moment-to-moment relationship was, in effect, a theme. Without the viewers' concentration, the work became a collection of individual phrases that had no relationship to one another.

(McDonagh 1974: 86)

McDonagh's description of Graham's dance resonates strongly with Wilfred Mellers's conception of Copland's *Piano Variations* as seeming to 'embrace all the physical and nervous energy of city life' (Mellers 1964: 86). Graham, as indicated above, stressed that dance should reflect the sharp jagged rhythms of industrial America, just as Copland wanted to create music that would relate to his experiences in the big city. As Graham was paring movement to the bones to release the energy of dance, so Copland was performing the equivalent reduction with music.

> [In the *Piano Variations*] It is because line, harmony and rhythm are so disintegrated that every facet must be serially related with such rigid fanaticism . . . the energy may be broken or distraught; but the 'disintegration' climax is liberated into stillness . . . It asks the question: Shall these bones really live?
>
> (Mellers 1964: 86)

Although Graham reworked *Dithyrambic* and it became a key feature of her concerts, it was dropped from the repertoire after several seasons when Graham went on to something new (see Martin 1933). It remained, 'a dance for the few and not for the many' (McDonagh 1974: 86). Martin considered that despite the difficulty of the dance, 'Dithyrambic served to crystallize the high regard of the public and to assure Martha Graham's position in the American arts' (Martin 1967: 198).

Despite the fact that Copland did not draw on native material in this period of austerity, he remained a staunch 'conceptual Americanist' (see Zuck 1980: 252–6). Copland's gift for organisation, and his desire to give American composers the opportunity to have their works played in concert, led him into a whole variety of extracurricular musical pursuits. In addition to lecturing, writing books and articles on music, he also organised contemporary composers' groups. The Copland-Sessions concert series (1928–31) provided an important forum for young American modern composers, at a time when home-grown works were seldom performed in the mainstream of serious concert music circles. Moreover, in the early 1930s, Copland brought together a number of talented young composers to form the Young Composers' Group. The Group was based on the French *Six* who had come together as a unit in order to provide a platform for their music, and whose work received a voice through a sympathetic critic. Copland invited Arthur Berger to become a member of the circle so that he could perform the same function as that of the French critic Collaer. Copland encouraged the Young Composers' Group to engage in discussions of their work and its relationship to the world outside, after the concert sessions.

Copland's development towards a simpler musical language emerged from the period of austerity in the early 1930s. During this time he became increasingly aware that his music was restricted to a very small public, while recent technological developments in radio, gramophone and film, had considerably increased the potential size of the musical audience (Copland 1968). Composers were no longer just writing in an industrial society; industrialism had entered their musical world, as it had entered the literary world in the nineteenth century with the development of mechanical reproduction in printing. He considered that it made no sense to ignore these developments 'and continue as if they did not exist' (Copland 1968: 160). In order to make contact with the increased audience, Copland decided to move towards a more simple style of music.

> I felt it was worth the effort to see if I could say what I had to say in the simplest possible terms.
>
> (Copland 1968: 160)

Berger (1953) has argued that it was not only the concern to reach a wider public that influenced Copland's change of musical style, but also his involvement with the leftish Group Theatre founded by Harold Clurman in 1931. Copland's association with the *Composers Collective* for whom he wrote the mass song *Into the Streets May Day First* (1934), has been cited as yet another influence on the composer's musical development (Zuck 1980).

The activities of the Group Theatre encompassed much more than that of a play-giving unit (see Clurman 1983 for a detailed history of the Group Theatre). Its ultimate aim was the creation of a permanent acting company in New York, that would give an alternative forum to playwrights, actors and directors who either eschewed the Broadway star system or were rejected by it. Clifford Odets, originally an actor in the Group, became heralded as the major new left-wing playwright of the 1930s, when his play *Waiting for Lefty* was produced by the Group Theatre in 1935. Throughout its brief ten years of existence, the Group held regular meetings to discuss not only the technical aspects of production but, more importantly, to develop a deeper understanding of the relationship of their craft to the life of the times. This latter concern, according to Clurman, led other artists not directly involved in the theatre to join in the Group's discussions.

> photographers like Paul Strand and Ralph Steiner, a musician like Aaron Copland, an architect like William Lescaze, and many others not directly connected with the theatre found these meetings, and the subsequent development of the group that emerged from them, both stimulating and relevant to their own fields of interest.
>
> (Clurman 1983: 34)

Copland encouraged the Young Composers' Group to engage in similar kinds of discussions, although of a less polemical nature than those of the Group Theatre (Berger 1953).

The Group Theatre's concern to come from the ivory tower and create works that were meaningful to their audiences in terms of both content and form, was reflected in other artistic fields: the *Composers' Collective*, the American scene and social-realist painters, and in dance. This movement was reinforced by the establishment of the WPA.

From around the mid-1930s to mid-1940s, Copland composed functional music for many different areas: for ballet and modern dance, as listed before; for radio *Music for Radio* (1937); for schools, the play–opera for the Henry Street Settlement, *The Second Hurricane* (1937); for orchestra, *Outdoor Overture* (1937); and for films, *Of Mice and Men* (1939), *Our Town* (1940) and *North Star* (1943).

The prevailing trend in this period of 'imposed simplicity' was towards the utilisation of folk material (Berger 1953). This musical simplification was not only reflected in the work of other American composers, but was also part of a wider international movement. In Germany, for example, this was exemplified in the *Gebrauchmusik* movement, with Paul Hindemith at the helm. In the mid-1920s, Hindemith, like Copland and other American composers a decade later, became concerned that contemporary music was increasingly isolating the composers from their audiences. In order to redress this balance, Hindemith began to compose functional music for students and sophisticated amateur musicians (Zuck 1980).

Gebrauchmusik was often composed for particular occasions or events and, like American music in the 1930s, frequently drew on folk-songs or popular tunes. Copland's commissioned scores for schools which Chase (1955) termed 'workaday music', broadly correspond to the concept of Gebrauchmusik. In America, this approach was strengthened by Marc Blitzstein's *The Cradle Will Rock* (1937), a contemporary play–opera whose theme of power and corruption was set in Steeltown, USA. Blitzstein dedicated the work to Bertolt Brecht, who collaborated with Kurt Weill, a leading exponent of Gebrauchmusik.

The Cradle Will Rock was scheduled for performance by the WPA Federal Theatre in New York in June 1937 (see Mathews 1967, Meltzer 1976, O'Connor 1972 for discussions of this production, the events leading up to it, and its aftermath). Washington viewed the work as political dynamite for several reasons. First, as was pointed out in Chapter 6, the Federal Theatre was notorious for its leftist orientation, and critics of the project were always ready to cite the Federal Theatre as a communist organisation that was taking funds from the American treasury. Second, Blitzstein's theme of corruption in Steeltown USA echoed the current battle between the steel industry bosses and the unions, which was making daily headlines in the press at that time. These factors made Washington very nervous, particularly at a time when the WPA was under threat of massive reductions in its budget. Despite the fact that 18,000 advance tickets had been sold, the Federal Theatre was informed by Washington, four days before the first scheduled performance, that the show could not go on. Orson Welles, who was to direct the show, tried to convince the officials in the capital that Blitzstein's work was an artistic venture, not a political one, but to no avail. Welles and the producer John Houseman decided that they would put it on under their own auspices, but the actors and musicians' union banned their members from performing with anyone except the Federal Theatre. On the evening of the first benefit performance the Federal Theatre's doors were closed to the awaiting audience. WPA guards were placed inside the theatre to prevent any unauthorised use of props, lighting, etc. Welles and Houseman, before going into the theatre, told the crowd that the show would go on regardless. A deal was made to open a disused theatre some streets away and the audience was informed that they should proceed to the new venue. The only item from the production that was taken to the new venue was Blitzstein's score, which Lehman Engel smuggled out under his coat. Throughout the whole performance the only person to appear on the stage was Blitzstein, who played his music on an old untuned piano. The actors and singers appeared everywhere in the auditorium, except the stage, and in so doing, did not defy their unions' ruling. The performance made front page news the next day with headlines calling it 'the Runaway Opera'. The performance was a huge success with the audience, which was in sympathy with the actors and the theme of the play. According to Copland, 'The opening night of "The Cradle" . . . made history: none of us who were there will ever forget it' (Zuck 1980: 209).

Although the first performance of *The Cradle Will Rock* made theatre history for numerous reasons, its approach to play–opera itself was significant at the time.

> Blitzstein turned to cops and capitalists and union organisers for his characters, and took action into night court, drugstore, hotel lobby, faculty, lounge, street corner and salvation mission. . . . His style was a mixture of realism, vaudeville and oratory. Blitzstein gave the man in the street a musical voice – the first serious attempt to do this in American musical drama.
>
> (Meltzer 1976: 40)

Apart from a brief excursion into tourist music with *El Salon Mexico* (orchestrated in 1936), Copland's main concern from the mid-1930s through to the 1940s was with American folk music (Berger 1953). This period also coincided with Graham's shift away from her 'long woollens' phase and towards the development of dance as a theatre piece and the utilisation of Americana material with the exploration of Puritanism and pioneerism in particular. It could be argued that Copland, in particular, compromised his musical standards by pandering to the market requirements of music at this time. In the 1930s, as discussed in the previous chapter, the dominant trend in all the arts in America was to turn away from Europe and look towards the home–grown culture for artistic inspiration. What began as a revolt in the 1920s became the vogue in the following decades. Indeed, some of the American abstract painters felt that their work was viewed with scorn because they did not conform to the dominant requirement to paint American themes in a figurative manner, but instead looked towards the work of modern European painters, such as Mondrian, for inspiration (Rose 1967). Copland has stated that he was well aware of this trend towards Americana in the 1930s: 'There was a "market" especially for music evocative of the American scene – industrial backgrounds, landscapes of the Far West and so forth' (Copland 1968: 162).

However, Copland (1968) has maintained that, even at this point in his development, he was still attempting to create a musical language, just as, indeed, Graham was striving to generate a dance language. In the 1920s, when Copland was drawing on jazz for his music, he was in the forefront of the modern music movement. Although the use of jazz had provoked a great deal of attention in the 1920s, it had also provoked cries of moral outrage from the mainstream of academic music and the majority of critics. The use of jazz elements in art music was also part of a wider international movement in modern music, as in the work of Stravinsky, Satie and Milhaud. Thus, the rejection of jazz in art music in America can be viewed as a rejection of modernism. However, jazz emerged from black American culture and not from the mainstream of the dominant white culture. Because black music was viewed traditionally as subversive, the cries of moral outrage that the introduction of jazz into serious music elicited, can be viewed as an attempt to maintain the status quo, and as implicit racism.

The later widespread interest in American folk material, however, did not provoke such moral condemnation as jazz did in the 1920s, in part because the former emerged from the dominant white cultural tradition. It is somewhat ironic that in their desire to achieve culturally specific art forms, many American artists turned away from the possibilities of modernism and instead drew on the very cultural tradition from which America had sought to differentiate itself, both politically and socially. By the 1940s, Copland was no longer in the avant-garde, but was moving with the prevailing trend and, indeed, he contributed to this vogue because, as Chase has pointed out, 'there were some Americans, and many foreigners, who heard these tunes for the first time in the engaging musical scores he wrote for the Ballets *Billy the Kid* (1938), *Rodeo* (1942) and *Appalachian Spring* (1944)' (Chase 1955: 499).

These three works, and in particular *Appalachian Spring*, were not only well received in their time, but they have also become modern American classics. In addition, they are, for dance, the most widely recognised

Americanist works of any period and Copland has been seen by some as the American Stravinsky (Berger 1953).

Not only did *Appalachian Spring* considerably enhance Copland's reputation, but also that of Graham. With *Appalachian Spring*, one of the most dominant figures in American modern dance and the most widely recognised American composer of this period came together for the first and only time. The work, in time, became a signature tune for both Copland and Graham. As such, it points to a particular significant moment in the history of modern dance and music in America and, therefore, is an appropriate object for sociological investigation.

Appalachian Spring was first performed along with two other works, *Mirror Before Me* (subsequently renamed *Hérodiade* at the request of the composer), and *Imagined Wing*, at the Library of Congress, Washington DC, on 30 October 1944. These three works and the respective scores by Copland, Hindemith and Milhaud, were commissioned by the Elizabeth Sprague Coolidge Foundation the year before. The set was designed by Noguchi, the lighting by Jean Rosenthal and the costumes by Edythe Gilfond. Graham danced the role of the Bride, Erick Hawkins the Husbandman, Merce Cunningham the Revivalist, and May O'Donnell the Pioneer Woman.

In his review of the Coolidge Festival, Martin (1944) stated that *Mirror Before Me (Hérodiade)* and *Appalachian Spring* were 'at once among the finest of Miss Graham's achievements', and the critic (Sabin 1944) in the *Dance Observer* considered that both these works were 'highly significant' in Graham's development.

> The first is dark and terrifying, the second radiant and affirmative, yet between the two exists a relationship which is not immediately apparent. For Miss Graham has developed them from the same cell, so to speak. 'Mirror' works inward, into the depths of the unconscious; 'Appalachian Spring' works outward into the basic experiences of people living together, love, religious belief, marriage, children, work and human society.
>
> (Sabin 1944: 120)

While *Hérodiade*, with its sombre psychologism, pointed to the direction that Graham would take in the third decade of her work, her psycho-mythological cycle, *Appalachian Spring* marked the high point of the second decade. The latter was a pivotal work for Graham in several respects (see Siegel 1979: 144–52). With this dance Graham's experiments towards a dance theatre reached a point of coalescence. The music, costumes and décor intertwined with the movement to create a functional unity. But it also foreshadowed the works of the later Greek cycle, in that a major focus of the dance constituted an exploration of the emotions of the female protagonist.

The pioneer spirit and the Puritan ethic permeated *Appalachian Spring*, as they did in many of the Americana dances. But this was the last of

Graham's dances on the Americana theme. With this dance, she rested her fight with Puritanism and not until she made *The Scarlet Letter* in 1975 did she return to that theme again (Siegel 1979). Graham's characterisations of Puritanism were drawn from her own biography and from Puritan writings (McDonagh 1974). The Ancestress in *Letter to the World* (1940) was founded on Graham's childhood memories of her great-grandmother, and the fire and brimstone sermons of Cotton Mather and Jonathan Edwards formed the basis of her creation of the Revivalist in *Appalachian Spring* (Graham 1991). The characterisations of Puritanism that emerged from Graham's work were not one-dimensional. The interpretations offered both the positive and negative consequences of the doctrine. For example, of the first part of *American Provincials* (1934), which was Graham's first explicit treatment of the Puritan theme, Martin wrote:

> 'Act of Piety' captures the essence of the ferocious Puritan tradition as it is rarely captured. It is a subject so often played with that it had become dangerously trite, but here it bursts forth with such new depths and such fresh inspiration that it becomes a truth told to us for the first time. Miss Graham never for one instant condescends to her subject. She measures it at its full value. There is no ridicule, no easy taunting of a dead victim. Her Puritan is a worthy enemy, a creature of heroic proportions.
>
> (Martin 1968: 17–18)

In *Letter to the World* (1940), the 'worthy enemy' took the form of the Ancestress. The dance was based on the life and poetry of the New England recluse poet, Emily Dickinson. As with all of Graham's dances, the theme was not treated in a literal manner (see McDonagh 1974: 148–50). Rather the characters in the dance were divided into those of the real world and those of the imagination and time was broken up so that the past and present were acted out in the same space at the same time. The character of Dickinson was divided between two dancers, the One Who Speaks (the rememberer) and the One Who Dances (the memory). The dance portrayed Dickinson as a woman caught between desire and duty who has to choose between them. The pleasure of the recollection of her love for a man was threatened by the Ancestress, the symbol of the Puritan spirit. In *Letter to the World*, Puritanism was victorious, duty and tradition triumphed over desire and love. But in the end, the choice was not simply a negation of the world because Dickinson endured through her art, her legacy to the future, in Graham's interpretation, her 'letter to the world' (McDonagh 1974: 149).

In *Appalachian Spring*, the 'worthy enemy' was characterised by the Revivalist. However, in this work, unlike *Letter to the World*, Puritanism's rejection of desire and its antagonism to all things sensual, were defeated. In the end, love succeeded over the preacher's sermon on the evils of indulgences of the flesh. At the same time, however, as will be discussed below, the character of the preacher was imbued with a certain ambiguity towards sexuality. Although he espoused the doctrine which denounced the flesh, he was also human enough to fall prey to desire himself.

Simply stated, on the surface level, *Appalachian Spring* tells of a young couple being married and taking possession of their newly built homestead (again see Siegel 1979: 144–53). It is set in a small community on the American frontier in the early nineteenth century. The source of stability and support in the small community is represented by an older pioneer woman. The wedding ceremony is presided over by the fervent itinerant revivalist preacher, who is accompanied by a congregation of four girl followers. The form of the work is episodic rather than that of extended narrative. The focus is directed towards the moods and feelings of the central characters, their strengths, religion, hopes, fears and aspirations for the future in the newly settled land. Attention is directed towards the intimacy of the occasion, and the frontier movement of taming the land for future growth and development of America.

Before Copland embarked on the score for *Appalachian Spring* in the summer of 1943, Graham, as was her standard procedure from the time of her pivotal work *American Document* (1938), prepared a script for him to consider (see Graham 1991: 226–31 for a description of how she worked with Copland). Although Graham preferred to sit with a composer and discuss her ideas, Copland was working at Goldwyn's studios in Hollywood at the time and, as often was the case, the collaboration between the dancer and the composer was conducted by letter. When Graham sent Copland the script it was without a title. She found that much later in a poem by Hart Crane entitled *The Bridge*. Thus Copland's score was not based on Crane's poem. On reflection Copland (1968) considered that he tailored the music to Graham's particular talents and personality. He originally titled it *Ballet for Martha*. Copland suggested some minor alterations to Graham's notes, which she accepted. He then began to create the music, taking a full year to complete it. After it was completed in June 1943, Graham began to absorb the music and choreograph the dance. Originally Graham had proposed a section of the dance with 'an Indian girl on whose lands the frontiersmen have settled. She was to represent a dream figure always at the fence of our dream' (Graham 1991: 226). In the end Graham dropped the ethnic element from the dance, considering that the dance sufficiently conveyed the ideas she wanted to express without it.

The apparent simplicity with which *Appalachian Spring* evoked both the intimacy of the wedding of two people and the frontier spirit of a young America, captured the audience's imagination.

> In *Appalachian Spring* audiences recognized a story that was simultaneously personal to a couple and their kin and an expression of a country's growth. The musical quotes from a traditional hymn that Copland incorporated into his score emphasized the warm, religious and joyful values expressive of the

sinew and heart of a young country that, though still struggling, was confident of a happy outcome.

(McDonagh 1974: 179)

It is important to note that although Copland's ballets drew on native folk music, he was not a folklorist. He did not re-present the music through exact quotations, but transformed the original tunes into his own setting (Zuck 1980). Similarly, Graham's use of religious dance ritual of south-west Amer-Indians, in *Primitive Mysteries* (1931) did not emerge as a reflection, but rather constituted an inspiring agent that is transformed in the work. According to Copland (1953):

> The use of such materials [musical Americana] ought never to be a mechanical process. They can be successfully handled only by the composer who is able to identify himself with, and re-express in his own terms, the underlying emotional connotations of the material. A hymn represents a certain order of feeling: simplicity, plainness, sincerity, directness. It is the reflection of these qualities in a stylistically appropriate setting, imaginative and unconventional and not mere quotation that gives the use of folk tunes reality and importance.

(Copland 1953: 104)

It is this transformational element, according to Barbara Zuck (1980) that distinguishes Copland's generation from previous Americanist composers and folklorists.

> Copland's use of musical Americana in *Appalachian Spring* is limited to a quotation of *Simple Gifts* in the finale. The quotation is not exact, for Copland has smoothed out a few melodic gaps and changed the first phrase to parallel the first. . . . The melody undergoes successive stylistic treatments characteristic of a set of variations, and is transformed from the almost lighthearted initial presentation by the solo clarinet to the majesty of the final tutti statement. The latter is reminiscent of a Bach chorale, particularly with the strong contra puntal low line in low register. The five variations are Baroque-like indeed, . . . for Copland has preserved the melodic and basic harmonic patterns while altering the orchestral and rhythmic values.

(Zuck 1980: 269–70)

Zuck's (1980: 167–272) analysis of *Appalachian Spring* refers to the full orchestral suite, completed by Copland in 1945, which has since become the standard concert version. Copland (1968) stated that he altered the original ballet score for 'choreographic purposes'.

Although the pre-existent music in *Appalachian Spring* is restricted to the quotation from *Simple Gifts*, a feeling of Americana pervades the whole work. The introduction of *Simple Gifts* seems to emerge naturally from the sections that have come before. The music achieves a unity on various different and related levels.

> Despite the sectional nature of the work, Copland's score is unified on several levels. First, cohesion is achieved by the recall of material throughout the

piece as a whole and within individual sections. . . . Second, the prelude forecasts much of the important thematic material of the entire work.

(Zuck 1980: 267)

The principal motif of *Appalachian Spring*, that appears first in the ninth bar of the prelude, a rising fourth followed by a major third, forms the basis of the major theme that permeates the work. By the time *Simple Gifts* is introduced in section seven, the melodic rising fourth is so familiar that the new melody does not seem an intrusion. Moreover, 'The first notes of the melody (Simple Gifts) are really an embellishment of the rising fourth and major third of the principal motive (*sic*) in the prelude' (Zuck 1980: 268). Thus, although Copland has transformed the quotation from *Simple Gifts* he has also shaped the score of *Appalachian Spring* around it.

The folk-like music of the third section to which the preacher and the followers perform a dance reminiscent of the Anglo-Saxon folk dance heritage, and which is recalled later in the dance, adds to the ambience of Americana, while the use of solo woodwinds recalled throughout the work, particularly in the more lyrical sections, lends an air of intimacy to the setting.

In *Appalachian Spring* Copland has captured what he considered to be the essence of a hymn, 'simplicity, plainness, sincerity, directness' (Copland 1953: 104). The apparent simplicity of musical forms that Copland has achieved in this work in fact is underscored by a complex web of inter-related musical elements that function on various levels throughout the score. Similarly, Graham's dance is one of her most accessible and easily assimilated works. However, as I hope to show in the following chapter, once the surface structure of *Appalachian Spring* is penetrated, a highly complex choreographic form is revealed that belies the apparent simplicity of the movement means.

Although Copland went through a variety of different styles in his musical development, as Berger (1953) has pointed out, it would be a conceptual mistake to separate his works into pigeon holes with the view that they fit neatly into particular categories.

> Though the lines of demarcation between the phases are in one sense distin-
> guishable . . . the works themselves resist rigorous separation into cubby-holes,
> because they are all distinguished by a pervasive and unmistakeable individuality.
>
> (Berger 1953: 37)

In terms of music analysis, there is a dominant thread that runs through all of Copland's work that denies any such strict segregation of particular works into closed boxes.

> What strikes analytical attention before almost anything else is his economy of
> means, the transparency of his textures, the preciseness of his tonal vocabulary.
> . . . With Copland, . . . one is immediately aware of the control, through the

way he aims at a moods essence, after paring away ramifications and the accidental.

(Berger 1953: 39–40)

Berger's comments lead to further considerations of the relationship between Copland's music and Graham's dance. Graham also went through a variety of styles and thematic treatments of materials: from the 'little blossom' dances reminiscent of Denishawn, to the abstract and economical style of the 'long woollens' period, through to the introduction of theatrical devices and a certain softening of movement in the 'Americana' period, and then on to the total theatrical works of the 'psycho-mythological' cycle. Despite the diversity of her work, Graham's dances, like Copland's music, were underpinned by the unmistakable stamp of her personality and by the paring away of excess movement frills to get to the essence of the order of a feeling or mood. As with Copland's music, the prevailing tendency in all of Graham's works, was towards an 'economy of means'.

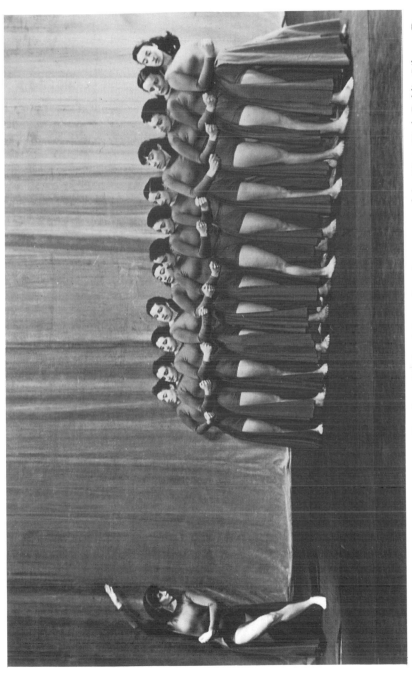

Plate 9 Helen Tamiris and her company in *How Long Brethren?* (reproduced courtesy of the New York Public Library Dance Collection).

Plate 10 Eric Hawkins and Martha Graham in 'Puritan Love Duet' from *American Document* (© Barbara Morgan).

Plate 11 Martha Graham Dance Group in studio demonstration (© Barbara Morgan 1991).

Plate 12 Martha Graham, May O'Donnell, Pearl Lang, Nina Fonaroff, Yuriko, Marjorie Mazia, Merce Cunningham and Erick Hawkins in *Appalachian Spring*, Elizabeth Sprague Coolidge Auditorium, Library of Congress (reproduced courtesy of the Library of Congress Collection).

9 APPALACHIAN SPRING

Thus far, the emergence of American modern dance has been examined in terms of the sociological context of its development. The aim has been to explain how modern dance is understandable as a feature of the socio-cultural milieu of its creation. This has entailed an exploration of the reasons why serious theatrical dance did not establish a sustained tradition in nineteenth-century America: a consideration of the changes that took place in American culture, which opened up a space in which the grounds for the emergence of a serious dance in America were made possible; and an analysis of the dominant features of American modern dance, involving a discussion of the relationship of the movement to the tradition of dance itself and to the other arts within the wider context of American culture. The analysis of American modern dance, then, has been viewed overwhelmingly from an *extrinsic* perspective. However, in order to point to the symbolic character of dance as art, the examination has also incorporated a consideration of the *intrinsic* properties of modern dance. As I argued at the beginning of the book, and have demonstrated at intervals throughout the historical analysis, American modern dance did not simply reflect the social conditions of its emergence, but it was also reflective *upon* those conditions.

When St Denis began her concert career around the turn of the century, dancers were considered to be beyond the pale of ordinary social discourse. However, by the early 1950s, the government of the United States had begun to view the indigenous art form of American modern dance as a cultural asset and Graham, among others, was asked by the State Department to represent the country abroad. Just as abstract expressionism was the painting style through which American art began to challenge the international art world, so American modern dance was the movement form that made America an innovator in the international dance field. The changing role of dance in American society from one of social outcast to that of cultural ambassador, as I have demonstrated throughout the preceding analysis, was achieved as a result of *intrinsic* processes of change in American dance as well as *extrinsic* forces. American modern dance facilitated the establishment of a new relation between dance art and American culture through its practice of separating art from entertainment and at the same time, by emphasising that American dance should be different from and not reducible to European dance in terms of movement or thematic content.

Appalachian Spring (1944), as I argued in the previous chapter, provides a point of reference for an examination of the history of modern dance and music in America because of the collaboration between Graham and Copland. Moreover, as I indicated towards the end of the first chapter, an examination of *Appalachian Spring* itself can be used to explore the relationship between the *extrinsic* and *intrinsic* perspectives through a consideration of the way in which the dance transforms everyday movement. With this in view, the intention here is to use *Appalachian Spring* as an exemplar to demonstrate that dance can offer interpretations of culture through its movement symbolism. As a result of this, I propose that the study of the internal dynamics of dance constitutes a significant resource for sociological enquiry.

There are two films of *Appalachian Spring* available for study, one made in 1958 and the other in 1976 (another film was made in the early 1970s which is held by the Graham organisation and is closed to the public). The 1958 film is in black and white and features Graham (at 64 years of age) as the Bride, Stuart Hodes as the Husbandman, Bertram Ross as the Revivalist and Matt Turney as the Pioneer Woman. The 1976 colour version was made for the *Dance in America* series. Here Graham's role is danced by Yuriko Kimura, Tim Wengerd dances the part of the Husbandman, David Hatch Walker the Revivalist and Janet Eilber the Pioneer Woman.

As John Mueller (1977) has noted, it is unusual to have the opportunity to compare two recorded performances of a major dance work. Indeed, according to Mueller, the release of the 1976 recording of *Appalachian Spring* constituted the first time that a 'complete major dance work' was available on a commercial basis in two different versions. This situation contrasts sharply with that of music where many recordings of an important work can be referred to for study.

The two versions have certain differences, which require elucidation. A comparison of the earlier film with the more recent recording demonstrates that while there are 'relatively few changes' in the choreographic structure, there are 'remarkable differences in characterisation' (Mueller 1977: 107). From his discussion of the two films, it is evident that Mueller prefers the earlier film. It is almost as if he takes the first film to be the original 'authentic' performance and the observable differences in the second version are then viewed as a deviation from the original (see also Hodes 1990/1).

> In general, the 1976 version is more athletically flamboyant, more decorative, more effusively and ingratiatingly theatrical. What gets lost is some of the

directness, simplicity and careful unhurried articulation that can make this dance masterpiece so deeply moving.

(Mueller 1977: 107)

In the introduction to the 1976 version, Graham states that *Appalachian Spring* is in essence a joyous dance, but that 'there are moments of darkness too'. For Mueller, the central character in the dance is the Bride and it is through her that this dualism is expressed best.

At times she (the Bride) fairly bubbles over with a dizzy giddy joyousness as she skitters in happy anticipation of her life on the frontier – of marriage, of creating a home, of children to come. At the same time there is fear – the sheer vastness of the space is an awesome, even terrifying challenge.

(Mueller 1977: 107)

Mueller concedes that Kimura in the 1976 performance expresses 'the giddy side' of the Bride better than Graham does in the earlier version, largely because Graham was 64 years old at the time of making the film. However, according to Mueller 'What is missing in Kimura's Bride is the darker aspect of the character and, accordingly, a major point of the dance work is missing' (Mueller 1977: 107). Alternatively, it could be argued that as Graham in the 1958 version does not express the other 'giddy side' of the Bride well, a major point of the dance work is absent in that film also. Graham was known principally for her power as a performer, and although small in stature her presence loomed large on the stage. In the 1958 film of *Appalachian Spring*, in addition to looking too old for the part of a young woman, Graham looks tiny and there is little indication of the power and magnetism that she consistently generated in live performance. What is often termed, 'the willing suspension of disbelief' in phenomenological analysis, is somewhat difficult to achieve when viewing the earlier film.

Mueller also notes that there are significant differences in the relationship between the Bride and the Husbandman in the two films. Although both films show that the couple care for and respect one another, the Graham–Hodes relationship posits these notions in a more 'archetypal' formal manner, while the Kimura–Wengerd relationship, for Mueller, is 'more fawning and cuddly', further emphasising the softer characterisation of the later work. In the 1976 film, the Husbandman seems much more openly emotionally responsive to the Bride's presence. In both films, during the Bride's first solo, he is standing with his arms leaning on the fence looking out with a smile on his face. The other characters are also still but alert in their respective positions. In the 1958 version the Husbandman remains fixed in his position while the Bride dances towards and away from him in her internal dialogue. In the later version, however, he breaks his position to smile and move towards her as she dances near him. Stuart Hodes (1990/1991: 92), who danced the role of the Husbandman from 1953–9, has also commented on the subtle differences of 'personal style' that Tim Wengerd injected into his role as the Husbandman.

A comparison of the two films also shows differences in the portrayal of the preacher and, again, Mueller considers that the later version, with Walker in the role, is lacking in certain respects.

> Bertram Ross's preacher in the 1958 version is brilliantly characterized, a carefully blended articulation of pompous self-righteousness and systematic humbug. Every pose, every inclination of the head, every posture seems to have been fully thought through.
>
> David Hatch Walker is one of the finest Graham dancers . . . but he doesn't give the role the happy inflections characteristic of Ross's performance. For example, there is a wonderful passage where the preacher, having struck a stern pose, is reluctantly but uncontrollably urged into a frolicsome little dance by a bubbling melody in the score: first his shoulders catch the rhythm, then his head, and soon his whole body. Ross does this clearly and cleanly; Walker blurs it.
>
> (Mueller 1977: 107)

At the same time, it can be argued that Walker brings to the role something that is absent in the earlier film: the darker side of power inherent in the characterisation of the Protestant ethic – that is, the right to chastise others in a most vociferous manner for doing something wrong, for failing in their duty to live for the Glory of God. Walker's portrayal of this aspect of the preacher's character in the chastisement solo, which shall be discussed more fully below, is much more convincing than that of Ross. He presents a terrifying figure while Ross's preacher is somehow much too pompous for his ministrations to be taken really seriously. Moreover, Edwin Denby (1986: 407) recalled that when Cunningham danced the role of the Revivalist, particularly in the sermon, 'everything about it was terrifying'.

There are comparatively few choreographic differences between the two filmed performances. One such difference, as Mueller points out, could suggest that Graham intended to alter the dualistic character of the Bride slightly in favour of a softer personality. Over half-way through the dance, during the Husbandman's solo, and prior to her second fearful solo, the Bride is sitting on the bench outside the house. In the earlier version, as Mueller notes, 'her pose is tense – one hand is placed firmly against her temple or, later, her forearm is pressed diagonally across her breast' (Mueller 1977: 107). In the 1976 version, the Bride remains in repose throughout, hands clasped in her lap.

This softer characterisation of the Bride in the 1976 version, however, is reversed somewhat at the end of the dance. In both films, after all the others have exited, the Bride and Husbandman are left alone on the porch. The Bride goes to sit on the rocking chair; he comes to stand behind her. He rests his hand on her shoulder and she puts her hand on his.

In the 1958 version she slowly raises her free arm, gesturing towards the vast space outside . . . instead of gesturing toward the space, Graham has the bride in the later version simply turn her head slowly to gaze out of it.

(Mueller 1977: 107)

The two images connote very different moods: the first is that of calm, while the second is somewhat disquieting. In the later version, the Bride does not seem to come fully to terms with her heritage and future on the land.

The differences between the two performances point to the fact that each and every performance of a dance is unique and cannot be repeated exactly. None the less, the fact that choreography remains relatively fixed – that is, it is the same for all practical purposes – means that we can look behind the dancers' individual interpretations of the characters into the wider framework of the choreographic scaffolding. The early modern dancers, as discussed above, emphasised that dances should be constructed in such a manner that they could be repeated. This does not mean that they considered that subsequent performances of a work should or could be exactly the same as the first, but, rather, that there should be a certain structure or framework to the dance which bound it together as a coherent entity. As Horst (Horst and Russell 1977) emphasised, it should be given form.

This examination of *Appalachian Spring* is based predominantly on the 1976 recording. A major part of it is directed towards an elucidation of some of the emergent meanings in the dance through an analysis of one particular section of the work, the Revivalist's solo. In this particular section of the dance the preacher's movement builds up into what appears to be a trance state in which he chastises the newly married couple against the indulgences of the flesh. The imagery that the movement connotes is that of a man who is trapped by the nature of his Puritan calling. Torn between the spirit and the flesh, he is not simply chastising the couple, but is also attempting to exorcise the flesh from himself.

However, in focusing primarily on this particular section, I do not wish to imply that it provides the key to the dance itself. Each individual section and the linking sequences in the dance, are of equal importance. Like the detail of a painting or a passage from a novel, a section of a dance can illuminate particular instances of form, but it does not exist outside the whole. Ultimately, its particular significance is subservient to the total dance. What has occurred before the preacher builds up into this trance state, the differing reactions that his ministrations create in the others, and how they are resolved are crucial to the viewer's understanding of the dance. The symbolism that dance engenders is not crystallised in any one section, nor in the relationship between one section and another. Rather, as Sheets–Johnstone (1979) has argued, it is always in the process of evolving into the unique dance – it is from beginning to end. In this sense, the totality, which is the dance, is always greater than the sum of its constituent parts. As such, any discussion of its parts should point to the integral relation of the whole. Hence, although the intention here is to illuminate how the preacher's movement in the afore-mentioned solo symbolises the dichotomy between mind and body, the spirit and the flesh, the discussion, where relevant, moves back and forth between other aspects of the dance. At the same time, however, as empha-sised throughout, dance does not exist outside the society in which it is created and performed, but stands in a relational tension to the social context. Consequently, other systems of relevance that exist outside the dance, but which are important to the interpretation of the movement, are also indicated.

Appalachian Spring, on first view, appears to be a relatively simple dance. Indeed, as soon as the set is made visible, the music begins, and the dancers appear one by one into the arena, the viewer is transported into its easily recognisable world. The dance centres on a brief episode in the life of a small community situated within the wider context of the American frontier. It is almost as if the viewer is witness to a private moment in people's lives – a wedding, within that wider framework. The dance, however, is not a reflection of an actual wedding, but is a transformation of the *idea* of a wedding in a small community in pioneering America in the nineteenth century. The dance, then, creates its own life-world in its own time and space. But its life-world is culturally specific and the ability to grasp the intended context is dependent on the viewer sharing a commonsense understanding of the external referents. The dance evokes a rememberance of weddings as we have known them in our time and place, and of how we might imagine a wedding to have been in the American frontier, with its small communities, pioneering spirit, non-conformist religion, expansive space and the harshness of life involved.

The attitudes and individual personalities of the four main characters in the dance – the Bride, the Husbandman, the Revivalist and the Pioneer Woman – are located and developed through the specific movement qualities they display. The preacher is accompanied by four girl Followers who, unlike the others, are not defined individually through their move-ment. The Pioneer Woman, the Husbandman and the Revivalist have a different kind of collective identity in that each appears as an archetype. Their individual personalities are collected under the wider identities of pioneerism, individualism and Puritanism. The Bride is rather different. She is almost, but not yet, a woman. Her emergent womanhood is conveyed at points through an ambivalence towards the frontier life and religion, and through her movement differences and similarities to the Pioneer Woman and the girl Followers.

The stage setting and the characters' relation to it, highlight the idea of building a home within a small community on the American frontier. The home and the frontier are central and related focuses in the dance. As with *Frontier*, Noguchi's setting for *Appalachian Spring* is suggestive rather than a literal representation. There is a sketch of a house, in the form of a simple wooden-framed structure which runs down stage right. A small section at the top is filled in with a bench attached to the outside of it. At the bottom of the house, there is a porch with a stylised rocking chair, which, in silhouette, takes on the image of a plough. The bench outside the house is used at various times throughout the dance by the Followers, the Bride and the Pioneer Woman. The Husbandman lifts the Bride into the inside of the framework of the house and out again on several occasions, and the Followers stand together inside the house during the wedding ceremony and the dance which follows. The boundary of the homestead is marked by a short fence, much like the one in *Frontier*, but at down stage left, beyond which lies the yet unchartered land of the prairies. In a sense the viewer is in the dance because he or she inhabits the frontier towards which the Husbandman, the Bride and the Pioneer Woman gesture, through their outward looks, from the porch or the fence. The dancers' costumes are also suggestive of their roles (the costumes, like the dance, did not remain exactly the same over the years; see Lloyd 1974: 72 for a discussion of the original costumes). In this production the Revivalist is dressed in a dark frock-coated suit, and a wide-brimmed hat and shoes. The Bride wears pumps and a long-sleeved yellow dress which is close fitting to the hips with an apron front and a pleated section at the back which allows for the expansive movement. The Pioneer Woman wears pumps and a long, dark reddish-brown dress, full from the hips, with dolman sleeves. The four Followers are dressed in long light-blue dresses − again full from the hips, with short puffed sleeves − bonnets, and pumps. The Husbandman is dressed in brown breeches, knee-length boots, light shirt, string tie and waistcoat.

Like many of Graham's dances, *Appalachian Spring* is punctuated by the processional. The dance begins with a procession with all the characters entering the stage one by one: the Revivalist first, then the Pioneer Woman, followed by the Bride, the Husbandman, and finally the four Followers. There is a procession in the middle of the work, which leads to the couple being blessed by the Revivalist. This is the only point in the dance where all the characters come together at the same time. There is a procession at the end of the dance with everyone leaving the stage, except for the couple, who remain together on the porch. 'Dance episodes are joined to realistic passages which set the frame' (Denby 1986: 314). During the dance, everyday gestures such as praying, walking and blessing are performed almost, but not quite, literally, giving the dance an air of simplicity or realism. Social-type dancing is brought in to convey a sense of occasion and place. The dancing space is never busy, the performers dance mostly in solo, duet, quartet or quintet, with an apparent simplicity of technical movement structure. But this seduction of simplicity and recognisability is underpinned by a complex choreographic form which evolves throughout the dance to reveal vivid psychological portraits of the characters in the dance, their relationship to each other, and to the place.

One of the issues that a sociological enquiry needs to address explicitly is *how* the viewer can make sense of this work. For example, how is it possible to understand that the Revivalist is chastising the couple, that he is building up into a state of trance, that his movement is revealing a pull between the mind and the body, the spirit and the flesh? That is, using a slighly awkward phrase: How is it possible to interpret the movement? As I argued in the first chapter, because of the reflexive character of dance movement, it is possible to gain some insight into the emergent meanings that dance generates by exploring the transformation of dance movement from everyday movement, which in itself is also an encoded system. With this in view, the following discussion of the Revivalist's solo in *Appalachian Spring* makes frequent use of the transformational character of dance movement from everyday movement.

The preacher's chastisement solo takes place after the couple have performed their celebration hoe-down to Copland's arrangement of the Shaker hymn *Simple Gifts*. The combination of the musical theme and their dance is significant in several ways to the solo that follows. The activity of dancing was an integral part of the Shaker ritual (see Andrews 1967: 1–8). As a sect, the Shakers were bound to a strict rule of celibacy. Indulgences of the flesh were considered evil and personal involvements with members of the opposite sex discouraged. Their dancing performed the symbolic function of 'shaking off the flesh' (see Andrews 1967: 144–5), to receive revelations and attain a greater purity. The form of dance evolved from ecstatic abandon, with the whole body shaking and convulsing, through to strict regimental formation, with unison movement, precise floor patterns and tiny shaking movements of the hands (see Andrews 1978: 3–12).

One of the devices used in the preacher's solo to enable the viewer to interpret that he is going into a trance state is this idea of 'shaking off the flesh'. The shaking movement begins small with the hand coming shaking in to the side of the body, and with the focus on the hand, the whole arm is raised, quivering, wide and high to the side. Even if the viewer were unaware that the idea of 'shaking off the flesh' had its origins in this particular American sect, he or she could still interpret this movement in this context as a possible indication of trance. In everyday life we speak of 'shaking with laughter' and 'shaking with fear', signifying a loss of bodily control. Shaking, in our culture, denotes the idea of involuntary movement. Trance is also an instance of loss of bodily control, which, along with other aspects of movement, is conveyed through shaking.

As discussed in the first chapter, in a rationally oriented society which extols the virtues of the head over the body, the loss of bodily control is normally treated as dangerous (Douglas 1970b). The idea of involuntary movement, and the dangers attached to it, are conveyed through the preacher's movements. In the solo, the build-up of the shaking movement from the hand to the whole arm being shaken away from the centre, symbolises the loss of control in one of the extremities. This, however, is contradicted in the other hand, which is clutched in a fist to the chest. The whole movement connotes the idea of attempting to free the spirit from the body, and at the same time of being pulled into the body of the self to regain control.

The couple's celebration dance, however, could not be interpreted as 'shaking off the flesh', but, rather, as the pleasure of personal involvement with each other. They are indulging in 'mixt' or 'gynaecandrical' dancing, the very form which the Boston ministers condemned in their tract of 1684 (Cole 1942), because they feared it would lead to lascivious behaviour. Thus, on the one hand, the Revivalist's ministrations which follow the 'couple' dance, can be interpreted as being founded on a typification of Puritanism's antagonism towards dancing. This can be consolidated further by pointing to the fact that Cotton Mather, who was the leader of the Boston ministers who wrote the tract against dancing, was a major point of reference for Graham's creation of the Revivalist.

The desire of the Bride and the Husbandman for each other is signified in their celebration dance through ease of bodily contact, reciprocal eye focus and open display of the self to the other. They are completely caught up in each other's space to the exclusion of everyone else, as often young lovers appear to be in everyday life. But, in dance, these taken-for-granted understandings are treated reflexively through transformational movement. The Bride and Husbandman move together, linking arms or hands; they separate, one stands still, with bodily attitude and gaze inclined towards the other who is displaying the self. Their intentions (the body) and their attention (the focus) are directed towards each other.

While the Bride and Husbandman are dancing, the preacher stands on his makeshift pulpit at centre-back of the stage, with feet apart, high bodily attitude, hands together at the waist, and head cocked up to one side. It seems that the dominant impression he is trying to convey is that he is apart from what is going on around him, his mind is on higher things. His bodily intention and attention are directed towards an other world. However, on close examination it can be seen that he is not altogether oblivious to the couple, and in particular the Bride. For when she moves into his line of vision, and stands quite still, with her focus inclined towards the Husbandman, the preacher slowly directs his gaze towards her. He follows her with his eyes as she moves away down stage towards the Husbandman, and then slowly lifts his head up to focus high in a different direction. This almost imperceptible movement is important to our understanding of the preacher's character. On the one hand, it can be interpreted that he is disdainful of this romantic involvement, and, on the other, it can point to his vulnerability to the opposite sex, to desire.

This ambiguity of character is visible in other parts of the work. The house and the fence, as I have indicated, are central and related focuses in the dance, symbolising the safety of the home in relation to the frontier wilderness. On the scale from near to far, which in proxemics can be seen to signify the range between intimacy and formality (Hall 1969), the preacher is often at the far end. He stands apart from the community, has no affiliation with the house, and does not go towards the fence to look out to the frontier as the others do. This apartness is also conveyed through his bodily attitude, which is stiff, with a backward tilt, and high head orientation. A similar bodily attitude in everyday life would be interpreted as a distancing of the self from others. But in this context, as we understand that he is a preacher, a man of God, his movement and lack of relation to the house or the fence can also be interpreted as a distancing of himself from the community in favour of an other worldliness.

This distant and otherworldly attitude is contradicted in other parts of the dance, particularly in relation to the four girl Followers. The latter are aptly named because they follow him eagerly whenever he summons them forth. Unlike the other characters in the dance, the Followers are not defined individually through their movement, they have a collective personality.

Generally speaking, because Graham made dances which focused attention on discrete characters, the sense of the social which emerges in her work is generated outwards from the individual (Siegel 1979). Humphrey, by contrast, usually began with the concept of the group and worked inwards to the individual. None the less, Humphrey's group work was defined by the individuality of the dancers (Cohen 1977b). When Graham composed for a group, however, as I discussed in Chapter 5, the dancers in the group functioned as multiples of one, rather like the traditional corps.

In his initial dance with them – which contains elements of the children's game 'follow my leader', social dance motifs, and praying gestures – the preacher shows that he too is vulnerable to the desires of the flesh. This occurs after the Followers have come to kneel in a square to pray, with the preacher kneeling in the centre top of the square. He raises both hands above his head, with palms leading through to forward and down onto the ground, he lowers his body down to the ground (in the 1958 version, the Revivalist does not raise his hand above his head at this point but instead places them down directly in front of him before lowering the body weight – thus, the sense of giving into the body weight is less vivid in the earlier version). From here he rolls over to lie face up on the lap of one of the Followers, who inclines the preacher's body close to hers by drawing her arm around him. He rolls back onto the floor and towards another Follower, who also cradles him in her arms. Then he transfers his weight onto his feet in the direction of a third Follower. He lifts the third girl high in the air above his head, focusing directly on her face, and holds her there for some moments, while the other Followers fall on their backs, covering their faces with one hand. Here the preacher's distant bodily attitude changes to one of intimacy (in the earlier version the camera does not linger on this lift and the sense of intimacy is not as striking).

In our everyday cultural interpersonal relations, close physical contact with another signifies intimacy and usually, with a gendered other, denotes sexual involvement (Hall 1969). At the same time, the physical taking hold of the upper body of a gendered other, and fixing the gaze towards that other in close face-to-face contact, is also understood as having sexual connotations (Hall 1969). As studies on the body (Birdwhistell 1973, Garfinkel 1984, Mauss 1973) have demonstrated, we learn the everyday techniques of the body that we normally take as being 'natural' (see Appendix), and this is particularly so with regard to gendered/ sexual behaviour. There are cultural rules for appropriate bodily behaviour in public places which vary according to whether the interactants seem to be 'significant others', acquaintances, passing strangers and so on (Goffman 1972). The cultural body is a site of restricted access. There are some areas of the body that can be touched with impunity by acquaintances and relative strangers, and there are others (like a woman's waist) that are usually percieved to be restricted to significant, or intimate, others. Moreover, some people have the power to touch and to look more directly and more frequently than others, by virtue of their dominant status or position (Henley 1977). The idea of giving in to nature, the earth, as expressed through the preacher giving in to the weight of his body, and by his coming into close physical contact with the Followers, enables the viewer to see an ambiguity in his personality. He can be distant and otherworldly, but he is also vulnerable to the desires of the flesh.

This ambivalent relationship between the mind and the body, the spirit and the flesh, is most powerfully expressed through the condensed movement form of the preacher's chastisement solo. It begins ominously with the preacher slowly lifting his hat above his head and placing it on the fingertips of the raised arms of the Followers, who are standing close together in a square in front of him. The viewer senses that he is about to deliver a sermon. On the basis of a shared cultural awareness of the form of revivalist preaching, or other similar non-conformist teaching, it is possible to anticipate that the ministrations which the viewer is about to witness will offer little reassurance or comfort to the assembled congregation.

The preacher's ministrations create fear and anxiety in the Pioneer Woman, the Husbandman and the Bride. Their reactions to this sermon lead to a greater unfolding of the personalities involved. For example, the Husbandman seeks and finds comfort, not in the Bride, but in the Pioneer Woman. It is she who directs his attention outwards towards the frontier, the imaginary symbol of the pioneering spirit, in order that he might re-establish his relationship to the land. This is the first and only time in the dance that the Husbandman steps out in front of the fence, the symbolic boundary of the homestead. Once this relationship has been reconsolidated, the Husbandman can then return to his religion and pray with all the others, except for the Bride who remains apart from them looking on. That the Husbandman does not seek comfort from the Bride, consolidates further the viewer's impression of her as almost, but not yet, a woman and, at the same time, strengthens the interpretation of the Pioneer Woman as a solid, encompassing person. Unlike the Husbandman and the Pioneer Woman, the Bride does not find comfort in the land or religion in the end, but she looks to her husband to allay her fears.

The Bride has three solos. The 'darker' side of her character emerges in the second solo and the dance stands in sharp contrast to the first solo where she introduces herself to the others and dances coquettishly in front of the Husbandman. The third solo retains echoes of the 'darker' second solo and elements of the first playful one. In the second solo she runs across the stage, stops short, looks around and then rushes off in the other direction (in the 1958 version the Bride does not begin her second solo by running across the stage space but performs some small agitated movements on the spot). The more expansive and agitated use of the stage space helps to convey the idea that the bride is frightened of the space, that she cannot find her space within it. It is as if she can find no stillness in herself. In this dialogue with herself (the idea of an internal dialogue is a feature of many of Graham's heroines), the Bride appears to be filled with fear and foreboding about her imagined future in the wilderness. She runs her hand down the house, rolls down the stairs of the porch and along the ground and rolls back again, as if she is trying to establish her relation to the land and the place. This solo occurs after the Revivalist's ministrations. It seems as if the preacher has tapped her inner insecurity. Graham, as I discussed before, considered that dance should be like a 'graph of the heart', and it is through the external choreographed movement that another facet of the Bride's psychological make-up is revealed.

The fear and anxiety that the Revivalist's sermon creates in the Pioneer Woman is different again. It can be interpreted as one of concern for others in her community, the Bride and the Husbandman. It is she who stops the preacher's chastisement of the couple by coming off the bench and creating a physically symbolic break between them. From the beginning of the dance the Pioneer Woman stands for an archetype of nineteenth-century American motherhood, a symbol of community and warmth. Her movement, which is very earthbound and open, conveys the idea that, unlike the preacher, she is at one with religion and the world. The support she offers after the Revivalist's sermon, to the

Husbandman in particular, consolidates further the idea the viewer has of her.

As soon as the Revivalist has placed his hat on the Followers' fingertips, he looks at the palm of his right hand and then, with a sudden movement of the head, he fixes his gaze on the couple who are together on the porch. From here, he draws the right hand slowly into a fist to his chest, and the left hand closes and moves down to the side to 'place'. It is as if something has made him angry: perhaps the sight of the romantic involvement between the Bride and the Husbandman displayed through their 'mixt' dancing, or the idea of immanent consummation of marriage, or what might be interpreted as his own desire for the Bride. A sharp movement of the head, directing the eyes to someone else, and subsequently clenching a fist towards the body, is not regarded generally as a gesture of friendliness. If a fist is drawn in towards the body it can denote the idea of trying to contain or hold the self together. But the fist can also be thrust out in anger and, here, the combination of sudden change of focus and the sustained movement of the hand clenching to a fist at the breast, conveys the idea that the couple will become the object of the preacher's ministrations.

In the Revivalist's solo, the meaning that is conveyed through the movement in one part of the body is contradicted constantly in another and, therefore, it is important not to isolate one element from the total movement. In everyday life, a hand opening to palm facing up, usually conveys the idea of pleading or giving. Its signification lies in the relationship of the self to the world. It is an opening movement away from the body, the self, towards someone, or something, else. In symbolic dance forms, such as *Appalachian Spring*, everyday gesture is not performed in a literal manner; rather, it is taken away from its point of origin and transformed through an idea into the dance context and developed through stylisation, sequencing and narrative structure. There are several points in the chastisement solo where this ordinary everyday gesture of giving is performed and is followed through with a change in the spatial-dynamic pull of the whole arm, which enables another meaning to come into play. On these occasions the Revivalist is travelling forward on his knees. As the weight is being shifted on to one knee, the opposite hand, opening to palm facing up, moves up and away to the side of the body, the fingers contort, and the whole arm, with the elbow leading, is pulled down across the diagonal in the direction of the knee that is taking the body weight. Diagonal movement in dance is highly expressive. When performed the body comes off-balance and, in so doing, connotes the idea of instability, of not being able to stop. Here the initial giving gesture is contradicted by the cross-diagonal pull of the elbow towards the ground. But the arm does not give into the ground; rather, the sense is that it is being forced towards it, with the palm remaining face up, but with the fingers contorted. The whole movement contributes to our understanding of the ambiguity in the preacher's personality. Graham, as I have already indicated, conceived of the ground as a symbol of life and energy, but in terms of the Revivalist's character this life-giving force is a symbol of danger, of the Fall. In one sense, it can be seen that the preacher is reaching out to another world, but in another, he is being pulled by gravity and nature. This idea of reaching out with one part of the body, with a counter pull in another, towards the floor, is prevalent throughout the solo.

Whenever the preacher chastises the couple he hurls his body round towards them, and with the hand coming in to a fist towards the shoulder, the whole arm is thrust out high, forward and down to shoulder level, with two fingers pointing at them. In everyday terms, when we speak of an individual 'rounding on' an other, it is understood that he or she is directing attention outwards in confrontation. It is not necessarily the case that the individual is physically rounding on someone else, rather, the body here is used as a metaphor for confrontation. The everyday gesture of pointing the index finger signifies making a point, and in the context of directing this action towards children it is usually associated with scolding. The spatial-dynamic force with which the preacher pivots his body round to the couple, and the thrusting of the arm out from the shoulder to point his fingers at them, leaves the viewer in little doubt that he is chastising them. This understanding is consolidated by the couple's reaction to his chastisement. During the build-up to this movement, the Bride is the first to turn her head to focus low in his direction and, then, she slowly lowers her head to the other side. Soon the Husbandman turns his head low to the side away from the preacher. At the end of the first chastising movement and the beginning of the second, they both transfer their weight on to their knees, bow their heads, and move their hands to a praying position. Almost like little children, they bow their heads in shame. They remain in these positions until the Pioneer Woman comes off the bench and runs downstage creating a barrier between them and the preacher.

The build-up into the trance state is conveyed through a gradual loss of control in the body. In the beginning of this section the preacher, with his right hand in a fist clutched at the chest, is in control of his body. He takes four long, slow steps towards the Bride and the Husbandman, bringing the right foot to place as he stops. From here the spine contracts suddenly, forcing the left foot into the floor, thrusting the head forward, the right fist into the chest, and the left arm making a sharp forward movement with the hand clenching, echoed by the right foot. The spine releases as the body returns to its original position. It is as if he is trying to walk forward but for some reason his foot is being riveted to the floor. This is the first indication that the preacher is not in total control of his body. Towards the end of the solo there appears to be a complete loss of bodily control. From raising his arms above his head, the body is lowered forward towards the floor, with the palms facing down and leading through to high-forward and then down towards the floor, and with the left leg gesturing towards high-back in the opposite direction. As the hands come down onto the floor, the arms flex so that the head touches the floor, the supporting leg flexes, lowering the knee down to take the body weight, and the left leg flexes down. From here the weight is pivoted round forcefully on the right knee, creating bodily imbalance, whipping the head round and to the back, and the arms swinging round to the sides. With the left knee stepping forward the body regains its balance, but the head is back and loose, and the arms swing at the sides as he scuttles forward on his knees (in the earlier version the Revivialist travels on his hands and feet at this point). Another of the indications of trance is a loss of focus. The preacher does not appear to know where he is going, his eyes lack an attention focus, he does not seem to be aware of the weight of his arms and he is scuttling forward with no sense of direction. The total movement conveys the idea that he is completely outside of his body, in a state of trance. In part, this is a curious direction for a Puritan to take because the doctrine of Puritanism emphasises control and reason and rejects trance. However, bodily disassociation and 'speaking with tongues' were aspects of nineteenth-century religious revivalist movements in America, and he is called the Revivalist. Moreover, the Shaker movement, which originated in Manchester in England and was an off-shoot of the Quakers, practised bodily abandonment in the early stages of its development (Andrews 1962). Thus, the characterisation of Puritanism that is being offered in *Appalachian Spring* is not, in itself, a literal one. Rather, it contains elements of other non-conformist sects which, in commonsense terms, are often deemed 'puritanical' in outlook. Consequently, at certain points the dance draws on commonsense interpretations of Puritanism.

The aim of the preceding discussion has been to demonstrate how, through its movement symbolism, *Appalachian Spring* generates a set of emergent meanings concerning American Puritanism, which, in turn, can provide for cultural interpretations of American history. The interpretation of Puritanism that the work engenders is multi-layered. It points to the oppositional pull inherent in the Puritan ethic between the mind and the body, the spirit and the flesh, culture and nature. It also indicates, as Hawthorne (1960) did in *The Scarlet Letter*, that the 'iron cage' of Puritanism has a human face in that it, too, can be vulnerable to the pleasures of life. But it also points to the power of the authority of Puritanism on American culture, and, as I discussed in Chapter 2, most cultural historians concur with this view. However, what is of import is that *Appalachian Spring* offers its interpretation of Puritanism, and pioneerism, and individualism, in terms of movement, not words.

10 CONCLUSION

I began this exploration at the end of the first chapter by posing several initial points of sociological interest concerning the development of American modern dance which proposed that the focus of analysis be conducted from two different frameworks: an *extrinsic* and an *intrinsic* perspective. The first point directed the focus of attention towards considering why nineteenth-century America did not establish a sustained art dance tradition. The second led to an examination of the socio-historical processes that helped to generate the appropriate conditions that made possible the emergence of a serious theatrical dance in America and its relationship to the other arts. The third directed the analysis towards an examination of the intrinsic features of modern dance that enabled it to generate a new relation between performance dance and American culture. Thus, the study proceeded by asking 'why' questions on the one hand and 'how' questions on the other.

The examination of the relation between theatrical dance and American society prior to the twentieth century pointed to the consideration that a combination of the legacy of Puritanism and frontierism in American culture, and a lack of city culture, helped to prevent the establishment of a sustained art dance tradition modelled on European ballet. Many of the features of the American character that Puritanism and frontierism promoted were a negation of the élitist character of European culture out of which ballet was forged. Moreover, unlike Europe, there were no established ballet companies or dance academies in America to aid the process of dance reproduction. The low status of dance in America was emphasised further by the fact that dancers were not socially acceptable in polite society, and unlike some of their counterparts in Europe and Russia in particular, they could not hope therefore to be treated seriously or to advance up the social scale.

In order for a serious art dance tradition to be generated in America, dance had to develop a different set of goals. Dance had to achieve a measure of respectability in the eyes of American society which hitherto had been denied it. It was argued that, as the evidence has demonstrated, American Delsartism and the feminist reform movement, both of which were principally middle-class women's movements, helped to create the impetus for this change by emphasising physical culture for women on a variety of pretexts such as health, aesthetic and spiritual grounds. The changes necessary to advance the cause of dance as an aesthetic mode of expression were given further impetus by the drive towards respectability in the variety theatre around the turn of the century. This was also one of the processes which contributed to the increasing entry of women into the realms of visibility in the modern city. Vaudeville created an opening for women from marginal middle-class backgrounds, e.g. Duncan and St Denis, to embark on a dance career, and for other women to see and enjoy dance and experience some of the pleasures of city life. Significantly, dancers such as St Denis and Duncan did not adopt the European model of ballet which had fallen into disregard, but began to create their own dance images on the basis of an anti-formalist aesthetic. At the same time, St Denis, in particular, stressed the spiritual value of the art which, in turn, helped to promote dance as a respectable pursuit for women to partake in and to watch.

Through the work of the forerunners of modern dance, especially Denishawn, the reproductive dance cycle, which was crucial for the development of a sustained tradition of dance in America, was set in motion. Thereafter, American dancers could draw on ideas and practices from local sources which were predominantly anti-formalist in expression, as opposed to drawing on European ballet. Of equal importance was the fact that the American dancers had the beginnings of a home-grown dance tradition against which they could begin to rebel and from there generate new forms which could then be built upon to advance the cycle of dance reproduction.

The examination of the intrinsic features of American modern dance as it emerged in the late 1920s and early 1930s pointed to the fact that modern dance was formed on the principles of non-conformism and individualism, as was twentieth-century American art in general. However, what made modern dance distinct from Denishawn, Duncan and other interpretive dancers was that it invoked systematically the need to draw on and to communicate to the American public, the unique American cultural and historical experience.

The fundamental claim of the dance modernists was unequivocally that dance should speak to, and of, its place and its time. Dancers like Graham and Humphrey thus sought to discover the 'first principles' of movement in order to generate a technique that would form the basis of a dance language, and, as the examination shows, the development of a technique was an important factor in the continuing process of dance reproduction. The search for first principles led the modern dancers to abolish all preconceptions concerning dance and to return to the natural impulses of everyday gesture as the starting point upon which to develop dance forms which stressed the 'firstness' of movement, 'the stuff' of dance.

The analysis that emerged from the exploration of the development of American modern dance raises certain concerns that are important for generating a sociology of dance. First, the issue of dance as an art form is raised as both a feature of the socio-cultural context of its emergence and creation, and as a reflexive practice which, in turn, offers a significant resource for sociological inquiry. Second, the issue of dance as primarily a mode of bodily communication points to the relation of dance movement to everyday movement and, hence, to body symbolism and representation as interdisciplinary features of the sociological analysis of dance. The final matter refers to the development of American modern dance in terms of an exploration of the American experience which helped to advance dance art and establish it as a significant feature of American culture. It is the second concern, the primacy of movement in dance, which forms the link between the points raised by modernism and contemporary culture in the context of the emergent complexity of the social structure of contemporary America. As such, it offers the basis for a paradigm for sociological inquiry into the ambiguous relation between dance art and society that is at the core of a sociology of dance: that is, the ambiguity of the social relevance of an art form which is marginalised threefold in western cultural formations as art, as a mode of communication which celebrates the body as its primary mode of expression and (re)presentation, and one in which women have been the central protagonists.

This thesis is unashamedly modernist in its orientation. Although I have argued for an interdisciplinary approach to the sociology of dance, nevertheless, there has been a concern to attend to the specificity of (American modern) dance. I would wish for dance's 'voice' to be heard (in this context the use of voice is appropriate) not as just one 'voice' among other 'voices'. Rather, I wish to explore what it (in its various manifestations) has to say and how it relates to or differs from other cultural practices. Moreover, the kinds of questions that I have asked, 'why' questions as well as 'how' questions, situate the discussion within a modernist, dare I say humanist framework. At the very moment when dance seems to be emerging out of the darkness in terms of academia, it seems such a pity to dissolve it in the melting pot of postmodernism or poststructuralism. But that, again, as they say, is another book!

APPENDIX

Each of the areas under discussion here – anthropology of dance, a particular approach to dance aesthetics and the social aspects of the body – constitutes a body of work in its own right. As with the discussions of feminism, postmodernism and poststructuralism, it is not my concern to provide a comprehensive summary of these fields. Just as I do not wish to give the impression of performing a sociology-type commando raid on these spheres, neither do I wish to borrow from them in an ad hoc manner (in the eclectic style of postmodernism). Rather, the consideration is to point to the ways in which they have informed the approach to the sociology of dance being forged through here (for a more detailed consideration of these fields see Thomas 1986). They are placed at the end of the book because I considered that such a lengthy discussion would detract from the flow of the narrative.

ANTHROPOLOGY OF DANCE

Although dance anthropologists bemoan the lack of interest in dance in the academy (Grau 1993, Kaeppler 1991), nevertheless, anthropologists from the beginning of this century have produced a considerable amount of data on dance on small-scale societies (see Royce 1980 for a detailed discussion of the various phases of development). Initially they were concerned with the search for the origins of dance. This was followed by a consideration of the function of dance in society, which emerged almost simultaneously from two different traditions of thought: on the one hand, the British structural functionalist school of anthropology (Evans-Pritchard 1976, Radcliffe-Brown 1964) and, on the other, the cultural trait approach stemming from the American cultural relativist school (Boas 1972). From there the concern centred on the meaning of dance and the formulation of classificatory schemes (Lomax 1968). In the 1960s and 1970s several of a new generation of American anthropologists (with dance backgrounds) sought to uncover the meanings in the various forms of dance under study through the application of communication and linguistic models and the consideration of the structure of human movement (see Hanna 1980, Kaeppler 1972, Williams 1977). Drid Williams (1976), for example, drew on Chomsky's theory of linguistics, particularly 'transformational' and 'generative' grammar, to analyse and understand the 'Deep structures of the dance'. The focus of Williams' analysis is directed towards uncovering the 'structures' that make any kind of dance possible. Thus, the search for meaning is not carried out at a surface level (signified). Rather, the concern is to articulate the kind of meanings that the grammar of dance could generate through its code. The aim, according to Williams, is to locate 'meaning' as a structural relationship which can be uncovered by the analysis of the syntagmatic plane. With the weakening of disciplinary boundaries in the 1980s, the issues that have come to the fore in anthropology (gender, identity, body, analysing the 'other', self-reflexivity) have also found their way into the work of dance and movement researchers (Cowan 1990, Grau 1993, Novack 1990, Sklar 1991). Dance anthropologists are also turning their anthropological gaze towards their own dance cultures (Novack 1990, 1993).

The American ethnologists/anthropologists of dance who began studying in the 1960s took their point of departure from the American and British traditions of anthropology (see Grau 1993, Kaeppler 1991, Williams 1991), as opposed to the European tradition of dance scholarship which has its roots in the folklorist tradition (see Lange 1980 for a discussion of this folklorist legacy). The difference between these two approaches may be characterised in terms of the former's preference for stressing the contextual aspects of dance while the latter focuses on the choreological aspects of dance or the 'end product' (Kaeppler 1991). The terms dance ethnology and dance anthropology are related, but again the focus of their attention is somewhat different. According to Kaeppler, dance anthropology or, more precisely, the 'anthropology of human movement' directs its attention towards 'system'; 'the importance of intention, meaning, and cultural evaluation' (Kaeppler 1991: 16). That is, the dance or the movement systems are examined in order to say something significant about the society in question. In dance ethnology, on the other hand, the focus is directed towards the dance and its development, and changes over time with the cultural context being brought in to elucidate the dance. Some anthropologists, such as Drid Williams (1991), Adrienne Kaeppler (1972), Judith Lynne Hanna (1980), Andrée Grau (1993), combine detailed analysis of the movement in their anthropological accounts while others, for example Jane Cowan (1990), evade any detailed discussion of the movement content.

Whether the focus is on the meaning or the movement content, dance anthropology is instructive in a way that cultural studies approaches to dance are not, because it directs attention towards dance as a serious topic of social and/or cultural inquiry. Most studies which draw on the American or British traditions of anthropology attempt to tackle issues that can facilitate a better understanding of dance as a cultural form. Some, such as Youngerman (1974), Williams (1977) and Kaeli'inohomoku (1983) have pointed to the incipient racism and ethnocentrism in many historical studies and dance histories in which dance is viewed explicitly or implicitly as a form of natural (instinctive and universal) behaviour which has developed from its starting point in 'primitive' culture into stylised western theatre dance, with the latter being venerated as the most 'advanced' civilised form. Often, these studies, as Youngerman and Williams have demonstrated, draw heavily from Curt Sachs's *World History of the Dance* (first published in 1937), largely, one suspects, because, for some time, it accorded dance a status worthy of investigation in a wilderness of non-attention in academia. Dance writers have used it as a form of legitimation and a source of data.

In his analysis of the origins of dance, Sachs adopted an ethological framework. He claimed that dance is an 'inherited pre-disposition' by citing accounts of the 'well known dances of the higher animals' (Youngerman 1974), thus reinforcing the idea that dance is natural and instinctive. Sachs adopted the dominant doctrine within German anthropology at the time, *Kulturkreislehre,* in his analysis of dance history. Although this theoretical approach was initiated in response to nineteenth-century unilineal evolutionary theory, it developed its own evolutionary momentum. In this framework, as Youngerman (1974) has argued, past cultures are conceived of in passive terms. Cultures are deemed only to change if they come into contact with other migrating cultures. This connotes the idea that those cultures which did not encounter others did not change. This further implies that 'primitive' cultures, as entities in themselves, have not changed to any significant degree and that they stand as the equivalent of man (*sic*) in his 'origins'. Thus, according to Youngerman (1974), in adopting this theoretical framework Sachs is led to conceive of modern 'primitive' man (*sic*) as the equivalent of 'primeval' man (*sic*). The net result is that contemporary 'primitive' cultures come to be seen as one amorphous mass, 'The Primitive Culture', denying their cultural variability, complexity and their individual cultural growth (Youngerman 1974). Despite the implications of Sachs's theoretical approach to the study of dance history, many scholars have persisted in drawing on his work as an exemplar of dance anthropology (see Novack 1990, Williams 1977, Youngerman 1974 for examples of these texts). Although they have often been concerned to reject Sachs's evolutionary framework, the ethnocentrism and evolutionism inherent in Sachs's framework are given voice through the very composition of these works, which usually begin with a discussion of primitive dance and only subsequently move on to, and discuss more fully, western dance. Implicit in this, as Youngerman (1974) and Kaeli'inohomoku (1983) have argued, is the notion that primitive dances exemplify the beginnings of dance and, therefore, are inferior to western dance – thus reinforcing the view of structurally simple societies as the denigrated 'other' to western 'civilised' culture. In warning against this treatment of dance in 'primitive' cultures as natural and ubiquitous, Kaeli'inohomoku invites us to turn the telescope round and, viewing ourselves with the self-knowledge of how we approach 'other' cultures, treat ballet as a form of ethnic dance. This requires us to call into question our commonsense assumptions of what we mean by 'dance', with the cognisance that the way in which we view dance in western culture will have implications for the treatment of dances of other cultures, and vice versa. In other words, we should look at our own culture as if it were 'anthropologically strange' (Garfinkel 1984). The ethnographer as a culturally embodied individual has to approach the area of study in a self-reflexive manner (Novack 1990, Sklar 1991, Thomas 1993).

Dance anthropologists such as Kaeppler (1991), Sklar (1991), Novack (1990) and Grau (1993), have adopted a cultural relativist position and stressed that the body in movement and dance is not natural but rather is socially constructed in 'concept and practice' (Novack 1990). They have demonstrated that dance is both aesthetic and social (Grau 1993, Novack 1990,). Because of the constant presence of the human body in dance, dance conjoins referential and formal qualities (Jordan and Thomas 1990, Novack 1990). That is, it speaks to something outside itself and it does so through formal principles: 'the dance combines form and reference, tying formal changes in technique to changes of meaning for the performer and audience through the body and movement of the performer' (Novack 1990: 15). Dance studies (Grau 1993, Hanna 1980, Kaeli'inohomoku 1979, Royce 1980) have demonstrated that dance does not simply reflect social relationships but can also contribute to shaping social relations and thus can contribute to change. Dance can thus be treated as a form of cultural knowledge (Sklar 1991). As such it is an appropriate area of socio-cultural inquiry. However, the concern is not simply to read the dance codes, but also to understand the context in order to be able to ask *how* does the movement mean?

DANCE AESTHETICS: THE PHENOMENOLOGY OF DANCE

The aesthetics of dance, as I indicated in Chapter 1, has been a marginal area of study within the tradition of the philosophy of art, which has been developed to analyse the conceptual framework intrinsic to art forms and the values attached to them, and to confer judgements upon them. The approach to dance which interested me and which, in large part, informed the discussion of *Appalachian Spring* (1944) in Chapter 9 is the phenomenological approach to dance, especially that expounded by Maxine Sheets-Johnstone (1978, 1979, 1984). The use of this perspective in this book could be usefully contrasted with certain other 'cultural' analyses of dance which draw on different aesthetic traditions such as Marxist aesthetics (Prickett 1992) or deconstructism (Foster 1986).

Sheets-Johnstone's (1979) study of dance 'as a formed and performed art', the first edition of which was published in 1966, takes its starting point from the philosophical method of phenomenology. The major exponent of this mode of analysis was Edmund Husserl (1965) whose work can be seen as a critical response to naturalism, positivism and historicism. Husserl viewed phenomenology as the first philosophy because, he maintained, it alone systematically sought to enquire into the structures of the realm of the subjective consciousness. His aim was to arrive at a *method* that would enable philosophy to grasp the essences of phenomena. The first step in the phenomenological method, according to Husserl, is the suspension of belief in the life-world: that is, bracketing out the objective reality. This reduction, or epoché, Husserl argued, enables the phenomenologist to become a disinterested observer. The phenomenological reduction was the means by which Husserl sought to radicalise the Cartesian method of philosophical doubt (see Schutz 1967: 99–106). What remains is the phenomenon in consciousness, not a pre-given objective reality. This leads back to 'intentionality' which, for Husserl, is the ultimate source of meaning of the experiential world.

Following Husserl, Sheets-Johnstone (1979: 10–11) considers that instead of describing experiences as the 'objective relationship of the man to the world', phenomenology seeks to bracket out both the man (*sic*) and the world and describe the direct experience as it is lived in the present, by direct intuition. Phenomenology attempts to describe the 'pre-reflective', 'pre-objective' encounter of man (*sic*) to the world as it is experienced to consciousness in the existential present as 'consciousness of something'. In accordance with Husserl, Sheets-Johnstone argues that phenomenology cannot give rise to theory because it is not concerned with theorising about phenomena, but rather with descriptions of their existence as they appear to consciousness in the 'vivid present'. That is, phenomenology seeks to develop a method which does not reduce experience to a reflection of taken-for-granted objectively given structures – 'the objective reality of man and the objective world' – but rather to 'illuminate' the lived experiences of the structures through which we orientate ourselves to the world through our consciousness of being in the world. This reasoning is underpinned by the notion of embodiment.

> Fundamentally, man is not an objective structure to be known, but a unique existential being, a unity of consciousness-body, which knows itself. Consequently any conception of man's relationship to the world must be based upon knowledge of his consciousness body in a *living* context to the world. Phenomenology is hence more method than system, for it engenders a particular point of view rather than a fixed body of beliefs.
>
> (Sheets-Johnstone 1979: 11–12)

Dance, according to Sheets-Johnstone (1979: 14–15) is often incorrectly defined as 'a force in time and space'. This conception does not, she argues, describe the 'lived experience of dance'. That empiricist idea is rejected on the basis that it presupposes separate objective categories in the dance 'with no unifying centre'.

> To conceive of them (force, time, space) as given objective factors beforehand is to overlook the very quiddity of dance: it is something which is created and which does not exist prior to its creation.
>
> (Sheets-Johnstone 1979: 14)

Following Jean-Paul Sartre's elucidation of temporality in *Being and Nothingness* (1956) and Maurice Merleau-Ponty's description of the phenomenological character of spatiality in the *Phenomenology of Perception* (1961), Sheets-Johnstone (1979: 15–29) sees that dance, as it is 'formed and performed' by the dancer, and experienced by the audience, is a 'cohesive moving form' which is never there at any one moment, but is always in the process of becoming.

> In short the dance appears as it has been created: a kinetic phenomenon whose spatiality and temporality are structures created with and inherent in the total global phenomenon itself.
>
> (Sheets-Johnstone 1979: 29)

Dance, from this perspective, as a consciously created movement phenomenon presented through the lived experience, exists in its *own* time and space, it creates its *own* life-world.

The central part of *The Phenomenology of Dance* elucidates and elaborates upon Langer's (1953) conception of dance as a symbolic form. Langer's phenomenological approach to the study of dance stemmed from Ernst Cassirer's philosophy of symbolic forms. Human beings, Cassirer (1953) maintained, are endowed with a symbol-seeking mind, and it is this that distinguishes us from the animals. The role of language, for Cassirer, is not to name a reality which is already pre-given, but to construct and inform it through conceptualisation and articulation. Verbal language, along with other symbolic forms such as religion, science, art, myth and history, informs on reality rather than reflects it. For Cassirer, the laws which govern symbolic forms are different from and thus not reducible to the rules of logic. Langer, following Cassirer, is concerned to maintain the difference between the verbal system and the artistic system, although they are both viewed as symbolic systems. Langer considers that if a symbolic form is to be an independent art it must have a 'primary illusion':

> The primary illusion of any artistic system is something created, and created at the first touch . . . the material must suffer transformation.
>
> (Langer 1953: 74)

The substance of the material force of dance is body movement, and movement becomes expression through gesture. Although gesture, as vital movement, is part of our behaviour, it is not dance, according to Langer. It is only when movement is taken away from 'actual spontaneous gesture and imagined' (ibid.), so that it may be performed apart from its original context, that it becomes an artistic element, a possible dance gesture. The difference between 'natural' gestures and dance gestures, for Langer, lies in the fact that the former are 'signals' of will, while the latter are 'symbols' of will.

The gestural character of dance movement, and the 'vital force' that dance gestures express, are illusory from Langer's viewpoint. The 'primary illusion' of dance is viewed as a 'virtual realm of power', not actual exerted power. It is from this position that Langer can criticise the view that dance is the direct self-expression of the artist. For Langer (1953), it is imagined feelings that govern dance, not actual emotional conditions. Dance gesture is not 'real' but 'virtual'. The movement is real enough but the self-expression is only virtual. Art, then, according to Langer transforms reality through the power of the imagination. It does not depict an already given reality, rather it creates its form through an illusion.

Sheets-Johnstone (1979: 33–5) considers that Langer's concept of the primary illusion of dance as a 'realm of virtual force' brings into focus the related structures of time and space. Langer, however, treats these as secondary illusions – a view which Sheets-Johnstone questions on the grounds that: 'it is phenomenologically as well as logically impossible for virtual force to take place in "real" time and in "real" space without thereby losing its virtuality' (ibid.: 36).

Sheets-Johnstone (1979: 33–5) argues that if dance were only an illusion of virtual force with the spatial and temporal structures as either outside or secondary to it, there would be little to distinguish between particular dances. Rather, she argues, all dances are different and their uniqueness 'relates in part to the highly individualised manner in which virtual force is temporalised and spatialised, in which virtual force is projected as a unique form in the making' (ibid.: 36).

Sheets-Johnstone (1979: 58–76) moves on to clarify what she sees as the two forms of abstraction inherent in the creation of the symbolic form (ibid.: 58).

> The first has to do with the forms of actual human feelings which are abstracted from their everyday context in order to be created and presented symbolically, and the second has to do with the movement which is abstracted from its everyday expressive context to become an expressive medium of dance.

Actual human feelings, in this framework, become symbolic of feeling, and movement becomes symbolically expressive as opposed to a sign. In other words, it is cut loose from its referential signification. These two aspects, however, are not to be seen as distinct, rather they occur at the same time, just as space, force and time are not separate objective entities of the dance. Separating or reflecting on specific aspects of the dance, for Sheets-Johnstone, necessarily entails losing the pre-reflective intuitive import of the dance as a whole continuous process of becoming itself. It denies the lived experience of the dance as a thing and an end in itself, 'a sheer form-in-the-making'. In the same way, she points out that if concentration is upon 'movement *qua* movement', what we are left with is a series of movements all out of context with each other and with the total dance.

While this notion of the illusion of the created symbolic form provides a critique of realist aesthetics, in that it entails the idea of the real-as-ism, an illusion of the real, it nevertheless raises problems in analysing other dance forms in which the focus is directed towards an exploration of movement for movement's sake. In the 1960s and 1970s a number of young American choreographers such as Yvonne Rainer, Steve Paxton and Trisha Brown, following the lead of Merce Cunningham, began to question the illusory quality of dance in dominant modes of performance. They sought to demystify the theatrical spectacle of dance, with its emphasis on extraordinary, non-literal movement, and return to everyday gesture, to discover its extraordinariness, in and of itself, not to make it artificial. Can this kind of phenomenological approach, then, deal with postmodern dance's denial of symbolic form in dance? Elsewhere, Sheets-Johnstone (1978) demonstrates that she is aware of this and that her earlier analysis was influenced by the dominant mode of modern dance in America at the time. She considers that the postmodern dancers' celebration of the mundaneity of everyday movement as an extraordinary activity of body in itself, can be viewed as a phenomenological exercise in that their intention was to return to the originary nature of dance, 'movement *qua* movement'. Hence, Sheets-Johnstone (1979: xiii–xiv) notes that a phenomenological analysis would have to take account of the differences between dances which operate in terms of a symbolic form and those which work on an existential basis.

The major part of this study is directed towards an examination of American modern dance in its early stages, and because the work emphasised 'form', Sheets-Johnstone's (1979) analysis of dance as a symbolic form is appropriate to that discussion. Moreover, the recognition of differences between dances which operate on a symbolic and an existential basis is conformation of the view taken here that questions such as, what *is* art? cannot be seen in isolation from what counts as art in a given society. In other words, as Wolff (1983) has argued, it points to the requirements of sociological aesthetics, which take account of both the specific qualities of the form/work itself and of its relation to the socio-historical conditions of its emergence and performace. At the same time, because phenomenology lays stress on embodiment in the sense of 'being in the world', it provides a 'complementary' perspective to the overtly textual and representational (Csordas 1993: 137) approach to the body that is to be found in the tradition on body symbolism, which also informs the discussion of *Appalachian Spring* (1944) in Chapter 9.

THE SOCIAL STUDY OF THE BODY: BODY SYMBOLISM

Although sociology has largely neglected focus on the body as a site of inquiry until quite recently, the social scientific study of the body, like the study of dance in society, has been the focus of attention of anthropologists and ethnographers since the late nineteenth century (see Polhemus 1975 for a detailed discussion of the various phases of development in the anthropology of the body).

Some, such as Edward Hall (1969, 1973), and Ray Birdwhistell (1973) have developed linguistic and communication models to the study of 'proxemics' (personal and social space) and 'kinesics' (everyday movement). The major concern within this avenue of research has been to show that the ways in which we perceive of our bodies and the ways in which we move are not just 'natural facts of existence', but rather they are socially constructed. The concern has been to demonstrate that the attention the body is afforded, and our perceptions of it, are largely dependent upon the type of society we belong to. However, within the dominant modes of discourse in this field until the 1970s, the relation between the physical body and the social body, or what we might call a sociological approach to the study of the body (body symbolism), had not been explored in any great detail (Polhemus 1975). In part, the reason for this is that those researchers who adopted a 'cultural' anthropological approach have been traditionally locked in debate with the proponents of social Darwinism who view bodily behaviour, and particularly facial expressions, as natural and/or universal (see Hinde 1972 for examples of neo-Darwinist approaches). As a result of their over-concern to prove their case against the students of animal behaviour, cultural anthropologists have tended to stress one of two related positions: the culturally relative character of gesture and posture (Hall 1969, 1973, La Barre 1978); or that bodily expression is learned (Bateson and Mead 1942, Birdwhistell 1975, Efron 1972), as opposed to directing their attention towards the development of a sociological framework – that is, exploring the relation between the physical body and the social body (Polhemus 1978).

A major exception to this rule within the dominant American tradition can be found in the work of Erving Goffman. In *Relations in Public* (1972), Goffman attempted to uncover the 'social rules' for appropriate bodily behaviour in public places and spaces. Goffman pointed out that he owed much of his insight into the social rules and norms of behaviour to the Durkheimian tradition of thought. Within that tradition, writers like Robert Hertz in 1909, Marcel Mauss in 1934 and much later Mary

Douglas (1970a, 1970b, 1975), pointed the way to achieve a sociological approach to the study of bodily expression which has nothing whatsoever to do with debating with the social Darwinists. Rather, their concerns have been directed towards an exploration of the social aspects of human bodily expression in order to elucidate, and say something significant about, the rules and the categories that are expressed in the social body or society. It is this tradition that has influenced my thinking on the role of the body in dance rather than that of Foucault, for example, or post-structuralist feminist writers like Irigaray, Cixous or Kristeva which I cited in Chapter 1.

Although this tradition of body symbolism has its roots in sociological theory of Emile Durkheim, it was through anthropology rather than sociology that this tradition of body symbolism was generated. For reasons given in the Chapter 1, Durkheim, as one of the founders of sociology, was not interested in the body. As Bryan Turner (1991: 8) has argued, '. . . whereas the body had entered anthropology at the fundamental level of ontology, sociology, partly evolving theoretically along the notion of rational economic action, never elaborated a sociology of the body'. However, as it was Durkheim's theoretical insights into the power of society revealed in symbolic forms that provided the impetus for this tradition of body symbolism, it is important to at least indicate his approach to symbolic forms.

Durkheim (1964) was concerned to show how society moulded the individual in its own light. Although he did not deny the existence of the individual or of individual ideas, Durkheim maintained that the whole (society) is always greater than the sum of its parts (social institutions and individuals). He considered that society exists as a reality in its own right ('sui generis') and that social relations are different from and not reducible to individuals. Sociology, whose object, for Durkheim, is society, should be concerned to study social factors not individual manifestations (see Durkheim 1982: 34–47). In *The Elementary Forms of Religious Life* (1968), Durkheim set out to demonstrate the social basis of knowledge by seeking to explain the origin of religious beliefs from an examination of aboriginal classificatory systems and Amer-Indian 'primitive' religions. Durkheim argues that it was humanity's innate sociality that led to the development of a common set of symbols (language, rituals, rites). According to Durkheim, within each individual there is a part of society. In order to become conscious of it and thereby to organise themselves collectively, individuals had to communicate with each other. Symbolic forms and their potential for communally shared knowledge of the world have their roots in the social nature of human beings. Durkheim treats primitive belief systems as cosmological systems (Douglas 1975). They constitute forms of knowledge that stem from the social realm. Thus, for Durkheim, knowledge, far from existing independently of the social realm, is generated from within the society itself; it is socially constructed.

Durkheim, however, did not apply this foresight to the study of 'modern' western industrial cultures largely because, as Douglas (1975: ix–xx) has argued, he presumed that western culture occupied a radically different space from that of primitive cultures and he believed that science constituted an objective form of knowledge. These assumptions prevented Durkheim from pushing his theory to its logical conclusion of cultural relativism. Moreover, by insisting that only science, through its methods, provides the tool for the uncovering of the essential sociality inherent in cosmological systems, Durkheim, by implication, treats 'primitive' cosmologies as partially illusory. As Douglas (1975) has pointed out, however – despite his concern to exclude scientifically oriented forms of knowledge from his analysis – the theoretical impact of Durkheim's work remains, particularly if we refocus our attention and view ourselves in a similar light as the traditionally perceived denigrated 'other'; primitive cultures. That is, forms of knowledge do not exist outside of society; they are generated from and organised within the social realm and they are voiced in and through the various aspects of everyday experience. Mauss (1973) and Hertz (1973) sought to apply Durkheim's ideas on the social construction of knowledge to the study of the body. Hertz turned his attention to the study of left/right body symbolism and gave rise to a great deal of debate in that area (see Needham 1973). Mauss focused on the learnt character of everyday techniques such as swimming, running, walking, etc. Hertz in 'The Pre-Eminence of the Right Hand' (1973) is concerned with both the physical and social factors concerning the 'pre-ponderance' of right-handedness in many societies. He argues that the apparent resemblance between the right and left hand is not borne out by society. The right hand is elevated and revered in the eyes of society, whereas the left is lowered and despised. Hertz accepts the anatomical theory (which was prevalent at the time of writing) which claims that there is a 'natural' slight disposition towards right-handedness, which results from the greater development of the left side of the brain. However, he argues that this, in itself, would not be enough to bring about the absolute preponderance of the right hand 'if these were not reinforced by other fixed influences extraneous to the organism'. Hertz, like Durkheim, sees that the individual is constrained by society. For the former it is the coercive power of society which guarantees the pre-eminence of the right hand. In examining 'primitive' cosmologies Hertz finds that their categories are formed around the polar opposition of the sacred and the profane. All the categories that are subsumed under the sacred symbolise that which is noble and precious, whereas those under the profane symbolise that which is common and despised. The profane contains all that is harmful to the sacred. In order to protect itself the sacred is hedged by rules and bound by sanctions. Hertz concludes from this that the primitives categorised the right side of the body under the sacred and the left under the profane. Because of this, he argues, the right side is elevated and revered in the eyes of societies and the left side relegated to a subordinate position. Thus the slight anatomical disposition towards right-handedness was developed fully through the classificatory scheme of society. The body, for Hertz, is a symbol of society.

Durkheim and Hertz both shared the same illusion as Sachs (1937), that the origins of modern western thought are to be found in the examination of more 'primitive' religions. The data that Hertz drew upon for his analysis of primitive religions, like that of Sachs (1937), is rather dubious. Moreover, his assumption of the pre-eminence of the right hand throughout societies has been called into question (see Needham 1973). However, the consideration behind the analysis is important. He was concerned to explain that the way we perceive of the body and the way we move in everyday life is not just a natural non-social fact of existence, rather it has a social significance. For Hertz the physical body stands in the same relation to the social body, as the individual does to society. The physical body is a microcosm of the social body. The notion of natural behaviour does not imply behaviour that is physically natural in the sense of 'non-social' behaviour. Rather, Hertz sees that there are certain natural characteristics which the body has: left side/right side, back/front, top half/bottom half, hair, nails, etc., to which society can and does give meaning. The natural (non-social) characteristics of the human body are given a symbolic loading by society and these, in turn, are conceived of as natural (non-social). That is, there is a transformation from the natural into the terms of the social system and this is transformed back again through the social categories into the natural.

Although Mauss's 'The Techniques of the Body' was written in 1934 it was only translated into English in 1973. In this 'gem of a paper' (Douglas 1978), Mauss shows that our ordinary routine bodily behaviours, from waking to sleeping, from movement to stillness, are socially controlled. He also maintains that what we ordinarily conceive as natural behaviour in relation to the body is also socially bound, such as the right amount of sleep the body requires to stay healthy.

Mauss, unlike Durkheim and Hertz, does not restrict his analysis to primitive cultures, but draws on available ethnographic data and his own experiences. Moreover, he seeks to 'move from the concrete to the abstract' (Mauss 1973: 70). He advances the claim that of all the elements involved in the art of using the body, education is most important. By considering the bodily techniques of different cultures in areas such as obstetrics and giving birth, sleeping, swimming, running, etc., Mauss sees that throughout our lives we learn to use our bodies in appropriate ways, particularly with regard to the learning of sexual (gendered) behaviour.

> The big moment in the education of the body is, in fact, the moment of initiation. Because of the way our boys and girls are brought up we imagine

that both acquire the same manners and postures and receive the same training everywhere. The idea is already erroneous about ourselves – and it is totally false in so-called primitive countries . . . for men as for women, the decisive moment is adolescence. It is at this moment that they learn the techniques of the body that they will retain for the whole of their adult lives.

(Mauss 1973: 80)

However, Mauss recognises that since he is concerned with movements of the body, the biological and psychological aspects must be considered. He emphasises that the study of the body should be viewed within symbolic systems – 'it is a triple viewpoint, that of "total man" that is needed' (Mauss 1973: 73).

The education of habitual bodily techniques comes from without, it contains all the social element, while the imitative actions involved in education contain the psychological and biological aspects (Mauss 1973). Mauss treats the psychological as 'connecting cogs' between the physical and the social. The techniques of the body are, nevertheless, governed by society through its educational processes. For Mauss, there is no such thing as a natural (non-social) body.

Dance as a symbolic art form consciously attends to its bodily techniques through its encoded system. What Mauss seeks to show is that natural everyday movement is also a symbolic form with an encoded system, but that its form is treated by societal members as natural (non-social) behaviour. Mauss, like Hertz, points to the fact that the body as an image of society is an appropriate area for sociological investigation. Focus on the bodily expression can be used to draw out some layers of insight concerning everyday experiences in society.

Mary Douglas's work on body symbolism extends the analysis put forward by Hertz and Mauss (Douglas 1970a, 1970b, 1975). Her approach may be defined as a systematic attempt to take up Durkheim's insights into the power of society and push them to their logical conclusion of cultural relativism (Douglas 1975). Douglas (1970b) treats all forms of knowledge as cosmologies, and that includes western systems of thought based on scientific principles as well as traditional systems of knowledge based on magic and/or religion. Following Mauss, Douglas (1970b) argues that the body is always treated as an image of society. She attempts to demonstrate that the way we perceive our bodily functions, boundaries, margins, etc., mirrors the type of society we belong to.

The body is a model that can stand for any bounded system. Its boundaries can represent any boundaries that are threatened or precarious. The body is a complex structure. The function of the different parts afford it a rich source of symbols for other complex structures.

(1970a: 138)

For Douglas (1970a, 1970b), the body symbolises society and society symbolises the body. She maintains that this is not a one way process from society to the body; rather, each body, the 'physical body' and the 'social body' reinforce each other. Like Durkheim, Douglas (1970b) sees that we each have a part of society within us. The relationship between the individual and the social is one of reciprocity. For the most part, this reciprocity is unconscious. It is implicit in the way we use our bodies in everyday life and in the attention we afford them.

In *Purity and Danger* (1970a), Douglas considers the symbolic load carried in attitudes towards bodily waste, urine, faeces, etc., paying close attention to 'boundary maintenance' and social forces that influence ideas about pollution in society. Douglas argues that the social system's concern with boundary maintenance is reflected in the care taken by society to maintain the body's boundaries. Analysis of the differing ways in which a society seeks to maintain the body's boundaries, according to Douglas (1970a) can uncover something about the idea the social system has of itself. Ideas about dirt and pollution relate to society at a symbolic level: they do not expose 'actual social relations' but rather, speak of 'numerous designs and hierarchy and symmetry' which apply to the larger social system (Douglas 1970a: 3). People come to know their own society through the rules and rituals that are routinely enacted on the body and expressed in the care and attention that is afforded it.

> The rules enact the form of social relations and in giving these relations visible expressions they enable people to know their society. The rituals work on the body politic through the symbolic medium of the physical body.
>
> (Douglas 1970a: 153)

In *Natural Symbols* (1970b) Douglas develops her approach to body symbolism by attempting to provide a method for analysing ritual and body symbolism that would facilitate comparative analysis between different groups who share the same social environment. Here, she seeks to distinguish a 'natural tendency' to represent situations of a certain kind in an 'appropriate bodily style' (Douglas 1970b: 97). For Douglas, body as a symbol of society cuts across cultures; that is, all societies engage in body symbolism. To that extent the body is a 'natural symbol'. This is a point of departure from Mauss's (1973) idea that there is no such thing as a natural body. However, she argues that the ways in which the body is expressed, and the meanings that surround it, are culturally specific. Since this natural expression is culturally determined, Douglas (1970b: 97) insists that any consideration of the body as a natural symbol would entail paying careful attention to the 'social dimension'. Douglas's structuralism, unlike that of Lévi-Strauss (1978) for example, is oriented towards cultural relativism. The idea of the natural tendency for the body to express society forms the basis of her framework of structural universals, but she insists that the analysis must be directed towards the understanding of the particular social formation which the body expresses, rather than towards the universals.

Bodily expression in the Durkheimian tradition is treated as a sociological phenomenon that provides a rich source of empirical investigation into the analysis of society. Its theoretical framework is constructed in such a way as to attend to and illuminate the social aspects of the human body. The significance of this approach to the preceeding discussion is that it demonstrates that everyday movement is not quite as natural or as individual as we commonsensically perceive it to be. It offers an approach to the study of the human body and everyday movement wherein the body is treated as a symbol of society. As such, it is complementary to the insights of those dance anthropologists cited earlier who perceive of dance as a form of cultural knowledge.

BIBLIOGRAPHY

Adair, C. (1992) *Women and Dance: Sylphs and Sirens*, London: Macmillan.
Adshead, J. and Layson, J. (eds) (1983) *Dance History*, London: Dance Books.
Anderson, J. (1974) *Dance*, New York: Newsweek Books.
—— (1980) 'The Dance: "Appalachian Spring" ', *New York Times*, 4 May.
—— (1982) 'Dance: Copland Conducts for Graham', *New York Times*, 18 June.
Andrews, E.D. (1967) *The Gift to be Simple*, New York: Dover Publications.
—— (1978) 'The Dance in Shaker Ritual', in P. Magriel (ed.) *Chronicles of the American Dance*, (first published in 1948 edn), New York: Da Capo Press.
Armitage, M. (ed.) (1966) *Martha Graham*, New York: Dance Horizons.
Austin, R. (1980) *Images of Dance*, London: Vision Press.
Balanchine, G. (1980) 'The Dance Element in Stravinsky's Music', in C. Steinberg (ed.) *The Dance Anthology*, New American Library.
Balcom, L. (1944) 'The Negro Dances Himself', *Dance Observer* 11, 10: 122–4.
Banes, S. (1980) *Terpsichore in Sneakers*, Boston: Haughton Mifflin.
Barth, G. (1980) *City People: The Rise of Modern City Culture in Nineteenth-Century America*, Oxford: Oxford University Press.
Barthes, R. (1969) *Elements of Semiology*, New York: Hill and Wang.
Bateson, G. and Mead, M. (1942) *Balinese Character: A Photographic Analysis*, New York: Special Publications of the New York Academy of Sciences, 2.
Bauman, Z. (1992) *Intimations of Postmodernity*, London: Routledge.
Beiswanger, G. (1934) 'Music For The Modern Dance', *Theatre Arts Monthly* 18, 3: 184–90.
—— (1939) 'The New Theatre Dance', *Theatre Arts* 23, 1: 41–56.
—— (1944) 'New Images in the Dance', *Theatre Arts* 28, 10: 609–14.
Belo, J. (ed.) (1970) *Traditional Balinese Culture*, New York: Columbia University Press.
Benjamin, W. (1973) *Illuminations*, London: Fontana/Collins.
Benthall, J. and Polhemus, T. (eds) (1975) *The Body as a Medium of Expression*, London: Penguin Books.
Bentley, E. (1983) 'Martha Graham's Journey', in R. Copeland and M. Cohen (eds) *What Is Dance?*, Oxford: Oxford University Press.
Bercovitch, S. (1974) *The American Puritan Imagination*, London: Cambridge University Press.
Berger, A. (1953) *Aaron Copland*, New York: Oxford University Books.
Berger, J. (1972) *Ways of Seeing*, Harmondsworth, Middlesex: Penguin Books.
Best, D. (1976) 'Rhythm in Movement – A Plea for Clarity', *Journal of Human Movement Studies* 2: 271–8.
—— (1978) *Philosophy of Human Movement*, London: Allen & Unwin.
Birdwhistell, R. (1973) *Kinesics in Context*, Harmondsworth, Middlesex: Penguin University Books.

—— (1975) 'Background Considerations to the Study of the Body as a Medium of Expression', in J. Benthall and T. Polhemus (eds) *The Body as a Medium of Expression*, London: Penguin Books.

Blacking, J. (ed.) (1977) *The Anthropology of the Body*, A.S.A. Monograph: 15, London: Academic Press.

—— and Kaeli'inohomoku, J. (eds) (1979) *The Performing Arts, Music and Dance*, The Hague: Mouton.

Boas, F. (ed.) (1972) *The Function of Dance in Human Society*, New York: Dance Horizons.

Bourdieu, P. (1984) *Distinction: A Social Critique of the Judgement of Taste*, translated by R. Nice (ed.), London: Routledge & Kegan Paul.

—— and Passeron, J.C. (1990) *Reproduction in Education, Society and Culture*, London: Sage Publications.

Boyne, R. and Rattansi, A. (eds) (1990) *Postmodernism and Society*, London: Macmillan.

Brake, M. (1985) *Comparative Youth Culture*, London: Routledge & Kegan Paul.

Braun, D.D. (1969) *The Sociology and History of American Music and Dance*, Ann Arbor: UMI Research Press.

Brinson, P. (1983) 'Scholastic Tasks of a Sociology of Dance: Part 2', *Dance Research* 1, 2: 59–68.

Brown, J.M. (ed.) (1980) *The Vision of Modern Dance*, London: Dance Books.

Brown, M.W. (1955) *American Painting from the Armory Show to the Depression*, New Jersey: Princeton University Press.

Buckroyd, J. (1989) *Eating Your Heart Out*, London: MacDonald.

Cage, J. and Russell, W. (1939) 'Percussion Music and its Relation to the Modern Dance', *Dance Observer* 6, 8: 264, 274.

Carroll, N. (1984) 'The Return of the Repressed: the Re-emergence of Expression in Contemporary American Dance', *Dance Theatre Journal* 2, 1: 16 27.

Carroll, P.N. and Noble, D.W. (1977) *The Free and the Unfree: A New History of the United States*, Harmondsworth, Middlesex: Penguin Books.

Cassirer, E. (1953) *Philosophy of Symbolic Forms*, New Haven: Yale University Press.

Chambers, I. (1985) *Urban Rhythms: Pop Music and Popular Culture*, London: Macmillan.

Chase, G. (1955) *America's Music*, New York: McGraw-Hill.

Church, M. (1937a) 'The Dance in the Social Scene', *Dance Observer* 4, 3: 27, 30, 32.

—— (1937b) 'First Convention – American Dance Association', *Dance Observer* 4, 6: 61, 65.

—— (1939) 'Federal Dance Theatre', *Dance Observer* 6, 2: 171–2.

Clarke, M. and Crisp, C. (1973) *Ballet: An Illustrated History*, London: Adam & Charles Black.

Clurman, H. (1983) *The Fervent Years*, New York: Da Capo Press.

Code, G. (1939a) 'Dance Theatre of the WPA: A Record of National Accomplishment, Pt 1', *Dance Observer* 6, 8: 264–5, 274.

—— (1939b) 'Dance Theatre of the WPA: A Record of National Accomplishment, Pt 2', *Dance Observer* 6, 9: 280–21, 290.

—— (1939c) 'Dance Theatre of the WPA: A Record of National Accomplishment, Pt 2, Conclusion', *Dance Observer* 6, 10: 302.

—— (1940a) 'Dance Theatre of the WPA: A Record of National Accomplishment, Pt 3', *Dance Observer* 7, 3: 34–5.

—— (1940b) 'Dance Theatre of the WPA', *Dance Observer* 7, 6: 86.

Cohen, M. (1983) 'Primitivism, Modernism and Dance Theory', in R. Copeland and M. Cohen (eds) *What Is Dance?*, Oxford: Oxford University Press.

Cohen, S.J. (1966) 'Avant Garde Choreography', in W. Sorell (ed.) *The Dance Has Many Faces*, New York: Columbia University Press.
—— (ed.) (1977a) *Dance as a Theatre Art*, London: Dance Books.
—— (ed.) (1977b) *Doris Humphrey: An Artist First*, Middletown, Connecticut: Wesleyan University Press.
—— (1981) 'What Does the Dance of the Sugar Plum Fairy "Mean"?', *Dance Chronicle* 4, 3: 279–96.
—— (1982) *Next Week, Swan Lake: Reflections On Dance and Dancers*, Middletown: Wesleyan University Press.
Cole, A.C. (1942) *The Puritan and Fair Terpsichore*, New York: Dance Horizons.
Connor, S. (1989) *Postmodernist Culture: An Introduction to Theories of the Contemporary*, Oxford: Basil Blackwell.
Cope, E. (1976) *Performance – Dynamics of a Dance Group*, London: Lepus Books.
Copeland, R. (1983a) 'Merce Cunningham and the Politics of Perception', in R. Copeland and M. Cohen (eds) *What is Dance?*, Oxford: Oxford University Press.
—— (1983b) 'Dance, Photography and the World's Body', in R. Copeland and M. Cohen (eds) *What is Dance?*, Oxford: Oxford University Press.
Copland, A. (1953) *Music and Imagination*, Cambridge: Harvard University Press.
—— (1968) *The New Music 1900–1960*, London: Macdonald and Evans.
Courtney, R. (1970) 'On Langer's Dramatic Illusion', *Journal of Aesthetics and Art Criticism* 29: 11–20.
Cowan, J. (1990) *Dance and the Body Politic in Northern Greece*, Princeton: Princeton University Press.
Cowell, H. and Cage, J. (1939) 'Percussion Music and its Relation to Modern Dance', *Dance Observer* 6,10: 296–7.
Croce, A. (1977) *Afterimages*, New York, Alfred K. Knopf.
Csordas, T. (1993) 'Somatic Modes of Attention', *Cultural Anthropology* 8, 2: 135–56.
Cullberg, G. (1966) 'Television Ballet', in W. Sorell (ed.) *The Dance Had Many Faces*, New York: Columbia University Press, pp, 169–76.
Cunningham, M. (1968) *Notes on Choreography*, New York: Something Else Press.
—— (1980) 'Choreography and the Dance', in C. Steinberg (ed.) *The Dance Anthology*, New York: The New American Library.
—— (1985) *The Dancer and the Dance*, New York, London: Marion Boyars.
Daly, A. (1987, Spring) 'The Balanchine Woman Of Hummingbirds and Channel Swimmers', *The Drama Review* 31, 1: 8–21.
—— (ed.) (1992, Spring) 'What has Become of Postmodern Dance?', *The Drama Review* 36, 1: 48–69.
Dance Education and Training in Britain (1980), London: Calouste Gulbenkian Foundation.
Daniel, O. (1982) '*Rite of Spring*, First Staging in America: Stokowski–Massine–Graham', *Ballet Review* 10, 2: 67–71.
Darwin, C. (1969) *The Expression of the Emotions in Man and Animals*, Chicago: University of Chicago Press.
Dempster, E. (1993) 'Re-visioning the Body: Feminism and New Dance', *JADE Conference Proceedings, Nakano Zeno, Japan*: 174–83.
Denby, E. (1945) 'Martha Graham Notes', *New York Herald Tribune*, 20 May.
—— (1986) *Dance Writings*, London: Dance Books.
Douglas, M. (1970a) *Purity and Danger*, Harmondsworth, Middlesex: Pelican Books.
—— (1970b) *Natural Symbols*, London: Barrie & Rockliff.
—— (1973) 'Fashionable Diseases: Women's Complaints and Their Treatment in Nineteenth-Century America', *Journal of Interdisciplinary History* 4: 25–53.
—— (1975) *Implicit Meanings*, London: Routledge & Kegan Paul.

—— (1978) 'Do Dogs Laugh?', in T. Polhemus (ed.) *Social Aspects of the Human Body*, Harmondsworth, Middlesex: Penguin Books.

—— (1980) *Evans-Pritchard*, London: Fontana Paperbacks.

Dudley, J. (1992) 'The Early Life of an American Modern Dancer', *Dance Research* 10, 1: 3–20.

Duncan, I. (1955) *My Life*, New York: Liveright Publishing.

Duncan, I. (1970) *The Dance Technique of Isadora Duncan*, New York: Dance Horizons.

Duncan, I. (1983) 'The Dance of the Future' in R. Copland and M. Cohen (eds) *What is Dance?*, Oxford: Oxford University Press.

Durkheim, E. (1964) *Division of Labour in Society*, Glencoe: Free Press.

—— (1968) *The Elementary Forms of Religious Life*, London: Allen & Unwin.

—— (1992) *The Rules of the Sociological Method and Selected Texts on Sociology and its Method*, London: Macmillan.

—— and Mauss, M. (1970) *Primitive Classification*, Routledge & Kegan Paul.

Dyer, R. (1992) *Only Entertainment*, London: Routledge.

Eagleton, T. (1977) *Marxism and Literary Criticism*, London: Methuen.

—— (1983) *Literary Theory: An Introduction*, Oxford: Basil Blackwell.

Editorial (1936) 'Federal Dance Theatre', *Dance Observer* 3, 8: 87–8.

Efron, D. (1972) *Gesture, Race and Culture*, The Hague: Mouton.

Elias, N. (1978) *The Civilizing Process, vol 1: The History of Manners*, Oxford: Basil Blackwell.

Emery, L.F. (1988) *Black Dance in the United States from 1619–1970*, New York: Dance Horizons.

Engel, L.A. (1933) 'The Dance: A Critical Review', *Trend*, April–June, 30–1.

Evans-Pritchard, E.E. (1928) 'The Dance', *Africa* 1: 446–62.

(1976) *Witchcraft, Oracles and Magic among the Azande*, Oxford: Oxford University Press.

Fanchar, G. and Myers, G. (eds) (1981) *Philosophical Essays on Dance*, New York: Dance Horizons.

Fast, J. (1970) *Body Language*, London: Pan Books.

Featherstone, M. (1988) 'In Pursuit of the Postmodern: An Introduction', *Theory, Culture and Society* 5, 2–3: 195–216.

—— (1991a) 'The Body in Consumer Culture', in M. Featherstone, M. Hepworth, and B.S. Turner (eds) *The Body: Social Processes and Cultural Theory*, London: Sage.

—— (1991b) *Consumer Culture and Postmodernism*, London: Sage.

Featherstone, M., Hepworth, M., and Turner, B.S. (eds) (1991) *The Body: Social Processes and Cultural Theory*, London: Sage.

Feibleman, J.K. (1949) 'The Art of Dance', *Journal of Aesthetics and Art Criticism* 8: 47–52.

Filmer, P. (1978) 'Dickens, Pickwick and Realism', in D. Laurenson (ed.) *The Sociology of Literature: Applied Social Studies*, Keele: Sociological Review Monograph, University of Keele.

Fokine, M. (1963) in A. Chujoy (ed.) *Memoirs of a Ballet Master*, London: Constable.

Foster, S.L. (1986) *Reading Dancing*, Los Angeles: University of California Press.

Frank, A.W. (1991) 'For a Sociology of the Body: An Analytical Review', in M. Featherstone, M. Hepworth, and B.S. Turner (eds) *The Body: Social Processes and Cultural Theory*, London: Sage.

Frascina, F. and Harrison, C. (eds) (1982) *Modern Art and Modernism: A Critical Anthology*, London: Harper & Row.

Fraser, N. and Bastky, S.L. (eds) (1992) *Revaluing French Feminism*, Bloomington: Indiana University Press.

Frazer, Sir J.G. (1957) *The Golden Bough*, London: Macmillan.

Freedley, G. (1978) 'The Black Crook and the White Fawn', in P. Magriel (ed.) *Chronicles of the American Dance from the Shakers to Martha Graham*, New York: Da Capo Press.

Freud, S. and Bruer, J. (1974) *Studies On Hysteria*, Vol. 3, Harmondsworth, Middlesex: Penguin Books.

Frith, S. (1978) *The Sociology of Rock*, London: Constable.

Fuller, L. (1913) *Fifteen Years of a Dancer's Life*, New York: Dance Horizons.

Gage, M. (1930) 'A Study in American Modernism', *Theatre Arts Monthly* 14, 3: 229–32.

Garafola, L. (1993, Spring) 'Book Review: *Martha: The Life and Work of Martha Graham* by Agnes de Mille, New York: Random House 1991; *Blood Memory: An Autobiography* by Martha Graham, New York: Doubleday 1991; *The Techniques of Martha Graham* by Alice Helpern', *Studies in Dance History* 2, no. 2 (Spring/Summer 1991) 59pp.; '*Martha Graham: The Evolution of Her Dance Theory and Training 1926–1991* edited by Marian Horosko, Pennington, NJ: Capella Books 1991; *Louis Horst: Musician in a Dancer's World* by Janet Mansfield Soares, Durham: Duke University Press 1992', *The Drama Review* 37, 1: 167–72.

Garfinkel, H. (1984) *Studies in Ethnomethodology*, Cambridge: Polity Press.

Geertz, C. (1975) *The Interpretation of Cultures*, London: Hutchinson.

Gell, A. (1979) 'On Dance Structures: A Reply to Drid Williams', *Journal of Human Movement Studies* 5: 18–31.

Gelpi, A. (1980) 'White Light in the Wilderness: Landscape and Self in Nature's Nation', in J. Wilmerding (ed.) *American Light: The Luminist Movement 1850–1875*, New York: Harper & Row.

Gershwin, G. (1930) 'The Composer in the Machine Age', in O. Sayler (ed.) *Revolt in the Arts*, New York: Brentano's.

Gibbs, A. (1945) 'The Absolute Frontier', *New Yorker* 23, No. 45.

Giddens, A. (1971) *Capitalism and Modern Social Theory*, Cambridge: Cambridge University Press.

—— (1972) *Politics and Sociology in the Thought of Max Weber*, London: Macmillan.

Gilbert, K.E. (1945) 'Mind and Medium in the Modern Dance', *Journal of Aesthetics and Art Criticism* 1: 106–29.

Gilfond, H. (1936) 'Public Hearing, Federal Dance Theatre', *Dance Observer* 3, 9: 1.

Gilroy, P. (1987) *There Ain't No Black in the Union Jack*, London: Hutchinson.

Goffman, E. (1971) *The Presentation of Self in Everyday-Life*, Harmondsworth, Middlesex: Pelican Books.

—— (1972) *Relations in Public*, Harmondsworth, Middlesex: Pelican Books.

—— (1979) *Gender Advertisements*, London: Macmillan.

Goldberg, R. (1979) *Performance: Live Art 1909 to the Present*, London: Thames & Hudson.

Goodman, N. (1983a) 'The Role of Notation', in R. Copeland and M. Cohen (eds) *What is Dance?*, London: Oxford University Press.

—— (1983b) 'Modes of Symbolization', in R. Copeland and M. Cohen (eds) *What is Dance?*, London: Oxford University Press.

—— (1983c) 'Afterword – An Illustration', in R. Copeland and M. Cohen (eds) *What is Dance?*, London: Oxford University Press.

—— (1990 November) 'Copland Musical America', *Dance and Dancers* 21–3.

—— (1991) 'Martha's Actors', *Dance Magazine* July: 64.

Graff, E. (1990 Summer) 'The Many Faces of Martha', *Ballet Review* 18, 2: 45–7.

—— (1994) 'Dancing Red: Art and Politics', *Studies in Dance History*, Vol. 1: 1–13.

Graham, M. (1930) 'Seeing an American Art of the Dance', in O. Sayler (ed.) *Revolt in the Arts*, New York: Brentano's.

—(1953 February) 'All Dance is Contemporary and There Are Only Two Kinds – Good and Bad', *Musical America* 43, 3: 4, 152.

—— (1968a) Graham 1937, in M. Armitage (ed.) *Martha Graham*, New York: Dance Horizons.

—— (1968b) 'Affirmations: 1926–37', in M. Armitage (ed.) *Martha Graham*, New York: Dance Horizons.

—— (1973) *The Notebooks of Martha Graham*, New York: Harcourt Brace Jovanovich.

—— (1991) *Blood Memory*, New York: Doubleday.

Grau, A. (1993) 'John Blacking and the Development of Dance Anthropology in the UK', *Dance Research* 25, 2 Fall.

Greenberg, C. (1961) *Art and Culture*, Boston: Beacon Press.

Greer, G. (1971) *The Female Eunuch*, London: Paladin.

Grossbard, J. and Merkel, R. (1990) 'Modern Wheels Liberated the Ladies 100 Years Ago', *Dress* 16: 70–88.

Habermas, J. (1985) 'Modernity – an Incomplete Project', in H. Foster (ed.) *Postmodern Culture*, London: Pluto.

Hall, E.T. (1963) 'Proxemics, The Study of Man's Spatial Relations', in I. Goldston (ed.) *Man's Image in Medicine and Anthropology*, Bloomington: Indiana University Press.

—— (1969) *The Hidden Dimension, Garden City*, New York: Anchor Books.

—— (1973) *The Silent Language*, New York: Anchor Books.

Hall, F. (1983) 'Dance Notation and Choreology', in R. Copeland and M. Cohen (eds) *What is Dance? (Readings in Criticism and Theory)*, London: Oxford University Press.

Hampshire, S. (1956) *The Age of Reason: The 17th Century Philosophers*, New York: Mentor.

Hanna, J.L. (1980) *To Dance is Human: A Theory of Nonverbal Communication*, Austin: University of Texas Press.

Harding, S. (ed.) (1987) *Feminism and Methodology*, Bloomington, Indiana and Milton Keynes: Indiana University Press and Open University Press.

Harvy, D. (1989) *The Condition of Postmodernity*, Oxford: Basil Blackwell.

Haskell, A. (1968) *Ballet Russe: The Age of Diahilev*, London: Weidenfeld & Nicholson.

Hastings, B. (1978) 'The Denishawn Era (1914–1931)', in P. Magriel (ed.) *Chronicles of the American Dance from the Shakers to Martha Graham*, New York: Da Capo Press.

Hauser, A. (1982) *The Sociology of Art*, London: Routledge & Kegan Paul.

Hawthorne, N. (1960) *The Scarlet Letter* (1906), London: Dent.

H'Doubler, M.N. (1977) *Dance: A Creative Art Experience*, Wisconsin: University of Wisconsin Press.

Hebdige, D. (1979) *Subcultures: The Meaning of Style*, London: Methuen.

Heinemann, M. (1980) *Puritanism and the Theatre*, London: Cambridge University Press.

Helpern, A. (1991/2) 'The Technique of Martha Graham', *Studies in Dance History* 2, 2 Spring/Summer: 1–59.

Henley, N.M. (1977) *Body Politics: Power, Sex and Nonverbal Communication*, Englewood Cliffs: Prentice-Hall.

Hertz, R. (1973) 'The Pre-Eminence of the Right Hand: A Study in Religious Polarity', in R. Needham (ed.) *Right and Left*, Chicago: University of Chicago Press.

Hewes, G. (1955) 'World Distribution of Certain Postural Habits', *American Anthropologist* 57: 231–44.

Higham, J. (ed.) (1963) *The Reconstruction of American History*, London: Hutchinson.

Hinde, R. (ed.) (1972) *Non-Verbal Communication*, Cambridge: Cambridge University Press.

Hirst, P.Q. and Wolley, P. (1982) *Social Relations and Human Attributes*, London: Tavistock Publications.

Hitchcock, H.W. (1969) *Music in the United States: A Historical Introduction*, New Jersey: Prentice-Hall.

Hodes, S. (1990–1991 Winter) 'Three Brides in "Spring" ', *Ballet Review* 18, 4: 91–4.

Horan, R. (1978) 'The Recent Theater of Martha Graham', in P. Magriel (ed.) *Chronicles of the American Dance from the Shakers to Martha Graham*, New York: Da Capo Press.

Horosko, M. (1991a) *Martha Graham: The Evolution of Her Dance Theory and Training 1926–1991*, Chicago: Cappella Books.

—— (ed.) (1991b) *Martha Graham: The Evolution of Her Dance Theory and Training*, Pennington, NJ: Cappella Books.

Horst, L. (1929) 'Bars and Steps – The New Allies', *The Dance Magazine*, December, 16–17, 63.

—— (1930) 'Modernistic Music – Modernistic Dancing', *The Dance Magazine* 33, 54.

—— (1969) 'Consider the Question of Communication', in M. Van Tuyl (ed.) *Anthology of Impulse: Annual of Contemporary Dance 1951–1966*, New York: Dance Horizons.

—— (1979) *Pre-Classic Dance Forms*, New York: Dance Horizons.

—— and Russell, C. (1977) *Modern Dance Forms*, New York: Dance Horizons.

Hughes, G. (1951) *A History of the American Theatre, 1700–1950*, New York: Samuel French.

Humphrey, D. (1959) *The Art of Making Dances*, London: Dance Books.

Hunter, S. (1972) *American Art of the 20th Century*, New York: Harry N. Abrams.

Husserl, E. (1965) *Phenomenology and the Crisis in Philosophy*, New York: Harper & Row.

—— (1970) *The Crisis of the European Sciences and Transcendental Phenomenology*, Evanston: Northwestern University Press.

Hutchinson Guest, A. (1984) *Dance Notation: The Process of Recording Movement on Paper*, London: Dance Books.

Huyssen, A. (1986) *After the Great Divide: Modernism, Mass Culture, Modernism*, London: Macmillan.

Jackson, G. (1966) 'The Living Dolls', in W. Sorell (ed.) *The Dance Has Many Faces*, New York: Columbia University Press.

Jameson, F. (1985) 'Postmodernism and Consumer Society', in H. Foster (ed.) *Postmodern Culture*, London: Pluto.

Jones, S. (1988) *Black Culture, White Youth*, London: Macmillan.

Jordan, S. (1986) 'Music as Structural Basis in the Choreography of Doris Humphrey, with Special Reference to Humphrey's use of Music Visualisation Techniques and to the Historical Content of her Work', unpublished Ph.D. Dissertation, University of London.

—— (1992) *Striding Out*, London: Dance Books.

—— and Allen, .D. (eds) (1993) *Parallel Lines: Media Representations of Dance*, London: John Libbey.

—— and Thomas, S. (1994, Autumn) 'Dance and Gender: Formalism and Semiotics Reconsidered', *Dance Research* 12, 2: 3–14.

Jowitt, D. (1977) *Dance Beat*, New York: Marcel Dekker.

—— (1984) 'The Return of Drama – A Postmodern Strategy?', *Dance Theatre Journal* 2, 2: 28–31.

—— (1988) *Time and the Dancing Image*, New York: William Morrow.

Kaeli'inohomoku, J. (1979) 'Cultural Change: Functional and Dysfunctional Expressions of Dance, a Form of Affective Culture', in J. Blacking and J. Kaeli'inohomoku (eds) *The Performing Arts*, The Hague: Mouton.
—— (1983) 'An Anthropologist Looks at Ballet as a Form of Ethnic Dance', in R. Copeland and M. Cohen (eds) *What is Dance?*, Oxford: Oxford University Press.
Kaeppler, A. (1972) 'Method and Theory in Analyzing Dance Structure with an Analysis of Tongan Dance', *Ethomusicology* 16, 2: 173–217.
—— (1991) 'American Approaches to the Study of Dance', *Yearbook of Traditional Music* 23: 11–21.
Kendall, E. (1979) *Where She Danced*, New York: Arnold A. Knopf.
Kermode, F. (1983) 'Poet and Dancer before Diaghilev', in R. Copeland and M. Cohen (eds) *What is Dance?*, Oxford: Oxford University Press.
Kesselman, A. (1991) 'The "Freedom Suit" ', *Gender and Society* 5, 4: 495–510.
Khatchadourian, H. (1978) 'Movement and Action in the Performing Arts', *Journal of Aesthetics and Art Criticism* 37: 25–36.
Kirkland, G. with Lawrence, G. (1987) *Dancing On My Grave*, New York: Jove Books.
Kirstein, L. (1967) *Three Pamphlets Collected*, New York: Dance Horizons.
—— (1968) in M. Armitage (ed.) *Martha Graham*, New York: Dance Horizons.
—— (1969) *Dance*, New York: Dance Horizons.
Kisselgoff, A. (1974) 'Dance: Attracting the Young and Old', *New York Times*, 18 April.
Kraus, R. and Chapman, S.A. (1981) *History of the Dance in Art and Education*, Englewood Cliffs: Prentice-Hall.
Kriegsman, S.A. (1981) *Modern Dance in America: The Bennington Years*, Boston: G.K. Hall & Co.
Kristeva, J. (1978a) 'Gesture: Practice or Communication', in T. Polhemus (ed.) *Social Aspects of the Human Body*, Harmondsworth, Middlesex: Penguin Books.
—— (1978b) 'Ray Birdwhistell: "Kinesics" ', in T. Polhemus (ed.) *Social Aspects of the Human Body*, Harmondsworth, Middlesex: Penguin Books.
—— (1980) *Desire in Language*, Oxford: Basil Blackwell.
Kroeber, A. (1925) 'Handbook of Indians in California', *Washington DC, Smithsonian Institution*, Bulletin 78.
Kurath, G.H. (1960) 'Panorama of Dance Ethnology', *Current Anthropology* 1, 3: 233–54.
Laban, R. (1971) *The Mastery of Movement*, 3rd edn revised by L. Ullman (ed.), London: Macdonald & Evans.
La Barre, W. (1978) 'The Cultural Basis of Emotions and Gestures', in T. Polhemus (ed.) *Social Aspects of the Human Body*, Harmondsworth, Middlesex: Penguin Books.
Lange, R. (1980) 'The Develoment of Anthropological Dance Research', *Dance Studies* 4: 1–23
Langer, M.M. (1989) *Merleau-Ponty's Phenomenology of Perception: A Guide and Commentary*, London: Macmillan.
Langer, S.K. (1942) *Philosophy in a New Key*, Cambridge, Massachusetts: Harvard University Press.
—— (1953) *Feeling and Form*, New York: Shribner.
—— (1957) *Problems of Art: Ten Philosophical Lectures*, London: Routledge.
Leabo, K. (ed.) (1961) *Martha Graham*, New York: Theatre Arts Books.
Leatherman, L. (1965) '3 Graham Restorations', *Dance Magazine,* November 42–5.
—— (1967) *Martha Graham: Portrait of an Artist*, London: Faber & Faber.
Levi-Strauss, C. (1978) *Structural Anthropology*, Vol. 2, Harmondsworth: Penguin Books.

Levin, D.M. (1983) 'Philosophers and the Dance', in R. Copeland and M. Cohen (eds) *What is Dance?*, London: Oxford University Press.
—— (1990) 'Postmodernism in Dance: Dance, Discourse, Democracy', in H.J. Silverman (ed.) *Postmodernism – Philosophy and the Arts*, London: Routledge.
Lloyd, M. (1968) 'Lloyd 1935', in M. Armitage (ed.) *Martha Graham*, New York: Dance Horizons.
—— (1974) *The Borzoi Book of Modern Dance*, New York: Dance Horizons.
Loewenthal, L. (1993) *The Search for Isadora: The Legend and Legacy of Isadora Duncan*, Pennington: Princeton Book Company.
Lomax, A. (ed.) (1968) *Folk Song Style and Culture*, Washington, DC: American Association for the Advancement of Science, No. 88.
Luck, K. (1992) 'Trouble in Eden, Trouble with Eve: Women's Trousers and Utopian Socialism in Nineteenth-Century America', in J. Ash and E. Wilson (eds) *Chic Thrills*, London: Pandora.
Lundall, V. (1990) 'A Retrospective of Dance as Viewed by the Writers of *Dance Magazine* and *Dance Observer* between 1926–1934', *Dance: Current Selected Research* 2: 23–32.
Lyons, J. (1970) *Chomsky*, Glasgow: Fontana/Collins.
Lyotard, J.F. (1984) *The Postmodern Condition*, Manchester: Manchester University Press.
McCoy, D.R. (1977) *Coming of Age: The United States during 1920s and 1930s*, Harmondsworth, Middlesex: Penguin Books.
McDonagh, D. (1970) *The Rise and Fall and Rise of Modern Dance*, New York: Outerbridge & Dienstfrey.
—— (1974) *Martha Graham*, London: David & Charles.
McFee, G. (1991) *Understanding Dance*, London: Routledge.
McKayle, D. (1966) 'The Negro Dancer in Our Time', in W. Sorell (ed.) *The Dance Has Many Faces*, New York: Columbia University Press.
McMahan, A. (February 1930) 'Why Don't You Like To Dance?', *Dance Magazine* 59, 60.
McNay, L. (1992) *Foucault and Feminism*, Oxford: Polity Press.
McRobbie, A. (1984) 'Dance and Social Fantasy', in M. McRobbie and M. Niva (eds) *Gender and Generation*, London: Macmillan.
—— (1991) 'Dance Narratives and Fantasies of Achievement', in A. McRobbie (ed.) *Feminism and Youth Culture*, London: Macmillan.
Magriel, P. (ed.) (1978) *Chronicles of the American Dance from the Shakers to Martha Graham*, New York: Da Capo Press.
Manning, S.A. (1993) *Ecstacy and the Demon: Feminism and Nationalism in the Dances of Mary Wigman*, Berkley: University of California Press.
Marcuse, H. (1979) *The Aesthetic Dimension*, London: Macmillan.
Martin, J. (1931) 'Two Dancing Groups Give Joint Program', *New York Times*, 6 December.
—— (1932) 'Graham Program for the Benefit Recital of N.S. of S.R.', *New York Times*, 31 January.
—— (1933a) 'Dance: Native Talent', *New York Times*, 19 May.
—— (1933b) 'The Dance: Martha Graham's Art', *New York Times*, 26 November.
—— (1944) 'The Dance: Washington Festival', *New York Times*, 5 November.
—— (1945) 'Graham Dancers Open at the National', *New York Times*, 5 October.
—— (1967) *American Dancing*, New York: Dance Horizons.
—— (1968) 'Martin 1937', in M. Armitage (ed.) *Martha Graham*, New York: Dance Horizons.
—— (1972) *The Modern Dance*, New York: Dance Horizons.
Mates, J. (1985) *America Musical Stage*, Westpoint: Greenwood Stags.
Mathey, F. (1966) *The World of the Impressionists*, London: Thames & Hudson.

Mathews, J.D.H. (1967) *The Federal Theatre, 1935–1939*, New Jersey: Princeton University Press.

Matthiessen, F.O. (1969) *American Renaissance: Art Expression in the Age of Emerson and Whitman*, Cambridge: Cambridge University Press.

Mauss, M. (1973) 'The Techniques of the Body', *Economy and Society* 2, 1: 70–88.

Maynard, O. (1965) *American Modern Dancers: The Pioneers*, Boston: Little, Brown.

Mazo, J.H. (1977) *Prime Movers*, London: Adam & Charles Black.

Mead, M. and MacGregor, F.C. (1978) 'Growth and Culture: A Photographic Study of Balinese Childhood ("Conclusions")', in T. Polhemus (ed.) *Social Aspects of the Human Body*, Harmondsworth: Penguin Books.

Meglin, J. (1992) 'Fanny Elssler's *Cachucha* and Women's Lives: Domesticity and Sexuality in France in the 1830s', *Dance Reconstructed*, Conference Proceedings, University, New Brunswick, 16–17 October, Rutgers: 73–92.

Mellers, W. (1964) *Music in a New Found Land*, London: Barrie & Rockliff.

Meltzer, M. (1976) *Violins and Shovels: the WPA Arts Project*, New York: Delacourt Press.

Merleau-Ponty, M. (1961) *Phenomenology of Perception*, London: Routledge & Kegan Paul.

Mille, A. de (1980) 'Martha Graham (1894–   )', in C. Steinberg (ed.) *The Dance Anthology*, New York: The New American Library.

—— (1992) *Martha: The Life and Work of Martha Graham*, New York: Vintage Books.

Miller, P. (1956) *The American Puritans*, New York: Doubleday, Anchor Books.

Miller, P. and Johnson, T. H. (eds) (1965) *Puritans: A Sourcebook of their Writings*, 2 vols, New York: Torch.

Millman, M. and Kanter, R.M. (1987) 'Introduction to Another Voice: Feminist Perspectives on Social Life and Social Science', in S. Harding (ed.) *Feminism and Methodology*, Bloomington, Indiana and Milton Keynes: Indiana University Press and Open University Press.

Mitchell, J. and Oakley, A. (eds) (1986) *What Is Feminism?*, Oxford: Basil Blackwell.

Moore, L. (1969) *Artists of the Dance*, New York: Dance Horizons.

Morinni, C. de (1978) 'Loïe Fuller – The Fairy of Light', in P. Magriel (ed.) *Chronicles of the American Dance from the Shakers to Martha Graham*, New York: Da Capo Press.

Morris, D. (1979) *Intimate Behaviour*, Hertfordshire: Panther Books.

Mueller, J. (1977) 'Films: Martha Graham Then and Now', *Dance Magazine* December: 107.

—— (1982) 'Television Technology and the Future of Dance', *Ballet International* 8/9: 39.

Mungham, G. (1976) 'Youth in Pusuit of Itself', in G. Mungham and G. Pearson (eds) *Working Class Youth Culture*, London: Routledge & Kegan Paul.

Murdock, G. (1967) *Ethnographic Atlas: a Summary of Ethnology*, 6, 2: 107–236.

Nadel, M.H. and Miller, C.L. (eds) (1978) *The Dance Experience*, New York: Universe Books.

Needham, R. (ed.) (1973) *Right and Left: Essays on Symbolic Classification*, Chicago: Chicago University Press.

Nelson, P. (1936) 'The American Dancer', *Dance Observer* 3, 7: 76, 82.

Newton, M.S. (1974) *Health, Art and Reason*, London: John Murray.

Noguchi, I. (1967) *A Sculptor's World*, London: Thames & Hudson.

—— (1993) 'Ballet, Gender and Cultural Power', in H. Thomas (ed.) *Dance, Gender and Culture*, London: Macmillan.

Novack, C. (1990) *Sharing the Dance: Contact Improvisation and American Culture*, Madison: University of Wisconsin Press.

Nye, R.B. and Morpurgo, J.E. (1970a) *A History of the United States: Vol. 1 (The Birth of the USA)*, Harmondsworth: Penguin Books.
—— and Morpurgo, J.E. (1970b) *A History of the United States: Vol. 2*, Harmondsworth: Penguin Books.
O'Connor, F.V. (ed.) (1972) *The New Deal Arts Projects: An Anthology of Memoirs*, Washington DC: Smithsonian Institution Press.
O'Connor, J. and Brown, L. (eds) (1980) *The Federal Theatre Project*, London: Eyre Methuen.
O'Neill, J. (1985) *Five Bodies*, Ithaca and London: Cornell University Press.
Padgette, P. (ed.) (1974) *The Dance Writings of Carl Van Vechten*, New York: Dance Horizons.
Parsons, T. (1951) *The Social System*, New York: Free Press.
Phillipson, M. (1985) *Painting, Language and Modernity*, London: Routledge & Kegan Paul.
Polhemus, T. (1975) 'Social Bodies', in J. Benthall and T. Polhemus (eds) *The Body as a Medium of Expression*, London: Penguin Books.
—— (ed.) (1978) *Social Aspects of the Human Body*, Harmondsworth, Middlesex: Penguin Press.
Pomeroy, E. (1962) 'The Changing West', in J. Higham (ed.) *The Reconstruction of American History*, London: Hutchinson University Library.
Poole, R. (1975) 'Objective and Subjective Meaning', in J. Benthall and T. Polhemus (eds) *The Body as a Medium of Expression*, London: Penguin Books.
Preston–Dunlop, V. (ed.) (1979) *Dancing and Dance Theory*, London: Laban Centenary Publication.
Prickett, S. (1989) 'From Workers' Dance to New Dance', *Dance Research* VII, 1: 47–54.
—— (1990) 'Dance and the Workers' Struggle', *Dance Research* VIII, 1: 47–64.
—— (1992) 'Marxism, Modernism and Realism: Politics and Aesthetics in the Rise of the American Modern Dance', Unpublished Ph.D. Dissertation, Laban Centre for Movement and Dance, CNNA.
—— (1994) 'Reviewing on the Left: The Dance Criticism of Edna Echo', *Studies in Dance History*, Vol. 1: 65–104.
Radcliffe–Brown, A.R. (1964) *The Andaman Islanders*, New York: Free Press.
Ramey, P. (1980 November) 'Copland and the Dance', *Ballet News* 2, 5: 8–12, 40.
Redfern, B. (1983) *Dance, Art and Aesthetics*, Cecil Court: Dance Books.
Reid, L.A. (1965) 'Susanne Langer and Beyond', *British Journal of Aesthetics* 5, 4: 357–67.
—— (1969) *Meaning in the Arts*, London: Allen & Unwin.
—— (1970) 'Movement and Meaning', *Laban Art of Movement Guild Magazine* 45: 5–31.
Reis, C. (1947) *Biographical Sketches of Living Composers with a Record of their Works 1912–1937*, New York: Macmillan.
Review, 'Aaron Copland: *Appalachian Spring* (1945) RCA', *Record Review*, p. 1.
Roberts, H. (1977) 'The Exquisite Slave: The Role of Clothes in the Making of the Victorian Woman', *Signs* 2, 3: 554–69.
Robins, D. and Cohen, D. (1978) *Knuckle Sandwich*, Harmondsworth, Middlesex: Pelican Books.
Roeder, G.H. Jr (1980) *Forum of Uncertainty: Confrontations with Modern Painting in Twentieth Century American Thought*, Studies in American History and Culture: 22, Ann Arbor: UMI Research Press.
Rolley, K. (1990) 'Fashion, Femininity and the Fight for the Vote', *Art History* 13, 2: 47–71.
Rose, B. (1967) *American Art since 1900*, London: Thames & Hudson.

Rosemont, F. (ed.) (1981) *Isadora Speaks*, San Francisco: City Lights.
Rosenberg, H. (1962) *The Tradition of the New*, London: Thames & Hudson.
—— (1967) 'The Mythic Act', *New Yorker* 43: 162–71.
—— (1972) *Discovering the Present*, Chicago: University of Chicago Press.
—— (1976) *Art on the Edge*, London: Secker & Warburg.
—— (1982) *The Anxious Object*, Chicago: Chicago University Press.
Royce, A.P. (1980) *The Anthropology of Dance*, Bloomington: Indiana University Press.
Rubridge, S. (1984) 'New Criteria New Alternatives', *Dance Research Journal* 2, 4: 36–8.
Rust, F. (1969) *Dance in Society*, London: Routledge & Kegan Paul.
Ruyter, N.L.C. (1979) *Reformers and Visionaries: The Americanization of the Art of Dance*, New York: Dance Horizons.
Sabin, R. (1940) 'Music for the Dance, An Interview with David Diamond', *Dance Observer* 7, 6: 82–3.
—— (1944) 'Dance at the Coolidge Festival', *Dance Observer* 11, 10: 120–1.
Sachs, C. (1937) *World History of the Dance*, New York: Norton.
Sagolla, L.J. (1990) 'The Influence of Modern Dance on American Musical Theatre Choreography of the 1940s', *Dance: Current Selected Research* 2: 47–68.
Sanchez-Colberg, A. (1993) ' "you put your right foot in, then you shake it all about . . . ": Excursions and Incursions into Feminism and Bausch's Tanztheater', in H. Thomas (ed.) *Dance, Gender and Culture*, London: Macmillan.
Sartre, J.-P. (1956) *Being and Nothingness*, translated by H. Barnes (ed.), New York: Philosophical Library.
Saussure, F. de (1974) *Course in General Linguistics*, Glasgow: Fontana/Collins.
Sayler, O. (ed.) (1930) *Revolt in the Arts*, New York: Brentano's.
Schlatter, R. (1962) 'The Puritan Strain', in J. Higham (ed.) *The Reconstruction of American History*, London: Hutchinson University Library.
Schlundt, K. (1972) *Tamiris: A Chronicle of her Dance Career, 1927–1955*, New York: New York Public Libraries.
Schutz, A. (1967) *Collected Papers 1: The Problem of Social Reality*, The Hague: Martinus Nijhoff.
Segal (1987) *Is the Future Female?*, London: Virago.
Senelick, L. (1989) 'Spectacle and the Kiralfys', *Dance Chronicle* 12, 1: 149–54.
Shaw, L. (1988) 'Ephemeral Signs: Apprehending the Idea through Poetry and Dance', *Dance Research Journal* 20, 1, Summer: 3–8.
Shawn, T. (1974) *Every Little Movement*, New York: Dance Horizons.
Sheets-Johnstone, M. (1978) 'An Account of Change in Dance in the U.S.A.', *Leonardo* 11: 197–201.
—— (1979) *The Phenomenology of Dance*, London: Dance Books.
—— (ed.) (1984) *Illuminating Dance: Philosophical Explorations*, Lewisburg: Bucknell University Press.
Shelton, S. (1981) *Divine Dancer: A Biography of Ruth St. Denis*, New York: Garden City, Doubleday & Company.
Shilling, C. (1993) *The Body and Social Theory*, London: Sage.
Shipman, M. (1974) 'A Sociological Perspective of Dance', *Association of Teachers in Colleges and Departments of Education, Dance Section* 1–6.
Siegel, M.B. (1977) *Watching the Dance Go By*, Boston: Houghton Mifflin.
—— (1979) *The Shapes of Change*, Boston: Houghton Mifflin.
Silbermann, A. (1968) 'Introduction: A Definition of the Sociology of Art', *International Social Science Journal* 20, 4: 568–88.
Sklar, D. (1991) 'On Dance Ethnography', *Dance Research Journal* 23, 1: 6–10.
Smart, B. (1993) *Postmodernity*, London: Routledge.

Sommer, S. (1975 March) 'Loïe Fuller', *The Drama Review* 19, 1: 53–67.
Sommer, S. R. (1982) 'Loïe Fuller's Art of Music and Light', *Dance Chronicle* 4, 4: 389–401.
Sorell, W. (1966a) 'In Defense of the Future', in W. Sorell (ed.) *The Dance Has Many Faces*, New York: Columbia University Press.
—— (1966b) 'Two Rebels, Two Giants: Isadora and Martha', in W. Sorell (ed.) *The Dance Has Many Faces*, New York: Columbia University Press.
—— (1981) *Dance in its Time: The Emergence of an Art Form*, New York: Anchor Press/Doubleday.
Sparshott, F. (1983) 'Why Philosophy Neglects Dance', in R. Copeland and M. Cohen (eds) *What is Dance?*, London: Oxford University Press.
—— (1988) *Off the Ground: First Steps to a Philosophical Consideration of the Dance*, Princeton: Princeton University Press.
Spencer, H. (ed.) (1980) *American Art: Readings from the Colonial Era to the Present*, New York: Charles Scribner.
St Denis, R. (1939) *An Unfinished Life*, New York: Dance Horizons.
—— (1966) 'Religious Manifestations in the Dance', in W. Sorell (ed.) *The Dance Has Many Faces*, New York: Columbia University Press.
Stanley, L. (ed.) (1990) *Feminist Practice*, London: Routledge.
Stebbins, T.E. Jr (1980) 'Luminism in Context: A new View', in J. Wilmerding (ed.) *American Light: The Luminist Movement 1850–1875*, New York: Harper & Row.
Sterns, L. M. (1977) 'Towards a Structural Approach to "Symbolism in Dance"', Ph.D. Dissertation, University of Wisconsin.
Stodelle, E. (1962a) 'Before Yesterday, the First Decade of Modern Dance: Martha Graham', *Dance Observer* 29, 1: 5–7.
—— (1962b) 'Midstream, the Second Decade of Modern Dance: Martha Graham', *Dance Observer* 29, 5: 69–71.
—— (1962c) 'Midstream, the Second Decade of Modern Dance: Martha Graham', Pt 2, *Dance Observer* 29, 9: 117–19.
—— (1964) *The First Frontier: The Story of Louis Horst and the American Modern Dance*, Cheshire, Connecticut: Ernestine Stodelle.
—— (1984) *Deep Song: The Dance Story of Martha Graham*, New York: Schirmer Books.
Straus, G.B. (1978) 'The Aesthetics of Dominance', *Journal of Aesthetics and Art Criticism* 37: 73–9.
Susman, W.I. (1984) *Culture as History: The Transformation of American Society in the Twentieth Century*, New York: Panther.
Swift, M.G. (1980) *Belles and Beaux on their Toes: Dancing Stars in Young America*, Washington, DC: University of America Press.
Sydie, R.A. (1987) *Natural Women, Cultured Men: A Feminist Perspective On Sociological Theory*, Milton Keynes: Open University Press.
Synott, A. (1993) *The Body Social*, London: Routledge.
Tamiris, H. (1966) 'Present Problems and Possibilities', in W. Sorell (ed.) *The Dance Has Many Faces*, New York: Columbia University Press, pp. 200–7.
Taylor, L. (1971) 'Review of Birdwhistell's "Kinesics and Context" ', in *New Society*, September.
Taylor, R.G. (ed.) (1956) *The Turner Thesis: Problems in American Civilization*, Boston: D.C. Heath.
Tawa, N.E. (1984) *Serenading the Reluctant Eagle*, New York: Schirmer Books.
Terry, W. (1953) 'American Dance', *New York Herald Tribune*, 17 April.
—— (1956) *The Dance in America*, New York: Harper Brothers.
—— (1960 Winter) 'The Legacy of Isadora Duncan and Ruth St Denis', *Dance Perspectives* 5: 3–61.

—— (1975) *Frontiers of Dance: The Life of Martha Graham*, New York: Thomas Y. Crowell.

—— (1978) *I Was There*, New York: Marcel Dekker.

Thomas, H. (1986) 'Movement Modernism and Contemporary Culture: Issues for a Critical Sociology of Dance', unpublished Ph.D. Dissertation, University of London.

—— (1991) 'The Sociology of Dance: Themes and Perspectives', in M.L. Harris (ed.) *The Joan Russell Memorial Journal*, United Kingdom: Dance and the Child International.

—— (ed.) (1993) *Dance, Gender and Culture*, London: Macmillan.

Thompson, K. (1982) *Emile Durkheim*, Sussex and London: Ellis Horwood & Tavistock.

Thompson, O. (1945) 'Graham Presents Copland's Ballet', *New York Sun*, 15 May.

Thompson, V. (1945) 'Two Ballets', *New York Herald Tribune*, 20 May.

Todd, E.W. (1993) 'Art, the "New Woman" and Consumer Culture: Kenneth Hayes Miller and Reginald Marsh on Fourteenth Street, 1920 1940', in B. Melosh (ed.) *Gender and American History since 1890*, London: Routledge.

Turner, B.S (1984) *The Body and Society*, Oxford: Basil Blackwell.

—— (1991) 'Recent Developments in the Theory of the Body', in M. Featherstone, M. Hepworth and B.S. Turner (eds) *The Body: Social Processes and Cultural Theory*, London: Sage.

Turner, F.J. (1945) *The Frontier in American History*, New York: Henry Holt.

Tylor, E.B. (1958) *Religion in Primitive Culture*, New York: Harper & Row.

Van Tuyl, M. (ed.) (1969) *Anthology of Impulse: Annual of Contemporary Dance 1951–1966*, New York: Dance Horizons.

Veblen, T. (1970) *The Theory of the Leisure Class* (first published in Britain in 1925), London: Unwin Books.

Vincent, L.M. (1979) *Competing With the Sylph*, New York: Andrews & McMeel.

Walsh, D. (1972) 'Varieties of Positivism', in P. Filmer *et al.* (eds) *New Directions in Sociological Theory*, London: Collier–Macmillan.

Ward, A. (1993) 'Dancing in the Dark: Rationalism and the Neglect of Social Dance', in H. Thomas (ed.) *Dance, Gender and Culture*, London: Macmillan.

Warner, M.J. (1984) *Laban Notation Scores: An International Bibliography*, New York: ICKL.

Watkins, M.F. (1931) 'The Work of Martha Graham Excels in Recent Dance Repertory Theatre', *New York Herald Tribune*, 22 February.

—— (1932) *New York Herald Tribune*, 22 February.

Weber, M. (1976) *The Protestant Ethic and the Spirit of Capitalism*, London: Allen & Unwin.

Wheeler, M. (1990) 'New Dance in the New Deal Era', *Dance: Current Selected Research* 2: 33–46.

Williams, D. (1976) 'Deep Structures of the Dance, 1. Constituent Syntagmatic Analysis', *Journal of Human Movement Studies* 2: 123–44.

—— (1976–1977) 'The Nature of Dance: An Anthropological Perspective', *Dance Research Journal* 9, 1: 42–4.

—— (1991) *Ten Lectures on Theories of the Dance*, Metuchen: Scarecrow Press.

Williams, R. (1977) *Marxism and Literature*, Oxford: Oxford University Press.

—— (1981) *Culture*, London: Fontana.

Willis, P. (with Jones, S., Canaan, J. and Hurd, G.) (1990) *Common Culture*, 1st edn, Milton Keynes: Open University Press.

Wilmerding, J. (ed.) (1980) *American Light: The Luminist Movement 1850 1875*, New York: Harper & Row.

Winter, M.H. (1974) *The Pre-Romantic Ballet*, London: Pitman.

—— (1978) 'Juba and American Minstrelsy', in P. Magriel (ed.) *Chronicles of the American Dance from the Shakers to Martha Graham*, New York: Da Capo Press.

Wolff, J. (1975) *Hermeneutic Philosophy and the Sociology of Art*, London: Routledge & Kegan Paul.

—— (1981) *The Social Production of Art*, Basingstoke: Macmillan.

—— (1983) *Aesthetics and the Sociology of Art*, London: Allen & Unwin.

Wollen, P. (1987 Spring) 'Fashion/Orientalism/The Body', *New Formations* 1: 5–34.

Worth, S. and Adair, L. (1975) *Through Navajo Eyes*, Bloomington and London: Indiana University Press.

Wright, E. (ed.) (1967) *American Themes*, London: Oliver & Boyd.

Youngerman, S. (1974) 'Curt Sachs and his Heritage: A Critical Review of World History of the Dance with a Survey of Recent Studies that Perpetuate his Ideas', *Cord News* 6, 2: 6 17.

Zaner, R.M. (1971) *The Problem of Embodiment*, The Hague: Martinus Nijhoff.

Ziff, L. (1967) *The American Nineties: Life and Times of a Lost Generation*, London: Chatto & Windus.

Ziff, P. (1981) 'About the Appreciation of Dance', in G. Fancher and G. Myers (eds) *Philosophical Essays on Dance*, New York: Dance Horizons.

Zuck, B.A. (1980) *A History of Musical Americanism, Studies in Ethnomusicology, no. 19*, Ann Arbor: UMI Research Press.

AUDIO-VISUAL MATERIAL

Air for the G String [choreographed by D. Humphrey 1928], (motion picture), USA, 1934.

American Document [choreographed by M. Graham 1938], excerpts in Martha Graham Dance Company 1938–1944, (motion picture), USA, 1940.

Appalachian Spring [choreographed by M. Graham 1944], excerpts in Martha Graham Dance Company 1938–1944, USA, 1944.

Appalachian Spring, orchestral suite [composed by A. Copland in 1945], (music score), Boosey & Hawkes Ltd, London, 1945.

Appalachian Spring complete ballet [composed by A. Copland 1944], (gramophone record), Columbia, ML 5157, 1957.

Appalachian Spring [choreographed by M. Graham 1944] (motion picture) USA, presented by WQED-TV, Pittsburgh, in cooperation with National Education Television and Chatham College, 1958.

Appalachian Spring [choreographed by M. Graham 1944], in Martha Graham Dance Company (video tape), WNET/13 Dance in America Series, New York, 1976.

Billy the Kid, Ballet Suite [composed by A. Copland 1938], (gramophone record), RCA Victor, LM 1031, 1950.

Bird, B., *The Early Technique of Martha Graham*, recorded interview with H. Thomas, 1984.

A Dancer's World (motion picture), WQED-TV, Pittsburgh, 1957.

Denishawn Dance Film (motion picture), Los Angeles, 191–.

Gruen, J., *Interview with Aaron Copland*, Radio Station WNCN-FM, New York, 1975.

The Flute of Krishna [choreographed by M. Graham], (motion picture), Eastman Kodak Studios, Rochester, New York, 1926.

Frontier [choreographed by M. Graham 1935], excerpts in Martha Graham Dance Company 1938–1944, (motion picture) USA, 1938.

Frontier [choreographed by M. Graham 1935], (motion picture), by D. Godwin under a grant from the Lena Robbins Foundation, USA, 1964.

Frontier [choreographed by M. Graham 1935] in Martha Graham Dance Company (video tape), New York, WNET/13 Dance in America series, 1976.

Incense [choreographed by R. St Denis 1906], (motion picture), Phillip Baribault, USA, 1953.

Lamentation [choreographed by M. Graham 1930], (motion picture), Pictorial Films, USA, 193?–.

Lamentation [choreographed by M. Graham 1931], (motion picture), S. and H. Moselsio and the Harmon Foundation, USA, 1943.

Lamentation [choreographed by M. Graham 1930], in Martha Graham Dance Company (video tape), New York, WNET/13, Dance in America series, 1976.

Letter to the World [choreographed by M. Graham 1940] in Martha Graham Dance Company 1938–1944 (motion picture), USA, 1941.

The Modern Dance (motion picture), Pictorial Films, USA, 193?.

Morgan, B., *Martha Graham: Sixteen Dances in Photographs* by B. Morgan, Duell, Sloan & Pearce, New York, 1941.

Primitive Mysteries [choreographed by M. Graham 1931] (motion picture), by Dwight Godwin, under a grant from Lena Robbins Foundation, USA, 1964.

Radha [choreographed by R. St Denis 1906], (motion picture), by Dwight Godwin, Massachusetts, 1973.

The Shakers [choreographed by D. Humphrey 1931], (motion picture), by Dwight Goodman for The Jerome Robbins Film Archive, New York, 1972.

Sherman, R. (1982) *Interview with Anna Kisselgoff and Walter Terry*, Radio Station WQXR, New York.

Tillers of the Soil [choreographed by R. St Denis and T. Shawn 1916], (motion picture), Phillip Baribault, USA, 1948.

Tobias, T. (1979) *Interview with Isamu Noguchi*, (phototape) recorded at Noguchi's home in Long Island, New York.

White Jade [choreographed by R. St Denis 1926], (motion picture), by Phillip Baribault, USA, 1948.

NAME INDEX

SUBJECT INDEX

204   *Dance, modernity and culture*

Frontier (Graham) 115, 116, 117–18, 131, 154, 155
frontierism 25–6, 27, 30, 43–4, 46, 68, 86, 118, 141, 143, 154, 163, 164
functionalism 10; in dance and art 26, 45, 46, 68, 86

gender 3, 4–5, 168
Germany: dance in 48, 60, 66, 70, 102, 111; *Gebrauchmusik* 140
Greece, ancient 50, 53, 66, 64, 66, 71, 87, 115, 143
Greenwich Village, NY 61, 103, 107
Greenwich Village Follies 92, 100
group dances 54, 95–6, 102, 158
Group Theatre 139–40

harlequinades 36
harmonic gymnastics 49, 50
health reform movement 48, 50–2, 53, 71, 80, 165
Heretic (Graham) 95–6
'high' culture 2 *see also* art
hootchy-kootchy 73
How Long Brethren? (Tamiris) 122, 123, 124

identity 168
illusion, theatrical 37
Independents 76, 105
individualism, in dance and art 26, 30, 45, 46, 66, 68, 76, 85–6, 106, 118, 154, 163, 165
interactionism 3
International Exhibition of Modern Art (1913) 104–6, 107, 126
interpretation, dance as 28, 150
interpretive dance 71, 81, 110, 111, 112
interpretive sociology 23
Italy, influence on dance 41

Japanese prints/design 57–8, 59, 79
jazz 104, 112, 113, 126, 134, 135, 136–7, 142
jazz dancing 82

kinesics 28, 175 *see also* everyday movement
kootch 73

Lamentation (Graham) 115, 116–17
lighting, use of 37, 55, 56, 57, 133

literature 33–4, 78–9, 88
Maid with the Flaxen Hair (Graham) 93
Marseillaise (Duncan) 67
Martha Graham Dance Group 95–6, 111
Marxist aesthetics 171
Marxist sociology 12, 18
men, dancing for 94
Metropolitan Opera Ballet School 112
Metropolitan Opera House 40, 82, 112
mind/body dualism 6–7
minstrel shows 25, 35, 40, 118
modern dance 2, 5
modern dance, American 1, 20, 22, 23–30, 66, 67, 68, 165–6; beginnings 46, 47, 65, 73, 82, 85–99, 165; development and relationship to modernism 100–13; forerunners 47, 53–84; from 1930s 115–28; influence of Denishawn 84, 85
modern dance, German 48, 102
modernism: in American arts 1, 20, 26, 66, 76–7, 89, 100–13, 125–8, 142 (*see also* fine art; modern dance, American; music, American); European 76, 104, 105–7, 126–7, 142
modernism/postmodernism debate 12–14, 16, 17
modernity/postmodernity debate 12, 16–17
movement *see* body; everyday movement; non-literal movement
music: dances without 98, 102, 112; Fuller, Duncan and 56, 60, 63; Puritans and 33; relationship of modern dance to 93, 116, 129–48
music, American 83; art music 103–4, 128, 129–48; in Depression and 1930s 120, 121, 125; influence of Europe 41, 104, 119
music hall 56, 58
music visualisation 68, 81, 89, 95

National Dance League 122
Negro spirituals, use in dance 113
Neighborhood Playhouse 103
Neighborhood Playhouse School 110
New Deal Federal relief projects 67, 68, 120–5, 127–8, 140–1
New Masses, The 107